Miracles

Miracles

Wonder and Meaning in World Religions

David L. Weddle

NEW YORK UNIVERSITY PRESS
New York and London

NEW YORK UNIVERSITY PRESS
New York and London
www.nyupress.org

© 2010 by New York University
All rights reserved

Library of Congress Cataloging-in-Publication Data

Weddle, David L. (David Leroy), 1942–
Miracles : wonder and meaning in world religions / David L. Weddle.
p. cm.
Includes bibliographical references and index.
ISBN-13: 978-0-8147-9415-9 (cloth : alk. paper)
ISBN-10: 0-8147-9415-7 (cloth : alk. paper)
ISBN-13: 978-0-8147-9416-6 (pbk. : alk. paper)
ISBN-10: 0-8147-9416-5 (pbk. : alk. paper)
[etc.]
1. Miracles. 2. Religions. I. Title.
BL487.W45   2010

202'.117—dc22   2009053830

New York University Press books are printed on acid-free paper,
and their binding materials are chosen for strength and durability.
We strive to use environmentally responsible suppliers and materials
to the greatest extent possible in publishing our books.

Manufactured in the United States of America
c   10 9 8 7 6 5 4 3 2 1
p   10 9 8 7 6 5 4 3 2 1

Dedicated to the memory of
Daniel Mark Weddle
(1965–2005)
per aspera ad astra

Note about the Cover

Since every book begins before it begins, I invite you to close this one and review the cover. We enter this account of miracles in world religions through a painting by René Magritte (1898–1967), the Belgian artist who created startling images by placing familiar objects in strange juxtaposition, as if in a dream. Magritte called this work *Le Pays des Miracles* (*The Land of Miracles*, 1964). The painting is surreal in that it depicts an excess of reality by collapsing two worlds: the ordinary world imposed on—or is it disrupted by?—a land of moonlit wonders.

At first glance the vase appears to contain a light blue flowering bouquet. Near the base is a nest with three eggs in orderly arrangement. Immediately, we must rule out the possibility that the nest fell, by accident, from the bushy plant. It has been placed, as if by design, as all things appear to be in the world of ordinary experience. Upon closer investigation, it appears that the jagged outline we thought to be flowers could be a tree with the vase forming its trunk and leaves or buds spilling over the edge of the container. But where is the rest of the plant? Is it covered by the dream scene of trees and clouds wanly illumined by a sliver of moon? Wait, that scene is not in front; we are seeing the country(side) of miracles *through* the plant. But, if so, is the bouquet transparent or has it been destroyed? Was our peephole to the world beyond, with its delicate lacy rim, ripped out of the brown background that is really the foreground?

The placid image with its soothing blue is surcharged with traces of violence. How could it be otherwise? Can miracles break into our world in any other way, except as transgressions, violations (as we often say) of the laws of nature? So it has seemed to those who are accustomed to viewing the world as the orderly creation of God or the regulated unfolding of evolutionary process. But for others, the world in which miracles occur is the greater reality that supports their lives and provides them hope and faith to aspire to flight beyond the routine cycles of the nest—even if they know of miracles only by distant report or fleeting glimpse, as if in a dream. The country of miracles does not lie brightly before us, clearly illuminated by full sunlight, but rather in the haze of the waning crescent of the moon. Magritte's painted image stops time just at the moment when the scene of the other world is fading from view, perhaps on awaking from a dream or in the hour before dawn. As viewers, we are invited to consider our arrangements on the flat tabletop of domestic life as fragile and artificial, vulnerable to shattering incursions of possibilities imagined, dreamed, and believed, from the country of miracles.

Contents

Preface

The story of miracles begins with the miracle of story: the power of narrative to draw readers into alternative views of reality. As some theorists of religion argue, one of the creative achievements of religious faith is the construction of "religious worlds."[1] Among the most powerful tools in that enterprise is the miracle story. For many believers, miracle stories reveal the poverty of conventional views of reality and demonstrate that human existence is not confined to the repetitive predictability of material forces in their blind and pitiless operation. Stories of miracles are dispatches from beyond the horizon of the physical universe; they are intimations of the transcendent. The accounts of "signs and wonders" retold in religious traditions across the globe are a primal form of anecdotal evidence: raw, naïve, and dramatic. Stories of miracles make belief in divine agency or infinite consciousness seem reasonable, even empirical. To enter imaginatively into their narratives is to begin to consider the wonders they recount as real possibilities for human life. For that reason, stories of miraculous healings strengthen the faith of the sick, accounts of casting out demons encourage those oppressed by injustice to imagine themselves freed, and stories of ascending masters inspire spirits to soar with hopes of liberation or resurrection.

Like other means of representing the transcendent, such as systems of doctrine or ritual performance, miracle stories contribute to the formation of many religious communities. The stories may seem to be little more than quaint tales, but when invested with meaning drawn from the communities in which they are treasured, they become "signs" pointing beyond themselves to transcendent power at work in this world producing novel and disruptive effects. Miracle stories, then, are central to the way some religious traditions construct their visions of reality because miracles are signifiers of what a tradition holds to be *transcendent*.

That word is admittedly vague, but it has the advantage of avoiding the problems associated with even less satisfactory categories, like "supernatural" or "sacred." The English verb *transcend* derives from a combination of

Latin roots, meaning "across" and "climb." The image of a *climb* puts us in the semantic range of ascent, one of the oldest forms of religious discourse. Many religions begin, we might say, with the glance upward. The preposition *across*, however, indicates lateral movement from one location to another, not necessarily above, but different. To reach the transcendent, then, one must climb (or clamber, for there are obstacles) across to a different site. In religious usage, that site is other than the material world. The transcendent may be in heaven (many religious traditions use that language), but it may also just be "elsewhere."[2] However transcendence is understood, it seems indispensable to religious views of reality, implying at the very least possibilities not otherwise available in this world.[3]

The problem with miracle stories, of course, is the seeming impossibility of integrating miracles into the modern scientific account of reality which does not admit their possibility. While contemporary theorists do not describe nature any longer as a closed system ruled by immutable laws, neither do they admit causal agency into the world from "elsewhere." Even sophisticated theories of consciousness emerging from natural processes or of reality being constituted by the ceaseless interaction of natural and cultural networks do not admit exceptions to what the mathematician and philosopher Alfred North Whitehead stated as "the ontological principle," namely, "there is nothing which floats into the world from nowhere."[4] Belief in miracles is the confidence that, on rare occasions, events come into the world from "elsewhere."

If you are opening this book with the question, "Do miracles *really* happen?" let me suggest that you first consider the question, "So what if they do?" Suppose this book suddenly rose out of your hands, transformed into an eagle and—before your wondering eyes—flew away. What difference would that event make in your life? It may not even serve as an amazing story with which to entertain your friends because, in all likelihood, they would not believe you. Not even the fact that you saw the miracle with your own eyes would necessarily convince you it happened. You could very well walk away, shaking your head, unable to make sense of it. That is, as sheer anomaly in the customary order of things, disconnected from the patterns of causation that determine the behavior of inanimate objects in your world, the flying book would have no *meaning* for you. The event would present no new possibilities for your subsequent behavior: for example, you would not proceed to place all your other books in cages or begin to worship at the local library. This curious example is meant to show that an event that is merely puzzling does not constitute a *miracle* in the religious sense. A miracle is an *interpreted* event, set within a tradition's broader system of beliefs and understood as signifying something about transcendent reality.

Take as an example of miracle understood in this way a story from the Gospel of Mark. A man approached Jesus, pleading that his son be healed of the convulsive disease that threatened his life. The father was a reasonable man, but desperate. In response Jesus challenged him: "All things can be done for the one who believes" (Mark 9:23). Who would not declare faith under those circumstances? Most of us would claim to believe in the Jolly Green Giant if the confession would save our child. But this man cried out in utter honesty, "I believe, help my unbelief!" Jesus healed the son, but the story demonstrates a basic ambivalence miraculous power evokes, even in those who witness it. That ambivalence can be resolved—if ever—only by reconciling the tension between faith and doubt, wonder and skepticism, by locating the miracle within a more comprehensive view of reality, in this case, the Christian interpretation of Jesus's healing power as a sign of divine compassion present in him. (The tension is unresolved in Mark's story; we are not told whether the father came to "understand" the miracle in any terms, let alone those of later Christian tradition.)

The miracles considered in this book are events invested with deep significance by those who witness them or retell their stories. For religious believers, that meaning is determined within the world constructed by the narrative in which the miracle occurs and the social consensus that ascribes authority to the one with whom the miracle is associated. Thus, miracles have many meanings, depending on where and when they occur, who performs them, and who benefits from their power to uphold or disrupt established authority. This book interrogates five of the world's religious traditions to discover what wisdom they offer on the meanings of miracles.

Those meanings, however, do not go uncontested. We hear voices of faithful dissent to belief in miracles in every tradition, raising objections on religious grounds. These are believers who disbelieve in miracles and wish no help for their unbelief. Praying for a miracle, many of these critics contend, is the mark of immature faith: an inability to accept the hard fact that natural forces are indifferent to our needs and virtues. Adult faith must leave childish fantasies behind and, inspired by stories of spiritual heroes, seek justice, show compassion, and live in peace, trusting that our efforts will lead to salvation or liberation for ourselves and others. Some believers regard this critical line of argument as decisive against belief in miracles.

Most believers, however, do not accept such criticism; and their belief in miracles persists. In a recent survey taken in the United States, over 57 percent of the public polled said they believed that divine intervention could save a patient when medical treatment proved futile.[5] What is remarkable about the popular hope for miracles is that prayers for divine intervention are rarely answered, yet the hope endures. If it is a peculiar characteristic of hope that it requires some faint foretaste of its own fulfillment in order to be sustained,[6] how could one hope for a miracle, an event that by its nature cannot be experienced "in advance"? As a moment of discontinuity in the ordinary flow of events, a miracle could not be experienced in any fashion prior to its full-blown appearance on the scene. Despite these logical difficulties, many religious believers hope for miracles in their lives and struggle to form a coherent understanding of miracles past, performed by holy figures and recorded in sacred texts; miracles present, tantalizingly promised but rarely fulfilled; and miracles future, projecting radical reversal of the tragedies of history. This book is an attempt to enter imaginatively into that struggle.

In wrestling with this subject many have urged me on and a few have entered the ring for a few rounds. I want especially to acknowledge Charlotte Martin, Brian Daugherty, Richard Ball, Pratap Kumar Penumala, Louis Cicotello, and Paul Gray, who philosophizes with Nietzsche's tuning fork, always checking for hollow sounds; as well as former students who continue to teach me, Clanton Dawson, John McAndrew, Zach Simpson, Whitney Turk, and Sierra Fleenor; fellow teachers at Colorado College, who offered encouragement and helpful references, Joe Pickle, David Gardiner, Tracy Coleman, Sarah Schwarz, Peter Wright, Marion Hordequin, Rick Furtak, Jonathan Lee, George Butte, and Susan Ashley; and colleagues in the Rocky Mountain–Great Plains region of the American Academy of Religion and Society of Biblical Literature, who responded to preliminary papers on this subject. A sabbatical leave sponsored by Colorado College allowed me several indispensable months for research and writing. Most importantly, to my wife Sharon for unfailing support during the years this work took shape; to our daughter, Lisa, for wise counsel about what not to say; her husband, Chad; and our lively and lovely granddaughter, Ellyson Danielle Siebert. This book is dedicated to the memory of our son Dan, who faced the sudden, final horror of leukemia with courage and grace, accompanied by his wife, C. J. Matthews, whose fierce love endured when miracles failed.

Finally, it is customary for authors to thank editors for guidance and patience, but in my case it is no formality. This book would not have the measure of coherence it displays without the careful attention of Jennifer Hammer of New York University Press, who no doubt at times feared that the long-delayed completion of this work would require an example of its subject.

Preliminary Considerations

Why should anyone, living at the dawn of the twenty-first century, be interested in miracles? For three centuries the capacity of science to explain events as the result of natural forces has seemed to make reference to divine causes unnecessary, even harmful. In times of crisis, hoping for assistance from supernatural saviors seems a dangerous distraction from the challenge of solving our own problems. Yet, around the world stories of wondrous acts continue to be retold in religious communities where they are invested with profound meaning: Krishna straightening a woman's curved spine, Moses parting the Red Sea, Buddha levitating in the air while fire and water streamed from his body, Jesus walking on the Lake of Galilee, and Muhammad ascending into heaven from Jerusalem. Many religions were founded on accounts of miraculous events, acts of transcendent power remembered in stories that evoke transformative responses in readers. Further, belief in miracles receives fresh encouragement today in religious communities across the world with the rise of traditionalist forms of piety and action.

Meanings of Miracle Stories

What significance do contemporary readers find in these tales? The answer is complex. First, miracle stories support the hope that humans are not bound within the limits of the material world and that the future is not already fixed as the consequence of past events. For Hindus, the stories of Krishna's triumph over demons include their release from punishment for former deeds, encouraging present-day readers to hope that they too may escape karmic debt. The stories of Jesus's healings give Christians confidence that their own diseases may be cured or their addictions broken. For believers, miracles signify the ultimate freedom of the human spirit from the world of material forces. Miracle stories open narrative worlds in which what is impossible in the reader's customary experience becomes possible, even anticipated. Belief in miracles is the confidence that, at rare and wondrous moments, grace may overcome fate.

Second, miracle stories serve to confirm the belief that there is a reality that surpasses, or is transcendent to, this world and that manifests its power by altering material conditions. Belief in the transcendent in one form or another is basic to most religions; and miracles are often cited as warrant for that belief. For Hindus, the ability of fully concentrated yogis to levitate supports their claim to have achieved a transcendent state of consciousness. For Muslims, the miracle of the Qur'an as divine revelation to Muhammad, an "unlettered prophet," is demonstrated by its "inimitability" that prevents any human poet or philosopher from duplicating its language. Miracle stories signify that belief in transcendent reality is not private fantasy, but a claim capable of public verification.

William James (1842–1910), founder of the American school of philosophy known as pragmatism, argued that religion "is not a mere illumination of facts already elsewhere given, not a mere passion, like love, which views things in a rosier light . . . But it is something more, a postulator of new *facts* as well." He believed that this pragmatic view of religion "has usually been taken as a matter of course by common men. They have interpolated divine miracles into the field of nature, they have built a heaven out beyond the grave." Their view gives religion "body as well as soul, it makes its claim, as everything real must claim, some characteristic realm of fact as its very own."[1] For believers, miracle stories present "new facts" that could not be produced by, or deduced from, the world of ordinary experience and, thus, serve as evidence of the transcendent reality required for their explanation.

Third, miracle stories serve the pedagogical purpose of illustrating teachings or insights of a religious tradition and inspiring adherence to those teachings. When Buddha appeared to his kinsmen, floating above the river they were about to fight over, his levitation signified the necessity of rising above self-interest in order to achieve peace and bring an end to suffering. For a Muslim mystic, the truth that God is Supreme Reality is demonstrated by the ability, while in ecstatic trance, to appear and disappear at will. The mystic's passage from being to non-being and back serves to illustrate the Islamic teaching that everything is created by God from nothing in each moment. Those who witness or hear of this miracle are thus taught to maintain a spirit of unbroken gratitude to God for the gift of continuing existence.

Fourth, miracle stories give symbolic expression to a community's desire for political freedom. In the triumph of a deity or hero over demons, people often see a coded reference to their own authority to overthrow powers that oppose their well-being, including unjust rulers. In Tibet, the belief that each Dalai Lama is a divine incarnation, a living miracle, supports a sense of national identity under his leadership and encourages resistance to Chinese rule. Jewish mystic masters often exercised their miraculous powers to protect or deliver Jewish communities under persecution in Christian or Islamic states. Miracle stories, as narratives of power, reflect the political situations of the storytellers. But miracles are instances of disruptive power and, as such, signal revolutionary desire. For discerning readers these stories are not innocent fantasies.

Stories of miracles, then, signify hope in radically new possibilities for this world, express confidence in transcendent reality beyond this world, provide visual aids to instruct believers in the values and wisdom of their tradition, and sometimes inspire political action. The abiding appeal of traditional stories and popular interest in their contemporary parallels indicate that miracles continue to have meaning for religious believers today as signs of transcendent power. That the term *miracle* (and its many variants in other languages) also occurs in secular discourse about startling events, unprecedented developments, and inexplicable healings suggests it resonates in all human speech as an echo of a common yearning for freedom. The purpose of miracle stories is to make that freedom imaginable, even realistic.

Working Definition of Miracle

This book is a study of miracles and the meanings assigned to them in five religious traditions: Hinduism, Judaism, Buddhism, Christianity, and Islam. The discussion will focus on a few examples in each tradition that illuminate the significance religious believers assign to miracles. To fully understand the range of meanings miracles have in these different traditions, we will also explore the wider systems of ideas about reality that provide the intellectual rationale for belief in supernatural or transcendent power intervening in the world of ordinary experience. The purpose of this broader investigation is to show that belief in miracles is not arbitrary, but is grounded in some coherent view of reality. (Of course, not all religious believers are fully educated in the metaphysics of their traditions; but each tradition offers one.) For that reason, miracles have meanings specific to each tradition; yet across traditions they are commonly regarded as rare and wondrous signs of a domain of being that utterly surpasses the laws and limits of our world. So we begin with this working definition of *miracle*:

A miracle is an event of transcendent power that arouses wonder and carries religious significance for those who witness it or hear or read about it.

There may be two surprises in this definition. First, there is no mention of divine beings because in some forms of Hinduism and Buddhism there are no divine agents. In those traditions, miracles are manifestations of the power of the human mind to transcend natural limits. Second, there is no mention of benefits in the definition. In most of the miracle stories in this book, transcendent power manifests itself in ways that are helpful to human beings, but not always. Punishing acts of the gods also fit our definition of miracles as events of transcendent power that arouse wonder, particularly in apocalyptic visions. In the well-known Bible story of the parting of the Red Sea, the appearance of dry land that allowed the Israelites to escape from Egypt was no more miraculous than the closing of the waters that drowned Pharaoh and his army. Our definition is intended to include within the category *miracle* every event of transcendent power, whether enacted by gods or yogis and whether resulting in weal or woe.

Like every serious book, this one is also out to get you. That is, I do have a thesis to argue—and as you likely detected in the first paragraph, I do not assume at the outset that miracles are impossible or that the people who believe in them are irrational. Rather, my thesis is this: *Despite the dominance of scientific explanation in the modern world and despite powerful philosophical criticism, belief in miracles remains strong in all religious traditions and continues to call forth official regulation and faithful dissent.* By *official regulation* I mean that miracle claims are controlled by religious institutions because they are potent sources of authority that miracle workers sometimes use to support criticism of established powers. By *faithful dissent*, I refer to the resistance that develops within each tradition by a loyal opposition whose members pose *religious* objections to belief in miracles. We shall see that not all who believe in miracles are irrational, and not all who reject them are irreligious.[2]

How Miracle Stories Mean

The poet and teacher John Ciardi once said that the most fruitful way to interpret a poem is to ask not "What does it mean?" but "How does it mean?"[3] That is, how does the language accomplish the task of communicating the poet's experience and insight? The British philosopher J. L. Austin called such creative use of words "performative language," and we can say that miracle stories are instances of such language at work. The meaning of a miracle story may vary for each listener, depending on context, language, location (in time, space, history, and geography), and imagination, the wild card in the game of interpretation. The story of a miracle performs its effect in interaction with its audience and the power of the story depends upon the audience playing the role of what the literary theorist Wolfgang Iser called "the implied reader." That designation was invented to describe readers who can fill in the inevitable gaps in any text by means of imagination, a creative process of "reader-response." Such a reader "must think in terms of experiences different from his own; indeed, it is only by leaving behind the familiar world of his own experience that the reader can truly participate in the adventure the literary text offers."[4] But that participation cannot be a full immersion in the illusion of the text, as in the effortless escape into a mystery novel. The meaning of a literary or religious text is neither the reader's fantasy nor a transparent truth; rather, "it arises from the meeting between the written text and the individual mind of the reader with its own particular history of experience, its own consciousness, its own outlook."[5] Thus, even readers within a shared tradition may respond in quite different ways to a common story.

A miracle story, as performative language calling for a creative response from readers and listeners, is both like and unlike other kinds of stories. Is it like a myth or a poem or a folk tale? Are the stories of miracles like news reports or parables? If a miracle story is an enacted parable, then is its meaning limited to each individual's response to it? Christian scholars think that Jesus did not interpret his parables, let alone assign a single meaning to each of them. We also know that Zen Buddhist masters do not interpret *koans*, the puzzling statements they assign students to meditate on, leaving it up to each individual to discern the meaning. For example, if a master assigned you the *koan*—"What was your true face before your parents were born?"—it would be foolish to search a sonogram image of your mother as a fetus for a clue because the answer is private and must be uniquely your own. The koan does not have a public answer that could be provided by everyone in the same way. Thus, to the extent that a miracle story is like a parable or koan, it does not have a normative meaning.

On the other hand, miracle stories are social narratives: *narratives* insofar as they follow a plot line; *social* insofar as the response of readers or listeners is an essential element of the story. So, while a miracle story may challenge our view of the world in the way parables and koans provoke us to new perceptions and values, it seems to have significance that extends beyond individual hearers or readers. Richard Davis, teacher of Asian religious studies, notes that miracles "require an audience, a community of witnesses, who respond to the event with appropriate reactions of wonder, surprise, astonishment, and delight. Miracles also presume a set of socially shared expectations concerning what ought to happen, a common sense view of the normal way of things, from which the miraculous by definition deviates."[6] Miracles require witnesses for their performance, and the stories they tell must be read with attention to their construction as narratives.

Stories of wondrous events create worlds in which miracles signify possibilities of insight, action, and freedom that are not imaginable within the limits of a universe of implacable material forces. But creating narrative worlds is not an innocent enterprise. Contemporary readers are acutely aware of the layers of meaning, the strata of motives (conscious or not), and the maze of contexts (political, gendered, economic) involved in the construction of stories, let alone the worlds they project and sanction.[7] We shall discover that narrative worlds in which miracles occur are often constructed as imaginative alternatives to the social or political conditions of the storyteller's actual world. In these cases miracle stories are revolutionary proposals in disguise, sometimes aimed at competing views of reality within the storyteller's religious community. Every story is told for a purpose; and every miracle story plays a role in larger contests over knowledge and power. Inasmuch as miracles are "signs" they require interpretation—and that need inevitably raises the question of authority.

That question is relevant not only to the stories in this book but also to the book itself. Each chapter constructs a narrative adapted for the purposes of this study: an overarching story of a religious tradition focused on the meaning of miracles in the tradition. Each tradition is presented primarily from the standpoint of those who perform wonders: avatars and yogis, prophets and rabbis, bodhisattvas and lamas, saints and healers, prophets and shaykhs. This approach seems to me a more productive way to proceed than to develop a typology of miracles since the same kinds of wondrous events appear in all the traditions under consideration. For example, we find cases of levitation by Hindu yogis, Christian saints, and Muslim shaykhs. The narrated acts of suspending gravity belong to the same category of miracle, but their meanings vary greatly in light of the different ways these religious virtuosi function in their traditions. The meaning of a miracle, then, is not only derived from *what* the act is but also from *who* performs it. For the purposes of this study we regard every miracle as a sign of transcendent power, but the process of interpreting its significance as a miracle requires attention to "how it means" in the context of who exercises the power and who witnesses and benefits from its manifestation.

As a result, each tradition is by no means presented in its entirety but only in those aspects that illumine the meaning of miracles. The examples were chosen for the purpose of conducting this inquiry, so they should not be taken as representative in some general sense of the traditions from which they are drawn. Further, because each chapter tells a story in which miracle workers are central, it ignores or pushes to the background features of the tradition that many of its own adherents (and conventional historians) regard as far more significant than belief in miracles. So, while I have sketched in some of the beliefs and practices of each tradition, there was no attempt to provide a comprehensive survey of these world religions. Finally, because of the highly selective and intensely interested character of this study, the chapter narratives do not adequately account for struggles for dominance among various schools and branches of each tradition. While I have chosen a few examples of faithful dissent from each tradition, my selections serve to support my thesis that objections to belief in miracles may proceed from religious grounds as well as philosophical and ethical considerations. So, even when the analysis does consider internal discontinuities, it is guided by theoretical interests.

To focus on "how miracles mean" requires us to look at the narrative worlds in which they occur and the wider systems of signification in which the stories become credible. As the scholar Christoph Auffarth reminds us, "it is the task of the academic study of religion to examine miracles as social facts in their historical contexts, to analyze their social functions, and to seek to grasp the diverse ways in which miracles are perceived."[8] That task requires us to look beyond the literal meaning of miracle stories, and that method may well disappoint both believers and skeptics. The motives for the literal reading of religious texts are relative to the views of religion their readers hold. Devout Christians may insist that believing Jesus walked on water is essential to faith, while pious Muslims may hold that it is a test of faith to affirm that Muhammad rode a winged beast from Mecca to Jerusalem and then ascended into heaven. In these cases, literal readings are marks of respect for the texts as sacred revelation. On the other hand, unbelievers may insist on reading such stories literally so that they can confidently declare them absurd or superstitious and dismiss them as meaningless. Literal readings, whether by believers or skeptics, are often sadly devoid of empathy, respect, and imagination—not to mention humor. Ensconced in their own worlds, literalists comfortably explain everything foreign in their terms, claiming to know better than storytellers what their stories mean, thereby shutting the door to the narrative world the story opens.

In our examination of miracle stories, we will try not to reduce the worlds their narratives create simply to the social and political conditions of the cultures in which the stories were performed. That method would miss the point of envisioning novel prospects for changing life under those conditions. We will also assume that even the most traditional storytellers are aware that theirs is an imaginative enterprise, an exercise in interpreting events rather than simply reporting them. Because the process of interpretation involves relating stories to the ever-changing conditions of their audiences, storytellers produce adaptive revisions of miracle stories that sustain the relevance and credibility of new possibilities for personal and social life, while constraining disruptive or fantastic elements of the narratives. The meanings of miracle stories, then, emerge from the interplay among popular wonder, official regulation, and faithful dissent.

Popular Enthusiasm: Miracles in Religious Resurgence

Miracles occur only in worlds of belief and practice where miracles are possible. You may not be located in such a world, but billions of our neighbors on this planet are. If you think that claim an exaggeration, consider that among the six billion people on earth, there are one billion Roman Catholics whose Church teaches that a miracle occurs every time they participate in the ritual of the Mass, transforming bread and wine into the body and blood of Christ; one billion Muslims who believe that a miracle of divine revelation created the Qur'an; a half billion Christians who believe in miraculous physical healing; and another half billion Hindus who pray to personal deities for intervention in their lives. By this rough count, believers in miracles of one sort or another constitute half the world's population—and their presence in those areas with the highest birth rates and where traditional forms of religion are flourishing indicates that confidence in miracles will continue to be a central feature of global religious life for the foreseeable future.

That fact may surprise those who continue to believe in the myth of secularization, the narrative of modernity that projected the inevitable success of science (and more importantly, technology) to meet every human need and the corresponding erosion of belief in divine beings. Of all the dramatic developments of the late twentieth century, however, the least anticipated was the resurgence of traditional religions across the world. Since the mid-nineteenth century it has been fashionable in some intellectual circles to predict the end of religion: as the illusion of false security in a world of primal desires (Freud), as the narcotic that dulls the pain of exploited workers and the ideology that sanctions the profits of capitalists (Marx), as the mythic endorsement of human uniqueness that must yield to the evolutionary account of the origin of all species (Darwin), as the oppressive morality that constricts human creativity (Nietzsche), as the symbolic representation of societal values (Durkheim), or as the desperate claim to purpose in a meaningless universe (Russell). At the opening of the twentieth century, the philosopher A. J. Ayer famously issued his confident proclamation of "the end of metaphysics." His obituary notice was premature, despite recent strident denunciations of theism as irrational.[9]

What underlies recent attacks on religion is the assumption that return to traditional faith necessarily entails delusional beliefs and fanatical behavior. For Sam Harris, an independent scholar whose books criticizing religious faith have made best-seller lists, the connection is clearly demonstrated in the implacable opposition to modernity among Islamic traditionalists who insist that the Qur'an is the comprehensive and infallible guide to social and political life. As he sees it, the only hope for a truce in the "war" between Islam and the West is for most Muslims to abandon their loyalty to tradition the way liberal Christians have. "A future in which Islam and the West do not stand on the brink of mutual annihilation is a future in which most Muslims have learned to ignore most of their canon, just as most Christians have learned to do."[10] For Harris, who began writing his book called *The End of Faith* on September 12, 2001, religious faith must come to an end if global civilization is to have a future. Unfortunately, there are many aspects of the resurgence of traditional religion that provide ground for Harris's concern. But do they justify his charge that tradition is necessarily opposed to modernity?

Talal Asad, professor of anthropology, argues that the charge rests on a false dichotomy, as demonstrated by hybrid societies that are part modern and part traditional. He continues, "I think that one needs to recognize that when one talks about tradition, one should be talking about, in a sense, a dimension of social life and not a stage of social development. In an important sense, tradition and modernity are not really two mutually exclusive states of a culture or society but different aspects of historicity."[11] For example, Islamic traditionalists are not so much returning to the past as adapting elements of their heritage to the present. Asad helps us to see that tradition and modernity do not describe successive epochs in the historical development of culture, but that tradition is always being reconfigured according to present needs and, in that sense, becoming modern. As he put it in an influential work: "Religious traditions have undergone the most radical transformations over time. Divine texts may be unalterable, but the ingenuities of human interpretation are endless."[12]

We live in a time marked by the revival of old beliefs in new forms. Billions of our contemporaries continue to find religion the source of primary guidance in personal and social life and the ground of hope for a future radically different from the present. In the past fifty years, religious communities across the world have given rise to what are called "fundamentalist" movements, committed groups of believers demanding the restoration of traditional beliefs and practices identified through what historians of American religion Martin Marty and Scott Appleby call "selective retrieval of the past."[13] Among the beliefs so retrieved is that of divine intervention in human affairs. For some traditionalists that belief drives political action as they identify divine interest with human leaders and movements, often tied to specific national identities. Nevertheless, belief in miracles can also draw religious communities together, as when Hindus, Muslims, and Christians meet at a common shrine of healing power.[14]

While the conflicts generated by religious beliefs play out in complex relations among nations created by global communications, economic exchange, and political negotiation, a primary provocation in contested arenas is the claim to divine intervention. God cannot be "on our side" and remain inactive in heaven. To believe in divine agency exercised in the course of history for the purpose of establishing one political order or another is to believe in miracles. If a deity acts to cure a patient's illness, then that same deity could presumably determine the outcome of an election or a revolution. Thus, testimonies to miraculous healing and claims of divine authorization of a political program are different species, so to speak, of the same genus, that is, belief in divine intervention. This connection is one reason why miracle claims are viewed as potent grounds of authority and so subject to regulation in all traditions by established political and religious institutions.

Official Regulation: Test of Miracle Claims in Roman Catholicism

Belief in miracles is not, as many skeptics assume, merely unthinking acceptance of fantastic stories as a way of escaping hard realities of existence. On the contrary, no religious tradition encourages sheer gullibility but rather tests and regulates claims to miraculous power; and every religious founder warns against basing faith on miracles alone. Miracles are interpreted events, signs of transcendent power that acquire meaning from the response of witnesses, readers, or listeners; they are not performed for their own sake alone. They point beyond themselves, serving a revelatory or pedagogical purpose. To discern that purpose requires critical reflection and prudent judgment, not blind faith. The authenticity of miracle claims is, then, always in question, even among the faithful. Nowhere is that religious doubt more clearly exercised than in the process of canonization in the Roman Catholic Church in which miracle claims on behalf of candidates for sainthood must withstand rigorous criticism.

Pope John Paul II died on April 2, 2005. On June 2, a young nun in France, who had suffered for years from premature onset of Parkinson's disease, suddenly found that she was free from debilitating tremors and able to resume her work of caring for newborns. The other sisters in her community, at the direction of her superior-general, had been praying to the departed pope on her behalf. According to the monsignor charged with verifying the miracle, "Exactly two months after the death of the pope from one minute to another, the nun didn't show the symptoms of the illness any more."[15] Her healing was dramatic and entire. One moment she was shaking violently, and the next her hands lay calmly in her lap ready to receive, with delicate control, an infant. She was released from the power of the same degenerative nerve disorder that enclosed and defeated the body of John Paul, freeing her to continue the same vocation of nurturing life that sustained his soul. Restored to her role as surrogate mother, the celibate nun could resume her faithful imitation of the supreme virgin mother, Mary, to whom John Paul was deeply devoted. Through simple acts of caring for children on earth, the nun sustains reverence for the mother who is in heaven. The parallels are striking, and could be seen to suggest that John Paul chose to heal this nun, so close to him in flesh and spirit, as his first exercise of miraculous power from heaven. Seen in this way, the event was a sign confirming what most Catholics already praise as John Paul's heroic virtue.

At the funeral of the pope, thousands of the faithful in Vatican Square raised the chant, "*Santo Subito*, Sainthood Now!" Most in the crowd knew, however, that their enthusiasm alone could not carry their beloved *Papa* immediately into perfect sanctity. Saints may be discovered on the ground among the people, but they are made by higher authorities through a process that requires critical scrutiny of their blessedness. In the Roman Catholic system that scrutiny is conducted by the Congregation for the Causes of Saints, and among the evidence examined are claims of miracles performed posthumously. According to an official explanation of the process, two miracles "of the first class are required in case the practice of virtues in the heroic degree has been proved."[16] While there is no question among millions of Catholics that John Paul II is both an exemplar of virtue and a miracle worker like Jesus Christ whom he represented, their popular enthusiasm on both counts is subject to official constraint.

The procedure for declaring someone a saint is designed to be so rigorous that no candidate can be presumed to pass its tests beforehand. Thus, since the decrees of Pope Urban VIII in 1640, Catholics have been forbidden public veneration of people under consideration.[17] Popular piety, however fervent, cannot presume to run ahead of the careful evaluation of the claims to virtue and power of local favorites by the established leaders of the Church Universal.

Constraining proliferation of local cults of the saints is an old strategy for maintaining central authority and the integrity of hierarchical leadership. Accordingly, John Paul II insisted that the authority to canonize resided solely in the papal office: "The results of the discussions of the Cardinals and Bishops are reported to the Supreme Pontiff, who alone has the right to declare that public cult [veneration] may be given by the Church to Servants of God."[18] The act of declaring someone a saint has far-reaching effects on the worship of the faithful: every new saint adds a feast day to the Church calendar; statues and other images are commissioned; another name may be addressed in petitionary prayers; and hagiographical literature is written to inspire believers with details of the new saint's life and examples of his or her intercessory efficacy. Because canonization obligates the entire church—especially under contemporary conditions of global communication where not only the faces of John Paul II and Mother Teresa are recognized worldwide but also images of local priests and religious are quickly posted on the World Wide Web by their admirers—it is an enterprise that must be undertaken by the head of the Church Universal.

Religious traditions, including Roman Catholicism, also generate within their own communities loyal opposition to claims of supererogatory merit and miraculous power. For that reason, the process of canonization not only allows for, but insists on, including expert consultants who can establish the "scientific value" of any miracle claim and "a board of medical experts in the Sacred Congregation whose responsibility is to examine healings which are proposed as miracles."[19] Further, bishops are instructed to include any witnesses who have credible objections to the candidate.[20]

The ongoing cause of sainthood for John Paul II demonstrates the dynamic tension between faith and doubt in the case of miracles. The position of religious authorities requires balancing competing interests: to identify with the confirmatory power and community prestige of miracles and, at the same time, to constrain and regulate popular claims to that power and prestige. In earlier times, the balance had been struck at different points. For example, the medieval veneration of relics of Christian saints to whom miracles are attributed is often interpreted as the product of superstitious popular piety; but the historian Peter Brown demonstrated that the "cult of the saints" arose with enthusiastic support from educated classes and religious authorities in the early Church. He wrote, "In western Europe, the power of the bishop tended to coalesce with the power of the shrine."[21] By embracing wonder-working saints, Church authorities both appropriated their power and limited their range of influence.

Faithful Dissent: Objections to Miracles for Religious Reasons

The third element in every tradition that comes into play when miracles are at issue is the call to abandon belief in miracles altogether. These are the voices of faithful dissenters, a type similar to those the American cultural analyst Michael Walzer calls "connected critics."[22] It may seem paradoxical to talk of faithful doubt, but we hear in many traditions voices of protest against, or at least caution about, belief in miracles on religious grounds. Neither dispassionate stranger nor estranged native, the connected critic re-reads the tradition in ways that exclude belief in or reliance on divine intervention. The first usually requires a metaphysical interpretation; the second, a moral argument. The connected critic is more likely to convince the community to change than an outsider, provided the dissent is firmly grounded in the bedrock values of their shared tradition. While a social reformer may appeal to universal human rights or principles of just war that transcend the particular interests of an offending society, and a few sensitive consciences may respond, a religious critic must speak the common language of his or her tradition and appeal to its specific authorities, whether sacred texts, exemplary figures, or ritual practices. As connected critics, faithful dissenters from belief in miracles face a formidable and thankless task—even though they can often cite the founders of their traditions for support.

Buddha forbade his disciples to perform miracles in public; Jesus refused to demonstrate miraculous power on occasion and pronounced blessing on those who believe without seeing; and Muhammad taught that the only sign of God humans require is the miracle of the Qur'an itself (each verse of which is 'ayat, "sign"). Faithful to these original restraints, later dissenters in each tradition argue that reliance on divine intervention distracts believers from responsibility to serve their neighbors or fulfill their social duty or act with compassion. Thich Nhat Hanh, founder of "engaged Buddhism," writes, "When we take refuge in Buddha, we must also understand 'The Buddha takes refuge in me.' Without the second part, the first is not complete."[23] Far from passively resting on the hope of supernatural assistance, one who takes refuge in Buddha accepts responsibility for becoming the incarnation of Buddha's compassion. Thich Nhat Hanh insists that a Buddhist extend the embodiment of Buddha for the sake of others. As we observed earlier, not all who object to miracles are irreligious.

Miracle as Transcendent Event: A Response to Hume

As we have seen, religious significance is determined by a complex response to a miracle made by individuals in the context of a believing community. Even those who claim the benefit of a miracle in their private experience have already interpreted the event for themselves by placing it under that verbal sign. What others may see as luck or coincidence the believer names *miracle*, thereby declaring faith in its meaning as a transcendent event requiring a transformative response. For example, a miracle may initiate a radically new sense of moral duty: because God healed me of a disease the doctors called incurable, I give all my goods to the poor. The practical response is the enacted interpretation of the cure as miraculous. By my donation I declare that my interpretation of the event as a miracle is not a private fantasy, but a public act. To acknowledge an event as having religious significance, then, is not a theoretical exercise but a practical commitment.

So, on that basis, can *any* event be called a miracle? Most believers do not regard every stroke of good luck as miraculous. One may thank God for having an evening meal or winning the lottery, but those events do not require transcendent power. The odds may be better that one will have a satisfying meal than that one will awake tomorrow millions of dollars richer; nevertheless, both events are routine in the sense that millions of people have enough to eat (while other millions do not) and someone wins a lottery every week. While devout people may acknowledge that every good thing they experience is a divine gift, they do not regard every benefit as a miracle.

To take a sensitive example, some folks gush over a birth as "the miracle of life," but there are reasons to be more reserved. Human procreation is a natural process that adds another helpless resident to the planet thousands of times a day. The profligacy of nature hardly seems, at the current level of global overcrowding, evidence of divine wisdom. On rare occasions an individual may be born whose coming into the world is of religious significance: Krishna descended to teach eternal wisdom in a dark age, Buddha enlightened to lead the deluded to wisdom and compassion, Christ incarnated to save humanity from sin and death, and Muhammad chosen to bear the words of divine guidance to a disordered world. These births are events interpreted as miracles, manifestations of transcendent power and goodness. But most of us enter the world in far less glorious fashion, in births that do not require transcendent power and in conditions that do not reflect divine benevolence. If most births do not count as miracles, can we specify more closely what does?

We begin by turning to *The Oxford English Dictionary*, in which *miracle* is defined as:

> A marvelous event occurring within human experience, which cannot have been brought about by human power or by the operation of any natural agency, and must therefore be ascribed to the special intervention of the Deity or of some supernatural being; chiefly, an act (e.g. of healing) exhibiting control over the laws of nature, and serving as evidence that the agent is either divine, or is specially favoured by God.

True to its conventional meaning in English, *miracle* is here defined in theistic terms, specifically as an act by an intelligent and purposive being that exerts "control over" the laws of nature assumed to be the rules of the customary operation of physical forces. The editors avoided the older phrase "violation of" laws of nature indicating supernatural intervention that "breaks the rules" in order to fulfill a divine purpose. The philosophical problem with calling a miracle a violation of a law is that it seems incoherent to say that a law has exceptions. For example, if gravity can be occasionally suspended, then is it really a *law* that bodies cannot float in air? Further, defining a miracle as a violation of law seems to beg the question whether a miracle is an illegitimate intrusion.

In his classic criticism of belief in miracles, the Scot philosopher and skeptic, David Hume (1711–1776), was not as judicious: "A miracle may be accurately defined, *a transgression of a law of nature by a particular volition of the Deity, or by the interposition of some invisible agent.*"[24] The background for Hume's understanding of miracles is the central premise of eighteenth-century science, inherited from Isaac Newton: that the world is composed of physical objects and forces that operate according to exception-less laws, either imposed on matter by a divine Creator or inherent within matter itself. Hume did not assume this premise was true a priori because then miracles would be impossible by definition (a violation of an exception-less law constitutes a logical contradiction) and further argumentation would be unnecessary.[25] But he did consider a miracle to be a disruption or subversion of the customary order of things that would require extraordinary testimony to establish as a fact. He used language of *transgression*, closely related to *violation* or forcible and unlawful assault on the integrity of another. For Hume, a miracle is an act of violence committed by God against the body of the world: the rape of Dame Nature by her capricious Maker. In his definition of *miracle* Hume registered a sense of outrage that a willful deity, by "a particular volition," could subvert the system of nature which Hume and his colleagues had just secured within their intellectual grasp. After all, if God could transgress the boundary between heaven and earth and interfere with the rationality of natural order, then where would science and philosophy be? What would become of their joint enterprise to master the secrets of physical forces and human actions?

By calling a miracle a transgression Hume was saying, in effect, that God had no lawful right to act in the world. The world belonged to human understanding, and any event that defied that understanding was a trespass into a forbidden region. As God once expelled humans from paradise, so Hume exiled God from the world. God can transcend, *pass beyond*, but God can not trespass, *cross over*. By means of his deceptively simple definition, Hume put those who accepted miracles in the position of advocating transgressive acts on the part of God. That is, after Hume, to defend the occurrence of miracles one had to defend the *violation* of nature, the significance of *irrationality*, and the value of *disruption*. Then as now, believers in miracles were cast at best as gullible, at worst as fanatical or deceptive.

This unfortunate characterization is the result of Hume's literal reading of miracle stories. He seems incapable of imagining a miracle claim that does not constitute a pious fraud because he assumes that all miracle stories must be either erroneous reports or outright lies. Hume explicitly limited his criticism to miracles that purport to confirm the truth of a religion. In those cases, he insisted, the probability an event was caused by supernatural agency will always be lower than the likelihood that the event has a naturalistic explanation, no matter how numerous or reputable the witnesses. Hume asked, "And what have we to oppose to such a cloud of witnesses, but the absolute impossibility or miraculous nature of the events, which they relate? And this surely, in the eyes of all reasonable people, will alone be regarded as a sufficient refutation."[26] In Hume's calculus, when proof of religious miracles from human testimony is "subtracted" from proof of laws of nature established by experience, "this subtraction, with regard to all popular religions, amounts to an entire annihilation; and therefore we may establish it as a maxim, that no human testimony can have such force as to prove a miracle, and make it a just foundation for any such system of religion."[27]

While Hume could not rule out miracles in advance, he did dismiss the testimony of believers as always fully accounted for by "natural principles of credulity and delusion." Hume's assessment of religious testimony as invariably the product of deception or gullibility may not be a priori, but it is prejudicial. He was certain that testimony to a miracle is always tainted: "As the violations of truth are more common in the testimony concerning religious miracles, than in that concerning any other matter of fact; this must diminish very much the authority of the former testimony, and make us form a general resolution, never to lend any attention to it, with whatever specious pretence it may be covered."[28]

Hume's distrust of religious motives was matched by his confidence in the reliable order of nature, and at times he wrote as if he believed that natural laws were apodictic prescriptions of the geometry of the universe. With the advent of quantum physics, however, we lost certainties of that sort. At the level of packets of energy in the nucleus of the atom we enter what the Christian writer C. S. Lewis called disapprovingly the arena of "lawless Subnature."[29] Here legal order has little authority; as on every frontier, there is wild insecurity and unpredictable creation. We now speak of "laws of nature" as statistical probabilities, descriptions of what is most likely to happen under given conditions. But if natural laws are descriptive rather than prescriptive, then a reversal of what would be most probable in a given set of circumstances may be highly unlikely but not impossible. It is a simple logical conclusion: statements of probability can never constitute necessary truths. If the universe is not governed in every detail by laws that inexorably regulate all events, then some events may be produced by the trespass of transcendent power. As Lewis failed to note, Hume recognized that problem and shifted his critique from defending the invariability of nature to attacking the integrity of religious witnesses.

Richard Swinburne, a Christian philosopher of religion, is willing to play Hume's game on Hume's terms. Swinburne defines a miracle as "an event of an extraordinary kind brought about by a god and of religious significance," but he is also willing to defend the more abbreviated definition: "a violation of a law of nature by a god." Swinburne specifies "a 'violation' of a law of nature as a 'nonrepeatable counterinstance' to it, *i.e.*, an exception that would not be repeated under similar circumstances,"[30] and so does not disrupt the general operation of natural law. Rather, Swinburne proposes, a miracle introduces a novel event into the system of nature the explanation of which is the personal will of God. As an example, take the case of healing from a terminal disease. A scientist might explain the physical processes that reversed course and turned from cellular destruction to restoration. But that account would not answer the question: why did this particular patient recover at this time? The medical category, spontaneous remission, is not an answer to that question. For religious believers, the answer requires reference to personal intention and agency. Moved by infinite love and mercy, God acted to heal this person. Thus, Swinburne concludes, the event has a personal, but not a scientific, explanation.

Swinburne's claim that personal agency constitutes a type of explanation is highly problematic, not least because it assumes the existence of the divine agent whose acts it is supposed to explain. We might better think of what he calls personal explanation as a form of interpretation. While Swinburne may object to making subjective response an integral feature of a miracle, the element of interpretation is inescapable. Inasmuch as Swinburne defines a miracle as having religious significance, it must be viewed as a highly interpreted event—a point he illustrates by viewing miracles as intentional acts of a personal deity, moved by love and justice. That description is more a confession of Swinburne's Christian faith than an explanatory hypothesis, but it is, to him and his fellow believers, a deeply meaningful interpretation of what they consider acts of divine intervention. The element of interpretation in understanding the meaning of miracles is often overlooked by critics like Hume and believers like Swinburne, but it is essential in identifying the transcendent. Let me demonstrate the point by an unusual example.

Example: Kant's Noumenal Freedom

Let us consider a modern example of human experience interpreted as transcendent: the sense of moral duty as analyzed by Immanuel Kant (1724–1804), the chief philosopher of the European Enlightenment. According to Kant, every event we experience is determined by universal and necessary laws of nature. But our moral decisions cannot be so determined if they are truly free. Therefore, the choices of moral agents represent genuinely new achievements of value. Good acts, then, spring from nothing but the agent's free will. The problem is that the origin of free moral decisions, whether for good or evil, remains for Kant a mystery because human freedom cannot be demonstrated in the world of material forces. In Kant's technical language, as material beings we are *phenomenal* (what appears to the senses), but as moral agents we are *noumenal* (what is known only by rational inference). We cannot see freedom, but we can postulate it as a "necessary belief of reason."

It is our noumenal freedom that bestows upon us our dignity as persons. Because we each possess autonomy, the capacity to legislate rules of behavior for ourselves, Kant argued, every person should be treated as "an end in himself" and not merely as a means to serve someone else's purpose. In Kant's account, what is often overlooked is that autonomy is an attribute of the human person that draws its power from beyond the natural world in which every effect is the necessary consequence of an antecedent cause. Inasmuch as the freedom of a moral agent cannot be accounted for by reference to empirical forces or immutable natural laws, it is a miracle. While Kant would be scandalized by that conclusion, his category of the noumenal designates a domain of reality that is separate from the world governed by natural laws. Further, by participation in the noumenal human beings realize their distinctive capacity to act apart from the determined order of the material world. In these ways the noumenal functions in a way remarkably similar to the transcendent in religious language. Thus, it is appropriate to say that a free moral decision, in Kant's reflection, is a transcendent event—and to the extent that he infers from freedom the postulates of immortality of the soul and the being of God as supreme moral judge, that transcendent event carries religious significance.[31]

Even though Kant acknowledged that human beings labor under "radical evil," making it practically impossible to form a morally good disposition, and he insisted that we must do our best to pursue moral duty while "hoping that in his goodness God will supplement our weakness,"[32] he refused to accept the necessity of divine grace. Rather, he listed grace among four ideas he identified as "abutting" on moral religion, but vulnerable to such distortions that belief in them is practically dangerous and, given their resistance to rational explanation, theoretically useless. The four are grace, miracles, mysteries, and sacraments. The sanction of grace, Kant charged, leads to fanaticism; and belief in miracles leads to superstition.

The irony is that, on Kant's own analysis, every virtuous act is a miracle—in the sense of an instance of novelty, of genuine creativity, in the natural world. That is the deep connection between morality and miracles: each requires a rupture in the tight grid of natural order. The free moral agent acts without compulsion; thus, every act of virtue is original, that is, has its origin in the individual will. In that sense every act of virtue is creative and constitutes an effect that cannot be accounted for entirely in terms of precedent causes. Kant is very clear that any act in accordance with moral duty that arises from inclination or self-interest or antecedent temporal conditions does not qualify as good. Virtue is entirely symmetrical with evil: both are radical, arising from unconditioned freedom birthed in the noumenal realm beyond the reach of empirical observation or speculative explanation. Every moral act is an anomaly in the order of nature.

After all, if one can explain *why* the Samaritan in Jesus's parable stopped to help the man who fell among thieves, then one has demonstrated the necessity of his good deed and thus evacuated it of virtue. Every natural explanation derives its persuasiveness from the evidence that the event could not have been otherwise. But there is no merit in doing what one must do, just as there is no blame in doing what one cannot help doing. That is why moral philosophers, even those without religious interests, object to the view that all our actions are the result of material causes. They insist that what one ought to do cannot be deduced from what is. To put the point in other terms, moral acts require transcendent origin as much as miraculous events.

Miracles disrupt order and that subversive effect is precisely their attraction, especially to those for whom "order" is too often a code word for limitation, even suppression. Popular enthusiasm for miracles does not distinguish neatly between natural and moral order. If my spirit can be transformed, in an ecstatic moment of conversion, so that my addictive desires are forever stilled, why can I not also expect my withered optic nerve to regenerate and my lost vision to be restored? Why should the disruption of engrained habit, enforced by physical craving and worn neural pathways, be any less miraculous or require any less power of transcendence than the sudden reversal of organic deterioration?

Either everything is entirely explicable by the operation of natural forces or much is not. If the autonomy of moral agents in Kant's sense is utterly free from empirical conditions, its origin is beyond natural explanation. Yet the good and evil acts of moral agents are observable events in the world of common experience. So they are effects whose causes are not natural. If unconditioned virtue and radical evil emerge from the noumenal, that which is not seen, then why not other manifestations of the supernatural? This question, systematically suppressed by the very thinkers whose arguments give rise to it, is the recurrent underground inquiry of the modern era that finds affirmative answers in continuing popular interest in miracles.

Of course, believers' claims to have witnessed miracles do not require anyone else to accept their formulations of their experience or to agree that their experience requires a transcendent reality for its explanation. But believers in miracles must adopt some interpretive schema in order for the miracle or vision to be intelligible and thus "experienceable." What cannot be made intelligible cannot serve as a sign, cannot carry meaning beyond itself, and such communication of religious significance is a primary element in our definition of miracle. For that reason a miracle must stand out from ordinary routine and yet remain familiar enough for us to recognize it as part of our experience. That recognition begins with the shock of wonder.

Miracles as Occasions of Wonder

We now come to the third main component of our definition of miracle. We have considered what it means to call a miracle an *event of transcendent power*, and we have seen the central role of interpretation—both theoretical and practical—in assigning the event *religious significance*. Now we turn to the peculiar sort of response miracles evoke: *wonder*. The purpose of a miracle, the Christian philosopher Søren Kierkegaard (1813–1855) wrote, is to gain attention, not to create faith.[33] A miracle is an event that startles us into considering an expanded view of reality; it does not by itself bring us to believe in, much less regulate our lives by, that reality. Because a miracle introduces a radically new element into our experience, our initial response is sheer wonder: a response embedded in the etymology of the term.

The word *miracle* originates in Middle English and enters our vocabulary via Old French from the Latin *miraculum* or "object of wonder," derived from the root *mirari* ("to wonder"). From this linguistic background we note that in ordinary usage the word *miracle* denotes an act or event, but it emerged from a matrix of meaning that connoted a human response to particular acts or events: a sense of wonder. Thus, what we use as if it were a verbal sign pointing to an objective state of affairs points instead, reflexively, to our own subjective impressions and responses. So the question arises, is a miracle made wondrous by the one who performs it or by those who declare the performance wonderful? The question is a variation on the old philosophical chestnut: if a tree falls in a deserted forest, does it make a sound? If a miracle occurs in an empty theater, is it a miracle? If sounds require an audience, do miracles require spectators? From what we have argued so far, spectators are not only required, they must also do more than observe. Witnesses to miracles must respond to what they see—or imagine through the proxy sight of reading—with wonder.

But what sort of response is "wonder"? The word *wonder* is a variation on the Old English noun *wundor*, based on the verb *wundrian* and related to Dutch *wonder* and German *Wunder*. Beyond that, the trail grows cold; we are informed the word is of unknown ultimate origin. Perhaps it is appropriate that a term indicating amazement at what defies understanding should itself be occluded, but no words are more in need of demystification than those that refer to mystery. In the New Testament, miraculous acts of Jesus are described as "powers and wonders and signs" (Acts 2:22), a description that combines the elements in our view of a miracle as an event of *transcendent power* that *arouses wonder* and *carries religious significance*. A miracle is an occasion for discovering something about oneself (as subject capable of wonder) and about the world (as object with unexpected possibilities).

Richard Davis points out that beneath the cluster of meanings associated with *miracle* in Western languages there lies a root term from Sanskrit, the classic language of India: "The word 'miracle' itself derives from terms of response: Greek *meidian*, 'to smile,' and Latin *miraculum*, 'to wonder.' Etymologically, these are related to the Sanskrit root *smi*, also meaning 'to smile,' from which derives one of the most common Indic terms for an astonishing, wondrous event, *vismaya*."[34] Other Sanskrit terms specify more precisely the nature of a wondrous event:

> Some Sanskrit approximations stress the unusual character (*alaukika*) of an event, some emphasize the response of wonder and astonishment (*adbhuta, ascarya, vismaya*) it evokes, and still others might be chosen to point to divine or non-human agencies (*daiva, apauruseya, amanyusya*) believed to cause the marvel . . .for ancient Indians as for modern Westerners, things that departed from the normal way of things (*alaukika*) as they defined it would create surprise and wonder.[35]

Davis concludes that miracles are social acts because they can be acknowledged as disruptions in natural order only if there is a company of witnesses who share a common understanding of what constitutes ordinary reality. Davis argues that a miracle requires an audience and that this feature of a miracle is cross-cultural. In this sense *miracle* is the same in different cultural worlds: it designates an event that evokes wonder.

The rationalist philosopher René Descartes (1596–1650) characterized wonder as "a sudden surprise of the soul which brings it to consider with attention the objects that seem to it unusual and extraordinary."[36] Descartes laid out the etiology of wonder as a linear process: the object impresses the brain as unusual, the brain transmits that impression to the spirits, and they in turn flow back into the brain and pass into the muscles in a way that preserves the original impression. But here the line curves back and the circle is closed; the object evokes the passion, and the passion sustains surprise at the object.

The question raised by this circuitry of reflection is whether wonder is evoked by a quality of the object or by a disposition of the subject to wonder at unusual events rather than, say, investigate or analyze them. One person's miracle is, after all, another's coincidence or illusion. Regardless of one's interpretation of an alleged miracle, however, believer and skeptic share a common initial relation to a surprising event: the shock of anomaly. That is what Descartes calls "wonder" and which he distinguishes from other passions by its amoral character: "it has as its object not good or evil, but only knowledge of the thing that we wonder at" (II.71). Wonder is a "primitive passion" because it precedes moral interest in the object, and scientific curiosity about it as well. For Descartes to call wonder "primitive" means that in a state of wonder we are unaware of what benefit, if any, the object might yield us, or what knowledge of it we might gain. Wonder is sheer surprise at an object that is unusual and extraordinary. Like an unexpected blow, the wondrous is striking. But unlike a blow, it is without moral inflection.

This point is of considerable importance to our use of the term *wonder* in defining miracle. The response of wonder is more primitive, to use Descartes' term, than worship or admiration because those responses carry strong moral overtones and thus are already shaped by values attributed to the object rather than intrinsic to it. The etymology of *worship*, for example, suggests that its object is worthy and what we admire elicits our sense of its superior value. Wonder, however, is closer to what the Protestant theologian, Rudolf Otto (1869–1937), in his classic work *The Idea of the Holy*, called awe or dread: the ambivalent, amoral, and arational response to the *mysterium tremendum* (tremor-inducing mystery) that he argued is the source of all religious experience. Considerations of good and evil do not arise in response to the uncanny.

There is much in Otto's account that is vulnerable to criticism; but he was right to see that religious communities develop ethical categories to interpret a more primitive passion, just as we associate various forms of music with specific emotions, such as erotic desire, martial fervor, and lament. The auditory vibrations mean nothing in themselves, but their interpretation along a range of significance is remarkably consistent as a specific cultural pattern. Because the initial perception of a novel event or object carries no intrinsic meaning, Descartes insisted that wonder is without rational content and consists of "only knowledge of the thing that we wonder at." By wonder we grasp *that* the object is, but nothing about *what* the object is.[37] If wonder is aroused before observers determine whether the event brings them weal or woe, many miracles are simply shocking, causing the witnesses as much distress as comfort. It is for good reason that angels are often said to introduce themselves with the words, "Do not fear." That assurance is the beginning of the move from wonder to interpretation.

The utility of wonder, then, lies in its power to attract us to new objects of knowledge, simply because they are new to our experience. Without the promiscuous interest of wonder, we would remain ignorant of everything that did not directly serve our interests. Even more lamentably, we would be unable to entertain radically new events or objects—the way some people rejected reports of men walking on the moon because they had no way of understanding that possibility in their view of the world.

For all of Descartes' praise of wonder, however, he was quick to add that we should avoid "excessive wonder" lest it "entirely prevent or pervert the use of reason." For Descartes, wonder is good inasmuch as it arouses attention in the object, but bad to the extent it blocks rational investigation of the object. The problem of indulging in the habit of excessive wonder is that one loses the ability to discriminate between the trivially novel ("no two snowflakes have exactly the same crystalline structure") and the rarity that signals an important departure from our routine state of affairs ("men walking on the moon").

In sum, without wonder we move dully through a world of repetitive sameness, a wholly predictable round of events powerless to evoke the "surprise of the soul." On the other hand, with too much wonder we go through life agape at every object or event as if it were worth our full attention and intellectual respect. As a rationalist, Descartes was skeptical of miracle claims; but believers in miracles are also wary of excessive wonder and its power to overwhelm critical faculties of the mind. In religious traditions where belief in miracles is strong, there are also many methods of testing and questioning claims to them and many cautions against gullibility. In the case of a miracle, wonder serves to provoke interpretation, leading to assigning religious significance to the event.

If wonder at unusual events is a universal feature of human perception, it may explain why, in one recent definition of *miracle* we read, "Belief in miraculous happenings occurs in all cultures and is a feature of practically all religions."[38] Why? At the very least because people everywhere are attracted to the unusual and, under the influence of sheer wonder, tend to interpret what does not belong to the usual order of things as having a source in another order of reality. As Davis shows in the Hindu context, for example, there are many worlds in operation at the same time, "each adhering to different standards of normalcy." Thus, he writes, "What might seem wondrous to humans in their world could be perfectly expectable in the divine worlds of Indra or Brahman. Traffic between worlds, too, was relatively common, if we judge by classical Indian texts."[39] While Davis regards the cosmology of multiple worlds as a point of contrast between Indians and Westerners, believers in miracles in many cultural locations are committed to at least two worlds: the one of ordinary experience and the one of transcendent power that impinges upon ordinary order. Miracles occur when there is "traffic between worlds."

The greater range of vocabulary for describing this traffic in India, and the greater number of worlds which can meet in cosmic exchanges, requires the expansion of the meaning of *miracle* beyond its use in Western monotheisms to indicate an act of God. In Indian imagination a wondrous event may result from the initiative of a deity or from the power of a yogi, but in neither case is the event a violation of nature. The Western dualism between Creator and creation requires miracles to disturb or suspend the natural system, but in some Hindu and Buddhist cosmologies wondrous events are rather manifestations of one world, with its own laws of operation, in another. Perhaps all that is common across these cultural sites is the wonder with which such events are initially entertained.

Miracle as Category of Cross-Cultural Comparison

This observation will guide our use of *miracle* as a category of cross-cultural comparison. What people seem to mean when they designate an event a miracle is, at the least, that it evokes wonder. But we also observe that people add to that initial perception interpretations based on their understanding of the religious significance of the event. My argument is that the process of forming the judgment that an event qualifies as a miracle is similar across religious traditions. Wonder is the primary response that identifies an unusual event as transcendent and leads to interpreting the event as having religious significance. As we proceed along this line of perception and interpretation, we also move from a common human response to increasingly more specific designations of the event in the distinctive terms of a given religious community or tradition. For example, almost anyone would look twice at a person hovering unsupported in the air, but a Hindu might interpret the event in the vocabulary of yogic powers, while a Muslim might employ the terms of demonic possession and a Christian use the categories of saintly virtues. Thus, we employ our definition of miracle as a category of cross-cultural comparison with the important proviso that the wondering response to miraculous events may be universal, but the meaning assigned to them is shaped by the broader view of reality in the religious tradition in which they occur. This reservation constitutes what the influential scholar of comparative religion, Jonathan Z. Smith, calls a "rectification" of the comparative category.

In his recent collection of essays, *Relating Religion*, Smith recommends a method of comparison based on historicized morphology.[40] Smith's preference for morphology over phenomenology is grounded in the belief that there is a shared shape of things that makes comparative understanding possible. The formulation of that shared shape is not inherent in the data as such, but is a scholarly creation in the interest of some theory. While Smith insists that every religious phenomenon must be investigated with meticulous attention to its cultural and historical particularities, comparison of disparate phenomena is an inescapable component of human cognition. The trick is to keep in mind that comparisons are artificial, invented by scholars in order to illumine differences—in light of which hitherto overlooked similarities may be seen. He makes the point in one sentence: "Relations are discovered and reconstituted through projects of differentiation."[41] Finally, comparing religious phenomena requires *rectification* or correction of the academic category initially employed in identifying the examples as comparable (in our case, the definition of *miracle* by which we will recognize examples in different traditions). The study of miracles across traditions is an appropriate test case for Smith's method because events that are the same in appearance are assigned widely different meanings. That is precisely the condition that calls for rectification of the category to insure it does not obscure or distort distinctive features of the examples under comparison. We will seek to trace the shared shape of miracles across traditions by attending to the common process by which people identify and interpret events as exhibiting transcendent power.

Miracles as Responses to Universal Human Needs

There is another feature to the shared shape of miracles across traditions, not indicated in our definition, that we must also acknowledge: hope for miracles and the stories that nourish that hope are grounded in universal human needs and sustained by primary human aspirations. Miracle stories that appear in different cultural contexts consistently reflect concerns about illness, death, birth, and food.[42] Mahatma Gandhi famously remarked, "The only form in which God can appear to a starving man is as a loaf of bread." So Jesus said to the famished crowd he supplied with nourishment out of thin air, "I am the bread of life." Feeding miracles recur in religious texts because holy figures satisfy body and spirit. But the fundamental threat, of which hunger is the mere portent, is death. It is the universal anxiety that marks and haunts us as human, and against its inexorable necessity religious traditions tell and retell stories of levitation and resuscitation. Saints and sages float above the earth, free from the dust to which all lesser beings return. Saviors and gods, crucified, flayed, burned, and buried, arise from the dead and bring the promise of eternal life. Resurrection is not a possibility within the set order of things, of course, but stories of miraculous victory over death are expressions of a nearly universal hope that the order of things is not as set as it seems.

As the greatest unknown in human experience—what we cannot know, confined as we are to our narrow lanes in the linear dash through time and space—the future also requires supernatural light for its illumination. Here the miraculous figures in two ways: divine revelation of future events and divine intervention to bring about those events. Thus, both prophecy and apocalypse are miraculous events. Insofar as stories of miracles are told in relation to human hopes about illness, death, birth, food, and the future, they represent nearly universal responses to common human anxieties. But does that observation enforce the impression that belief in miracles is a naïve wish to have our basic needs met by power more reliable than our own, an escapist delusion that relieves us of the responsibility to care for ourselves?

Miracles and Reflective Faith

Objections to belief in miracles often echo the hope of the founder of psychoanalysis, Sigmund Freud (1856–1939), on the concluding page of *Future of an Illusion*, that once humanity receives a proper "education to reality" religion will be understood as the nursery rhyme it is and we will leave heaven to angels and sparrows. But the charge that believers expect divine intervention to release them from their duty to work for the improvement of the world is exaggerated. For most religious people, belief in miracles is not so much a deterrent to responsible action as it is the necessary, if not sufficient, condition of acting in the first place. After all, why should I be motivated to sacrifice self-interest in pursuit of ideals if the course of events, natural and historical, is immutably bound by principles in place since the birth of the universe? If genuine novelty is impossible, if there is no other order of reality capable of impinging upon this world, if in fact there is "nothing new under the sun" and all return to the dust together, then I may perceive all labor to realize new value as futile. Believers in miracles believe, on the contrary, that certain events in our common world signify human possibilities and divine powers that lie beyond the limits of ordinary reality. That belief need not be confirmed under ordinary conditions (indeed, how could it be?), yet it is central to their religious faith.

The American Presbyterian theologian William Adams Brown (1865–1943) once characterized a miracle as "a strange fact with a divine meaning—a luminous surprise."[43] The surprise of a novel event becomes luminous through interpretation. These two responses are dialectically related: wonder responds to absolute difference, while understanding requires comparative similarities.[44] Moving from one to the other is not a linear process, but both point to distinctively human characteristics. We are capable of surprise, but we remain unfulfilled by sheer novelty. For Brown it was a mark of progress when humans moved from receiving unusual events as wonders to understanding them as signs. At that point miracles become revelatory, not only of divine reality but also of human capacity. "In miracle man is conscious of some new accession of vitality and power. It is not simply that his questions have been answered, but that his resources have been enlarged." That is, to designate an event a miracle is not merely to engage in a naming exercise, it is to participate in the creative power that produced the event and to find one's own life enriched as a result. This is another way of expressing what we earlier called the performative effect of a miracle story, evoking in readers or listeners a lived response that draws them into the narrative world of the story.

We pause at this point to note important differences between telling/hearing a miracle story and performing/observing an act of magic. There is the usual self-serving distinction drawn within religious traditions: magic is the result of human deception or demonic influence, while miracles are caused by divine agency. For example, the magicians in Pharaoh's court who duplicated Moses' miracle of turning a staff into a serpent are denounced in Jewish tradition as opponents of divine purpose. In a reversal of judgment, the New Testament account of the Acts of the Apostles records that "God did extraordinary miracles through Paul," including the defeat of seven Jewish exorcists by a demon who acknowledged only Paul's authority. As a result, "a number of those who practiced magic collected their books and burned them publicly" (Acts 19:19). From a less apologetic perspective, we may say that miracles and acts of magic both evoke wonder; but entering the narrative world of a miracle carries the potential of permanently transforming the hearer's life. While an act of magic is puzzling, it is not necessarily life-transforming. The difference is that those who witness or read about a miraculous event attribute a meaning to it that they are willing to enact in their subsequent lives.

Further, there are techniques by which magicians create their illusions: incantations, potions, gestures, and objects endued with wondrous power. Miracles, by contrast, often occur without ritual means by a spontaneity that signals to believers their impetus from transcendent, not mundane, intention. Finally, if magicians are accomplished at their craft, they produce the same results from the same techniques. If not, they are judged to have failed at some point in their performance. Consistent efficacy is the test of a magician. Miracle workers, on the other hand, typically do not presume to control the manifestation of transcendent power.

Reflecting strong Jewish condemnation of sorcery and divination, early Christian thinkers drew what the historian Michael Bailey calls "the essential and stark Christian distinction between divine and demonic power" that shaped subsequent negative European perceptions of magic. Eventually, even those techniques designed to draw from the influence of astral bodies on earthly events—so-called natural magic—fell into disrepute under the double rejection of scientific investigation and theological judgment.[45] In the Islamic world as well, magicians were associated with spirits (jiin) who could lead humans astray.[46] In all three traditions, the term magic serves the polemical purpose of designating powers and rituals that are foreign to one's own deity and religious ceremonies.

In Hinduism and theistic forms of Buddhism, on the other hand, the semantic distinction between miracle and magic (both terms of Latin origin) is not linguistically available and the theological assumptions that support the distinction are not present. For example, Hindus affirm that everything appearing to us as real is the result of māyā (illusion) and, in that sense, our entire lives are lived under the spell of magic. According to the popular Hindu scripture called Bhagavad-Gītā, that condition can be good for those who take refuge in Krishna's "divine magic," but for those who fail to do so "their knowledge is ruined by magic, they fall prey to demonic power."[47] Divine and demonic agents both exercise transcendent power in creating wondrous acts that are most often called vismaya, the sight of illusion. When performed by supernatural agency, such events may be termed miracles or magic acts; the critical question is whether they contribute to the spiritual liberation of those who witness, hear, or read about them—or become further snares attaching one to this world.

Given the wide differences between the meaning and range of terms for wondrous events in religious traditions, let us be content at this point to observe that in the ordinary parlance of English speakers magic belongs to the powers of this world, while miracles are signs of transcendent reality. Yet the distinction becomes less bright in the modern turn of the miraculous from supernatural intervention in nature to transformation of human motivation.

William Adams Brown claimed that the form of creative energy that awakens wonder and calls for meaning shifts as human consciousness develops. "When life is simple and needs largely physical, miracle is sought and is found without—in the rain that saves the harvest, in the pestilence that destroys the enemy, in healing for the body, or water smitten from the rock; but where the conscience awakes and man . . . realizes that his worst foe and his most formidable dangers are within, the centre of interest shifts from the body to the soul."[48] We find similar judgments in other religious traditions: that the shift from outer to inner concerns, from power over the material world to mastery of spiritual reality, is a sign of religious maturity.[49]

Miracles of the sort that most attract popular attention—levitation, translocation, clairvoyance, and healing—are often proscribed by religious authorities and devalued by the very ascetics, mystics, and spiritual masters best qualified to perform them. Despite cautions from the highest authorities, however, ordinary believers flock to shrines, temples, mosques, and churches in search of wonders. For them the meaning of miracles consists primarily in their signifying possibilities of achievements of new value in a degenerate world, of freedom from the pitiless necessities of closed systems, natural or political or personal. Whether the breakthrough comes in immediate and unprecedented release from disease, imprisonment, addiction, or despair, it is a sign of ultimate freedom: a promise of access to divine power.

If there is a transcendent realm of being, a claim at the heart of most religious traditions, and if humans are able to know or participate in that realm, then miracles seem not only possible but also necessary as signs of that being. For Brown, the final psychological ground for belief in miracles was the desire for certainty about the reality of God, a confidence that requires for its greatest assurance confirmation in public form. "It is not only in the closet that man has met God face to face," he wrote, "but on the wider stage of nature and of history." Despite philosophical, scientific, and historical objections, religious belief in miracles remains strong both in the closet of inner transformation and on the stage of public display.

Inner and Outer Miracles

Miracles come in many forms: preternatural powers, such as levitation, control of weather, freedom from limits of time and space, transformations of nature, insight into the minds of others; healings of body and mind; visions of divine beings or of future events; and knowledge of reality beyond finite consciousness. As miracles occur in different ways, so believers testify to their presence in different domains of experience. Some may feel directly in their bodies a miraculous healing. Others may see with their own eyes a person rise from the dead or storms dissipate at the wave of a saint's hand. Still others may be filled with spontaneous joy or a sense of unconditional forgiveness or compassion embracing all creatures or inexplicable tranquility of soul in the midst of suffering or mourning. Believers interpret such states of enhanced awareness as gifts from beyond their own emotional and psychic resources. Whether experienced as deliverance from overpowering addiction when one has "hit bottom" or as release from paralyzing depression or as the centering of scattered thoughts and energies in a creative focus, these are some instances of what religious believers call miracles.

But there is another type of experience that we must also consider. Some believers claim to receive knowledge that surpasses the limits of human understanding through revelation. For Siddhartha Gautama, sitting in determined meditation, the clear realization of his true being transformed his consciousness. No longer deluded by ordinary human awareness, he became the "enlightened one," Buddha. The miracle in this case was not the result of supernatural agency, but of Siddhartha's discovery of reality beyond the world in which all suffer and die. On very different premises, St. Paul claimed to receive transcendent knowledge through revelation. He insisted that his gospel was "not of human origin; for I did not receive it from a human source, nor was I taught it, but I received it through a revelation of Jesus Christ" (Galatians 1:11b–12). That is, the insight he was given into the significance of Christ's death and resurrection did not come from other disciples, nor was the truth drawn from his own reason. The mystery he proclaimed had been "hidden for ages in God who created all things," and who now chose to reveal secrets kept since "the foundation of the world" to his chosen apostle (Ephesians 1:4). In both cases the miracle consisted of an event of disclosure, private apprehension of transcendent reality that inspired public teaching and proclamation.

Interestingly, Paul testified that his own prayer for a miracle of healing was denied, three times, until he finally gave up—content that the inner miracle of enlightenment was of higher value than the outer miracle of physical healing. On that principle, religious leaders often seek to confine popular enthusiasm for miracles to higher spiritual aspirations. For example, one Sufi saint declared, "It is better to restore one dead heart to eternal life than to restore to life a thousand dead bodies."[50] Perhaps, but the thousand mourners at the side of those dead bodies might well disagree. For them the miracle of receiving lost loved ones into their arms again in this world would be a far greater display of transcendent power and goodness, a more wondrous benefit, than the unseen transformation of an insensitive soul. Charles Dickens portrayed the melting of the miserly heart of Ebenezer Scrooge as a Christmas "miracle," but any parent knows that the healing of Tiny Tim is the true wonder of the story. When a miracle transpires in the secrecy of private experience, it loses its power to bestow wider meaning. It is no longer a social act that carries religious significance beyond the individual. Thus, despite cautions by officials and skepticism by critics, people of faith continue to believe in miracles as public displays and not merely personal benefits—even if most believers never see a miracle themselves.

Belief without Expectation

There is no more persistent feature of religious life than unanswered prayers for miracles. Believers across traditions pray for healing of their bodies and cures of loved ones, for rain on their fields and food on their tables, for knowledge of future events and visions of enduring reality beyond this world. In short, they pray for freedom from the constraints of limited existence within a fated natural order. They pray, however, with a history of death, starvation, and unforeseen disaster behind them. They pray, furthermore, with the paradox of confidence that a miracle *could* occur and reluctance to affirm that a miracle *must* occur. They pray for the best, they say, and prepare for the worst. They do not pray out of desperation for to be desperate, as the Latin root of the word indicates, is to be without hope, and they offer their prayers with courageous hope. But that hope is held in spite of the background knowledge that almost all prayers for miracles go unanswered.[51] In the nature of things, it could not be otherwise.

A miracle cannot be necessary because there is no system of causation, physical or moral, that could guarantee a miracle. Here is where religious traditions often draw another line between magic and miracle. A believer kneeling in prayer or bowing in worship is not performing a magic trick, but registering a need that cannot be met by any exercise of natural powers and awaiting a deliverance that cannot be scheduled or demanded. An attitude common among devotees of Krishna, disciples of Jesus, and servants of Allah is to leave the outcome to divine will. Similarly, some Buddhists and Hindus, who seek no relation with personal deities, do not regard ascetic denial or prolonged meditation as leading *necessarily* to spiritual liberation. In fact, ascetics in all traditions are famously scornful of those who offer shortcuts, let alone guaranteed programs, to enlightenment or holiness.

In whatever form a miracle is sought, there cannot be a direct relation between the way of seeking and certainty of attaining the end. Believers in miracles seem clearly to understand this discontinuity and are not unduly discouraged by it. Most pilgrims to Lourdes, including popes, return home with their medical conditions none the better. Most daily bathers in the sacred Ganges proceed on their way with prayers for health or fortune unanswered. Yet the lack of supernatural response neither precipitates a crisis of faith nor prevents a return trip. It appears that only skeptics consider such experiences as disconfirming faith. For believers, the rarity of miracles is essential to their capacity to evoke gasps of wonder and prayers of thanks.

Still, one might persist, how is it possible to sustain belief without expectation? If not the anticipation of personal benefit, provided at the moment of acute need, what other values could miracles realize? Why do people rush to sites of apparitions of the Virgin Mary or to milk-drinking statues of the Hindu god Ganesha, to witness what they believe is a divine intervention that offers them no immediate personal reward? Conventional answers play on public gullibility, political and economic interests, official deceit and manipulation—and it cannot be denied that these factors play a role. In fact, the frequency with which ordinary believers are duped by religious charlatans, whether priests, rabbis, or gurus, is great enough that all traditions develop safeguards against them, from official control to cautionary tales in oral culture.

But most believers in miracles are not fools; they are simply playing the odds. By its nature as an event of transcendent power, a miracle cannot be predicted or compelled by anything in the world, including human agency or need. Thus, one could never count on a miracle occurring, just as one cannot count on drawing the winning numbers in a lottery. Yet uncertainty about actually pulling the winning combination does not cancel the possibility of winning, assuming the lottery is not rigged. Similarly, one can believe that miracles happen, without assuming that the specific miracle one desires will occur. For example, even if it is possible that your heart disease will be miraculously healed, it is improbable. Therefore, you would be wise to seek the best medical treatment you can find. Praying for miracles does not guarantee their occurrence, and faith endures disappointment—still the believer hopes for that unexpected breakthrough that signals an event of transcendent power, wondrous in its startling newness and rich with meaning for the rest of one's life.

Talk about miracles across the five traditions we will consider in this book expresses a common desire for freedom from the merciless confines of time and space, from the inevitability of age and death, from the limits of body and mind. Perhaps at the most basic level, belief in miracles is the expression of our refusal to accept existence in a closed system of material forces and our hope that the future may be radically different from the past. Religious or not, I believe, we all desire the rare and striking wonder that will open our lives to new possibilities. Is that not, after all, a large part of what it means to be human?

Hinduism

Signs of Spiritual Liberation

Among the most widely read Hindu sacred texts is the *Mahābhārata*, an epic about a divided family and its tangled tragic history. Brought to the point of war, the righteous Pandava brothers confronted their evil cousins on the plain of Kurukshetra, near modern Delhi. Just before they launched into battle, the leader of the Pandavas, the renowned champion Arjuna, paused, reluctant to fight because those on the other side were members of his family. He wondered how he could fulfill his caste duty as a warrior without neglecting his duty to protect his family. Bewildered, Arjuna dropped his bow, deciding that it was better to be killed than to kill. At that decisive moment his charioteer, who was the god Krishna in human disguise, took the occasion to instruct Arjuna about the nature of duty in a world created by divine play—teaching that was fully effective only when Krishna provided his student with a vision inaccessible to human perception: a miracle of revelation.

According to the *Mahābhārata*, Krishna held undetected in his human form infinite powers as the source and end of all beings. Krishna's claim that "whatever is powerful, lucid, splendid, or invulnerable has its source in a fragment of my brilliance"[1] led Arjuna to a fateful request: "Just as you have described yourself, I wish to see your form in all its majesty . . . If you think I can see it, reveal to me your immutable self, Krishna, Lord of Discipline" (11.3–4). Arjuna asked for a direct vision of the divine, but Krishna explained that unobstructed sight of transcendent reality is impossible for the human eye; therefore, Krishna must provide not only the content of the vision, but also the condition for Arjuna to behold it: "I will give you a divine eye to see the majesty of my discipline" (11:8). Then Krishna revealed the entire universe in his body in a display that was magnificent and terrifying. Arjuna was astounded by what he saw as Krishna's "awesome, terrible form."

Seeing the many mouths and eyes of your great form,
its many arms, thighs, feet, bellies, and fangs,
the worlds tremble and so do I . . .
You lick at the worlds around you, devouring them with flaming
    mouths . . .
Tell me—who are you in this terrible form?
Homage to you, Best of Gods! Be gracious! (11.23, 25, 30–31)

"I am thrilled," Arjuna went on to exclaim, "and yet my mind trembles with fear at seeing what has not been seen before" (11.45). Arjuna's mixed reaction of fascination and terror was the stupefied recognition of what utterly surpasses human knowledge and being. Arjuna's blank wonder at the vision gave him no comfort because it revealed not only Krishna's eternality but also his own mortality: "Seeing the fangs protruding from your mouths like the fires of time, I lose my bearings and I find no refuge" (11.25).

For Arjuna to see the immortal divine reality—"you are eternity, being, nonbeing, and beyond"—was at the same time to be seen, in reflective self-knowledge, as a fragile and momentary being. Krishna revealed what is beyond even the distinction between existence and non-existence: what endures when everything returns to the primal source. With this insight Arjuna was released from the anxiety of killing others for they were no more permanent than he. Thus, Krishna urged him to battle in these words: "even without you, all these warriors arrayed in hostile ranks will cease to exist. Therefore, arise and win glory! Conquer your foes, and fulfill your kingship! They are already killed by me. Be just my instrument, the archer at my side!" (11:32–33).

The context for Krishna's wondrous display was an extended conversation, interrupting the furious action of the *Mahābhārata*, known as the *Bhagavad-Gītā* (*Song of God*). In this text Krishna urged Arjuna to fulfill his sacred duty in battle, while remaining "impartial to . . . victory and defeat" (2.38). Only by remaining unattached to the effects of his actions could Arjuna "escape the bondage of action" (2.39), that is, the weight of *karma* (cosmic law of cause and effect) that requires each deed to be punished or rewarded in a future rebirth. By giving up all interest in the outcome of actions, Krishna promised Arjuna he could be free from "the terrible wheel of rebirth and death" and reach the goal of spiritual quest: "a place beyond decay" (2.51).

That "place," the abode of Brahman (Supreme Reality), Krishna already occupies. Krishna claims to be the supreme manifestation of Brahman and thus the only worthy object of human devotion. Those who worship other gods will be rewarded with rebirth in the realm of the gods, but those who focus their minds on Krishna will receive liberation when "they know me at the time of death" (7.30). Those who devote themselves to Krishna are not reborn into the world of change, but "attain absolute perfection." At death one who takes the path to direct union with Brahman "ascends to the place of pure beginning" (8.28). The end of spiritual quest is to return to the eternal primordial source from which all beings are derived.

We see in this event of supernatural disclosure the primary purpose of miracle stories in Hindu tradition: wondrous acts are performed for the purpose of bringing spiritual liberation to those who witness or read about them. Whether the miracle is divine revelation, immediate healing, or triumphant levitation, it demonstrates the possibility of freedom from the limits of the material world and from the spiritual burden of the past. The specific moral lessons miracle stories impart may differ, but their common goal is to demonstrate the way to final release from this world, not only for the characters in the story but also for any readers. As we have seen, miracle narratives invite their readers to enter imaginatively into the worlds they create and thus reenact miraculous transformations in their own lives, freeing them even from the burden of karmic debt. Miracles in Hindu tradition are peculiar in this respect: even when supernatural power is employed against demons, the miraculous display results in spiritual liberation for the demonic being. Whether produced by divine manifestations (*avatars*) like Krishna or by humans through discipline and meditation (*yogis*) or devotion (*saints*) or learning (*gurus*), Hindu miracles break the bonds of this illusory world and open the way to ultimate freedom.

Avatar: Miracles of Krishna as Child and Lover

In Hindu theology the supreme reality, Brahman, has two forms: as the unseen origin of all beings and as the manifested powers of creation (Brahmā), preservation (Vishnu), and destruction (Shiva). In its nonmanifest form Brahman is without attributes; therefore, it is impersonal and unknowable. As the inexhaustible source of being, Brahman is unchanging and inactive as pure potentiality. Brahman exerts no providence and entertains no purposes for the cosmos. To attain the state of nonmanifest Brahman, deathless and free from rebirth, is the goal of yogic practice and of meditation in the non-dualist (*advaita*) school of Hinduism that teaches that Supreme Reality is one and that Brahman is the only enduring reality; all other beings are temporary manifestations of it. While that rigorous and cerebral route to liberation attracts many, most ordinary Hindus seek Brahman through one of its revealed forms as a personal deity.

In Hindu myths of creation, Brahmā, Vishnu, and Shiva represent powers required to compose and maintain any universe. What is created must eventually age and disappear to make way for what is new: birth without death would result in cosmic overload, just as death without birth would leave the world barren, inevitably sinking into the torpor of entropy—and without the grace of extended life there could be no growth or achievement. Thus, preservation of beings for different lengths of time and with varied capacities for creative advance is also necessary for the composition of any world worth making. In devotional practice, however, Vishnu and Shiva attract the most enthusiastic devotees who attribute to their chosen deity all the cosmic powers. Many Hindus focus their worship on one of the many forms Vishnu and Shiva graciously assume in the world. Among the most popular of these appearances, known as avatars, is Krishna.

The Sanskrit term *avatāra* has the root meaning "to descend or cross downwards." The avatar is a divine descent into the world, usually at a time of moral and spiritual decline, in order to combat evil and establish virtue. Krishna fulfilled that redemptive vocation by performing wondrous deeds, the most celebrated of which were those he performed as child and lover, as recorded in Book Ten of the *Bhāgavata Purāna*. Edwin Bryant, who translated the Sanskrit text into English, explains, "The word *purāna*, in Sanskrit, signifies 'that which took place previously,' namely ancient lore or legend."[2]

The *Bhagavata Purāna* opens at a gathering of sages to perform a sacrifice in recognition of the onset of the present evil age, called *kali yuga*, which commenced after the great battle recounted in the *Mahābhārata* and following Krishna's death and ascent from the earth. The sages invited Sūta, a skilled storyteller, to relate tales of Krishna's exploits which he in turn had heard from Śuka, an earlier storyteller, who had recounted them to King Parīksit. The king had survived the battle of Kurukshetra, but was cursed to die a week later. He abandoned his throne, withdrew to the bank of a river, and called upon Śuka to answer his questions about how best to prepare for death. Śuka responded by reciting stories about Krishna as the Supreme Lord. Sūta then recounted their dialogue in the later context of the ritual sacrifice. As in the case of the *Bhagavad-Gītā*, this text is a conversation within a larger narrative. By the setting alone we conclude that stories of Krishna's supernatural feats carry meaning for those facing the brutal limits of natural existence and provide insights into how to face death in an unjust world. For King Parīksit they were "the remedy for the material predicament" (1.4). For Sūta, "These narrations can destroy the sins of the age of *kali*" (1.14). How? What meaning do these stories of heroic wonders convey?

Krishna descended into the world at a time of trouble for the Yadu clan. Despite their devotion to the supreme lord of the universe, they suffered under the oppressive rule of a brutal king named Kamsa. Driven by jealous fear that a rival might arise from the family of Vasudeva, leader of the Yadus, Kamsa imprisoned Vasudeva and his wife Devakī, who was also the king's sister, and murdered each of six sons born to them. In that desperate situation Vishnu entered the mind of Vasudeva and empowered him to "deposit" Krishna in the womb of Devakī by "mental transmission" (2.18). The conception of Krishna was a supernatural act by which Vishnu was manifested in human form. The divine person in her womb caused Devakī to radiate with a glow that the ever-watchful king recognized as a threat to his power. Killing his pregnant sister in order to protect his throne, however, was too repugnant an act of cruelty, with such fearful karmic consequences, that Kamsa bided his time, awaiting the birth.

On the day Krishna took human form there were auspicious signs everywhere. Rivers ran with water clear as crystal, birds sang in harmony, and a pleasant breeze refreshed the entire land. The Brahmans' sacrificial fires burned brightly and "the minds of the ascetics and the gods were peaceful." At midnight, with stars filling the sky, Krishna emerged from the womb of Devakī, "his four arms wielding the weapons of the conch, club, lotus and discus." Already dressed in a yellow garment, the child was equipped for battle: "He was resplendent with a magnificent belt, and arm and wrist bracelets, and his profuse locks were encircled with a lustrous helmet and earrings made of . . . gems" (3.9–10). The warrior-savior arrived in a display of power that aroused the hope of freedom from the oppressive rule of Kamsa. Here is an instance of a miracle story that expresses both religious devotion and political aspiration. In the narrative world of the miraculous, there is no restriction on the exercise of transcendent power and its capacity to shape and modify every domain of human experience.

Krishna's father was overwhelmed by the sight of his son. Even though "his eyes were wide with amazement," Vasudeva "understood that this was the Supreme Being illuminating the birth chamber with his radiance. . . . He praised Krishna with body bowed, hands joined in supplication, and concentrated mind" (3.12). Vasudeva addressed his newborn son as "*Bhagavān*, God himself, the supreme being beyond the material world" (3.13), and continued in a hymn of praise, expressing the hope that Krishna "will destroy the armies arrayed for battle with millions of demoniac leaders masquerading as kings" (3.21).

Then Krishna indulged in a bit of masquerade himself by abandoning his divine form to assume the appearance of an ordinary baby. When Vasudeva took Krishna in his arms, the chains fell off his feet and the locked doors of his prison swung open, and in secret he carried the infant god to the city of Vraj. There he exchanged Krishna for the newborn daughter of Yaśodā, who was too drained by the exertions of labor to remember whether her infant was a boy or a girl. Vasudeva brought the daughter back to Devakī and refastened his shackles. The ruse was complete, but the paranoia of Kamsa was not assuaged. The next morning he arrived to find that his sister had given birth. Despite Devakī's pleas for mercy, Kamsa dashed the infant girl against a stone. To his astonishment, from the tiny crushed body arose a goddess "bearing weapons in her eight mighty arms," who warned the king that the champion who would defeat him had already been born (4.12).

This series of wondrous transformations and revelations demonstrates a primary rhetorical strategy of miracle stories: the reversal of hierarchies of power in this world by the administration of justice by transcendent power. Miracles not only modify material conditions, but also reverse unjust social and political orders: the seemingly helpless infant reveals herself as a formidable goddess with the authority to announce the death of a king. This disruptive power of miracles is what nurtures hope in the oppressed for radical reversal of fortunes.

To return to the story, Kamsa realized that he had acted despicably and asked Vasudeva and Devakī to forgive him. They graciously did so, and he comforted them with words that echoed Krishna's own teaching in the *Bhagavad-Gītā*: "do not grieve for your offspring who were destroyed by me. . . . For as long as one who does not see his real self thinks that the self is killed or is the killer, he remains an ignorant person" (4.20–21). While the forgiveness of Krishna's parents was genuine, his uncle's repentance was short-lived. After consulting with demonic advisers, Kamsa sent them into the countryside to kill every child under ten days old. To prevent the gods from interfering, he also instructed demons to destroy the worship of Vishnu by killing the priests who offered sacrifices, those who recited the Vedas, all ascetics, and even the cows that provided milk for ritual use. The king declared war on the gods.

One of the demons Kamsa dispatched was Pūtanā, "slaughterer of children," who roamed about devouring infants (6.2). She arrived by mystic flight at Vraj and transformed herself into an alluring seductress. The men of the city were agape at her voluptuous appearance. She took the infant Krishna into her lap, unaware of his cosmic powers hidden from view "just as fire is concealed in ash" (6.7). When she offered her breast, smeared with deadly poison, Krishna seized the opportunity to enact poetic justice. "Squeezing it tightly with both hands, the furious Lord sucked it, along with her life breath." The demon masquerading as a mother was killed by the god disguised as an infant. Pūtanā screamed for release and assumed her original form in its dreadful enormity. But her struggles were of no avail against the power of Krishna and her gigantic body fell to earth, crushing trees within a twelve-mile radius.

What is the meaning of Krishna's defeat of Pūtanā? At one level he defended his village against demonic forces directed by the unjust king Kamsa; the divine champion achieved an unambiguous victory of righteousness. Pūtanā as pure evil deserved to be destroyed, but then the narrative takes a surprising turn: "Even though a demoness, Pūtanā attained the celestial realm of the gods, the destination of mothers" (6.38). The story ends with the demon in heaven, demonstrating that the miracle was successful in leading her to a degree of spiritual liberation. Pūtanā was a creature of *māyā* or illusion as much as the infant body that Krishna indwelled. Her evil intention was consistent with her nature; she too was bound by destiny. Yet her maternal gesture fit a pattern of care that sustains life, and in a bizarre parody of motherly love she gave up her life for the child. Krishna literally sucked the life out of her and her unwilling sacrifice counted more, in the calculus of *karma* that regulates life in the transient and changing world, than her career of demonic iniquities. The story elicits the response of hope for liberation despite one's past deeds. If Krishna saved Pūtanā despite her deadly teat, there is hope for wicked step-mothers and their poisoned apples, and even murderous uncles like Kamsa.

Everywhere in the world one finds selfishness, cruelty, and illusions of lasting power, wealth, and life. It is true that illusion allows us to live in a world of order and purpose, but illusion also tricks us into thinking that some things are permanent. At least, we tell ourselves, our moral judgments are immune from reversal. But Hindu teaching provides no such confidence in the eternal validity of our distinctions between good and evil. In the story the evil demoness is elevated to the same heavenly realm as good mothers. She must, of course, pay her karmic debt and suffer an agonizing death, but then she is free. Krishna executed justice in her death, just as Arjuna fulfilled his caste duty by fighting against his own family members, but there is no cosmic finality about such punishment. No enemy is beyond redemption; and one must accept that fact even in the midst of mortal struggle.

One of the most famous stories of Krishna's childhood exploits is an incident when his playmates told his adoptive mother that Krishna had eaten mud. When Yaśodā scolded him, he protested that the accusations were false and invited her to investigate for herself. When she peered into his wide-open mouth, she saw "the universe of moving and non-moving things; space; the cardinal directions; the sphere of the earth with its oceans, islands, and mountains; air and fire; and the moon and the stars. She saw the circle of the constellations, water, light, the wind, the sky, the evolved senses, the mind, the elements. . . . Seeing Vraj as well as herself in the gaping mouth in the body of her son, she was struck with bewilderment" (8.37–38). Her initial response to this cosmic vision was to question whether it was an illusion or a manifestation of divine power. But she quickly offered homage to Krishna, who then erased her memory of the event so that she could return to her state of ordinary maternal affection.

As in the *Bhagavad-Gītā*, Krishna here disclosed that he is the ultimate source of all things and that the entire universe, in all its variegated parts and qualities, is united in the being of Krishna. As with all moments of revelation, Yaśodā's experience is a miracle of showing by Krishna and of seeing by his mother. What Yaśodā saw when Krishna opened his mouth could not be seen through the investigation of any particular feature of the universe. Her vision of the entire cosmos required a perspective she could not have from her location in time and space. It was only when she saw the world *as Krishna saw it*, from his universal perspective, that the final unity of being was visible to her.

Visions of ultimate truth, then, are always miracles because they depend upon a comprehensive angle of sight that is not available to anyone standing within the natural order. No part can ever see the whole from within the whole; therefore, statements humans make about the whole—the whole world, the whole truth, and the whole meaning—are always false. By our nature as finite beings we are always speaking of the whole in fragmentary and provisional accounts. There is no alternative because none of us can occupy a point outside the universe from which we could see, much less understand, the whole of reality. Thus, any claim about the origin or destiny of the world could be true only if supported by divine revelation—that is, only if the claim rests on miraculous access to the perspective of the gods. Yaśodā's response to the vision of the whole in the smudged mouth of her son was not comprehension but bewilderment. She responded to the vision as an event of transcendent power evoking in her a sense of wonder.

For the reader, however, the story discloses a central teaching of Hindu tradition that opens the way to liberation. If all beings are present in Krishna, then no being exists in its own right or for its own purposes alone. The story calls for a transformative response that frees the reader from anxiety about securing a permanent place in the universe and releasing one from attachment to temporary arrangements of possessions, family, and career. The vision of the universe in the mouth of Krishna was a miracle of revelation for Yaśodā, and the reader of her story may participate in her vision by living with detachment from self, a way of life Hindu tradition promotes as liberating—even for those whose concentration is intensified by hatred.

Krishna's evil uncle, the king, later plotted to have him killed in a wrestling match held in the royal city. The appearance of Krishna as a mere boy was an exercise of his play (*līlā*), but the disguise did not conceal his true identity. Kamsa recognized that this child held the power of destiny over him, and demanded that his relatives be expelled from the city and that his father be killed. In the face of Kamsa's unyielding hatred toward his family, Krishna rose from the ground of the arena to the royal dais, seized Kamsa by the hair of his head, and cast him down to the dirt below. The storyteller notes that "Kamsa's crown tumbled off" (44.37) and Krishna threw himself on the dead body, securing victory over his enemy with a final pin.

Krishna's victory over Kamsa fulfilled the promise voiced by Vasudeva at Krishna's birth: "You will destroy the armies arrayed for battle with millions of demoniac leaders masquerading as kings" (3.21). As such, the story is a tale of divine intervention that sustains hope in the triumph of justice—but it also has that twist that distinguishes these Hindu narratives from other stories of triumph over demonic evil: at the moment of his well-deserved death Kamsa attained the form of divinity. From the moment of Krishna's birth the king was obsessed with him—as much as the most adoring devotee—and for that obsession, notwithstanding its origin in fear and greed, Kamsa was reborn in Krishna's form. The grace bestowed upon Kamsa did not cancel the necessity of his later rebirth to suffer the consequences of his actions, but the story of his liberation does mean that his fate was not entirely fixed nor was his punishment everlasting in duration. Not even the demonic character of Krishna's opponents is a permanent feature of their identity. In the cosmic play of the Supreme Lord, demons and gods are temporary roles played by beings on their way to the final stage of realization, merging their identities with Krishna as intimately as lovers. Thus, the greatest miracle Krishna performs is to purify the soul and release it from the burden of *karma* and rebirth into this world.

Miracles of internal transformation are viewed as more important in Hindu tradition than wonders that suspend the operation of natural order. Because the central purpose of miracles is to provide occasions for spiritual liberation, how they change material conditions is of little significance. Whether levitation, transmutation, or knowledge of the future, miracles serve the end of liberating the subjects and those who read the stories from bondage to this world.

One final story about Krishna will illustrate how an outer miracle of healing and an inner miracle of spiritual liberation are related. On his way into the wrestling arena Krishna met a hunchbacked woman, named Trivakrā ("crooked in three places"), who prepared ointments for Kamsa. Smitten by the handsome features of Krishna and his brother, she smeared consecrated oil on both of them. In response to this spontaneous gesture of devotion (which was also a courageous act of defiance of the king and an impulsive act of infatuation), Krishna "decided to make the beautiful hunchback Trivakrā straight of form, thus showing what can result from seeing him." He stepped his foot on hers and, placing two fingers under her chin, pulled her body upright. "Trivakrā instantly became a most beautiful young woman, with large hips and breasts, and with her limbs straight and uniform" (42.7–8).

Trivakrā was so strongly attracted to Krishna that she begged him to satisfy her desire for him. He promised to return after the wrestling match and, when he did, she was waiting eagerly.

> Trivakrā embraced her lover with her two arms, and eased the pain of
> desire in her burning breasts, as well as the pain in her chest and eyes, by
> smelling the lotus feet of Ananta [the Eternal]. Krishna, the embodiment
> of bliss, placed himself between her breasts, and she gave up the intense
> yearning she had suffered for so long. (48.7)

The narrator of this steamy passage notes that Trivakrā was granted exclusive intimacy with Krishna "even though she had merely performed a token act of piety by offering him ointment." Śuka relates the rest of the story, that Krishna satisfied her passionate desire by staying with her for several days; but he adds the moral tag line: "One who chooses sensual objects after having worshipped Vishnu . . . is misguided. This is because the nature of sensual objects is illusory" (48.11). Śuka's caution is entirely understandable in light of ascetic restrictions in Hindu devotional practice, but it also reminds us that the story of this healing and the passion it aroused was not meant to be taken literally. The meaning of Krishna's realigning the woman's body by miraculous traction lies in its awakening her desire for Krishna. For Śuka the true healing, because it is of lasting value, is Trivakrā's deliverance from sensual desire altogether—and it is not mere prudery that leads him to this interpretation. The text informs us that in giving herself utterly to Krishna in self-forgetfulness, Trivakrā emptied herself of any further yearning. By allowing her passion to burst into full flame, she found that it burned every other object of desire except Krishna himself. The final end of Krishna's healing of Trivakrā's body was to purify her soul, and the souls of all who read her story.

The power of sacred narrative to draw readers into its representation of divine acts defines scripture in most traditions and distinguishes it from historical accounts of past events. In retelling stories about redemptive acts of gods, the original power is made present again to restore what has gone awry in human life. For example, every reader suffering with debilitating handicaps can find solace in the story of Trivakrā, in whom Krishna takes delight, re-forming her body, ravishing her senses, and finally liberating her mind. To enter into that narrative is to realize the illusion of physical form and the lasting reality of union with Krishna. Within that narrative all bodies are entrancing to the Lord and every reader can imagine exciting his passion and being embraced by his loving arms. The meaning of this powerful healing story is that anyone can experience the ecstasy of Trivakrā in devotion to Krishna. The stilling of her spiritual anguish was an effect more real than her physical healing because her ecstasy lasted longer than her ability to walk erect. For the contemporary reader the meaning is clear: whether one's body remains unmoving in a wheelchair or not, it is possible to unite with Krishna in spiritual healing that is eternal consciousness made present. That insight is what makes these stories a source of spiritual liberation for those who read and hear them.

Book Ten of the *Bhāgavata Purāna* ends with this promise: "By thinking about, reciting and hearing the beautiful stories of Mukunda [Krishna], which constantly become more in number, a person [attains to] his incomparable abode, and overcomes death" (90.50). That reassurance would be of particular significance to King Parīksit, who now understood that his most effective preparation for death was not to master the metaphysical teachings of Krishna but to enter imaginatively and with full devotion into the stories of Krishna's "amazing acts." In that way the king would be sure to leave this life with his mind fastened on Krishna and thus be liberated through union with the Supreme Lord.

The order of the phenomenal world, including its fearsome law that every being must die, has no final authority over the devotee whose consciousness is absorbed in adoration of the divine person. Miracles, as disruptions of natural order, confirm the arbitrary and transient nature of the world and reveal the transcendent power that sustains it. Healings, paranormal wisdom, even levitation, are made possible by divine energy at play in the world, awakening wonder, inspiring devotion, and liberating from constraining limits of body and mind. But for some Hindus that energy can be tapped without the aid of divine beings.

Yogi: Ascetic Power over Body and World

Within the Indo-European family of languages *yoga* and *yoke* are related terms; they both indicate a means of *discipline* that creates *union*. As a team of oxen are trained to work together under a yoke, so a yogi trains his body and mind by rigorous exercises to reach a state of total integration with the undifferentiated source of reality. In that indeterminate state of mind the yogi is neither an object in the system of physical forces nor a subject composed of pure consciousness, but a creative agent whose control of body and mind is so compelling that the world in which he exists must yield to his power rather than vice versa.

The revelatory significance of a yogi's power over his body is that he disrupts the order of nature that governs all bodies and thereby discloses the relative authority of the laws of this world. It is the view of nature as mutable that sustains the efforts of yogis to discipline their bodies, overcome physical desires, and finally attain utter freedom from the material world. One of the earliest references to release from the bonds of nature in Hindu sacred writing is a description of a long-haired ascetic in the *Rig Veda*, a set of texts dating from around 1200 B.C.E. The passage appears to be an account of ritual ingestion of a hallucinogenic drug in communion with Rudra, the warrior deity of healing remedies (2.33, 1–3). The benefits are dramatic.

> Long-hair holds fire, holds the drug, holds sky and earth. Long-hair reveals everything, so that everyone can see the sun. Long-hair declares the light.
> These ascetics, swathed in wind, put dirty red rags on. When gods enter them, they ride with the rush of the wind. (10.136, 1–2) [3]

Their formerly naked bodies now draped with ragged robes soiled by their own studied neglect, they cry out from their soaring height, "Crazy with asceticism, we have mounted the wind. Our bodies are all you mere mortals can see" (10.136, 3). The following verse reflects the standpoint of those still on the ground: "He sails through the air, looking down on all shapes below. The ascetic is friend to this god and that god, devoted to what is well done."

The "everything" the yogi reveals in this event is not, of course, comprehensive knowledge of every individual being. Gaining an encyclopedic inventory of all the variations of material existence would not only be tiresome, but pointless. Rather, in opening a crack between this world and another, the flying ascetic reveals the secret from which everything else can be worked out, namely, reality is not only shaped by mind, it is created by mind. Every possibility one can imagine, therefore, can be actualized. That is the world-shattering meaning of the ascetic's flight. By gaining control over his own body he also rules the world. To put the point in other terms, by becoming master of his body as microcosm, he gains power over (or freedom from) laws that govern the macrocosm. "Long-hair declares the light." That is, his levitation illumines the limited and mutable nature of everything.

Later in this hymn we read that the ascetic's flight is not the result of rigorous self-denial but the effect of imbibing what may have been an extract from pressed mushroom stalks, called Soma. "Long-hair drinks from the cup, sharing the drug with Rudra" (10.136, 7). To Wendy Doniger, scholar of comparative religion and the sympathetic translator of these Sanskrit texts, there is no question that the Soma drinker is metaphorically, not literally, high. She comments, "the poet may simply feel that he is flying, a frequent symptom of drug-induced ecstasy."[4] But why does the ascetic experience a sense of flying in the heavens under the influence of Soma rather than falling into the ocean or seeing his body transformed into the likeness of an animal? These are also experiences reported by people who ingest hallucinogenic drugs. Apart from the obvious significance of "rising above" as a symbol of superiority, why is flying the signifier of mastery over the world that we find in every religious tradition discussed in this book? While each tradition understands the meaning of the miracle of levitation differently, in the Hindu case it is a matter not only of mastery over the world but freedom from it. Taking flight is precisely the moment of release, of abandonment, of total renunciation. Accordingly, "Long-hair" is "swathed in wind," entering another world nude as a newborn. One can take nothing from one world into the next; what is true of the passage of death is true of the way of ecstasy.

The miraculous powers of yogis are signs they are liberated, not only from bondage to desire and illusion, but also from confinement by operational laws of the physical universe. Yet it is precisely the radical nature of spiritual freedom as release from self-consciousness that raises a question about the possibility of acting independently of natural laws. Here is the problem: If self-awareness vanishes in the trance state, then how can yogis who levitate or disappear or remain submerged in water for hours *know* that they are exercising marvelous powers (*siddhis*)? In an unconditioned state of consciousness one could not be aware of personal agency, yet without self-awareness or intentionality one could not be rightly said to exercise power. It would seem that insofar as a yogi is in the trance state he lacks the necessary condition to act in the world, and insofar as he acts in the world he cannot be in a state of unconditioned consciousness. This question arose early in Hindu reflection on yoga.

The first systematic treatise on the practice of yoga is the *Yoga Sutras*, a collection of 195 aphorisms written by a teacher named Patanjali, probably in the third century c.e. The text is often accompanied by explanatory commentaries that represent the progressive elaboration of the yogic tradition from authoritative but cryptic aphorisms to their primary interpretations. Patanjali devoted the third chapter to "attainments," marvelous powers the yogi achieves through mental effort. The highest state of consciousness, combining concentration, meditation, and contemplation, is called *samyama*. In it the yogi can bring under the control of his mind knowledge of previous lives, knowledge of other minds, power to become invisible, knowledge of the time of death by insight into the duration of karmic effects, understanding the languages of animals, appropriation of the powers of animals (strength of an elephant, flight of birds), clairvoyance, knowledge of heavenly bodies and the astral regions (including realms of the gods), control of the body (including autonomous functions), vision of heavenly beings, entry into other bodies, levitation, mastery over fire, translocation at will, and the power to determine the characteristics of physical objects.

This is an impressive list of powers that might nurture a sense of pride in anyone who attained them. But early in this chapter Patanjali described a yogi's consciousness as innocent of any trace of self-awareness: "When the purpose shines forth as if empty of own form, that indeed is *samādhi*."[5] What is required is a mental feat of abstraction that dissolves particularities into the primordial unity from which they emerged. By this mental discipline the yogi becomes capable of recasting features of the phenomenal world.

The power to control natural forces is no sooner attained, however, than it immediately comes under regulation. Since the exercise of *samyama* must be relative to the yogi's level of awareness, Patanjali insisted that as one ascends to higher levels (by which he seems to mean more comprehensive and unified states of consciousness), effecting changes in more limited and variegated fields of awareness becomes increasingly less important. "The trance modification of the mind is the destruction and rise of all-pointedness and one-pointedness, respectively" (III.11, Prasada translation). That is, the yogi's mind knows everything as one. That cognition, however, is not awareness of undifferentiated unity because then it would not be of every *thing*. Neither can it be focused knowledge of each item in the catalog of entities in the universe because then it would not be unified. The first would be the horror of a blank mind, the second the chaos of a distracted mind. Either would be closer to insanity than the perfection of consciousness. Rather, the relation between the two modifications of mind is dialectical, held together in contemplation.

We should remind ourselves at this point that our text consists of enigmatic aphorisms, but we might venture an inference from this passage about the source of the yogi's miraculous powers while in the trance state. If, for the yogi, present conditions in the world emerge directly from a state of cosmic latency, they cannot be subject to laws of nature, as present laws of physics do not hold in whatever state of affairs obtained before the present state of the universe. Therefore, the yogi's experience of present events is not determined by the order prevailing in past states of the material universe. That is, the yogi can act in the present free from the law of cause-and-effect. In the lawless freedom of the primordial source, the yogi enters the infinite reservoir of cosmic potentialities. Here nothing exists, yet everything is on the "event horizon."

It is at this location in the undifferentiated source that the yogi manifests marvelous powers, including the capacity to assume the characteristics of any object of meditation. Patanjali offers the example of a yogi's ability to levitate by meditating on the lightness of cotton, then proceeding to "passage through space." In the state of *samyama* the yogi's mind reduces all things to their elements and is free to reconstitute them as he wishes so that his body corresponds to whatever his mind is focused on: light as cotton or floating as a feather.

Patanjali believed that yogis are capable of wondrous acts, but extending those powers to modify conditions in the material world would be a distraction from the goal of meditation: "These are impediments to samādhi" (III.37, Chapple translation). Thus, the first authoritative treatise on the practice of yoga devalued the exercise of miraculous powers, even as it carefully explained how they can be attained. Patanjali's caution is a theme running through Hindu tradition: powers over the body and the physical world are demonstrable effects of yogic practice, but they are obstacles to spiritual advance because their intentional exercise requires the yogi to remain attached to the external world. Such attachment can lead yogis to betray their spiritual calling by indulging paranormal powers to curry favor with patrons or enhance their reputations. In either case they break the essential bond between meditation and morality.

For many Hindus religion and morality are inextricably linked. Thus, the acts of a *fakir* (poor wandering yogi) lying on a bed of nails or playing a pipe to charm a cobra from the basket at his feet are often regarded as performances to amaze and amuse but bereft of spiritual value or religious authority. Even acts like climbing a rope that uncoils in thin air or sustaining a state of suspended animation fail to convince not only Westerners but also doubting Hindus that the fakir is a holy man. What lies behind the skepticism is a sense that religion is demonstrated in moral leadership and not in power over forces of nature. In the matter of determining holiness, might does not make right. Many Hindus would agree that the test of a yogi's authority is ethical purity, and they can be skeptical of yogis who perform wonders for profit or sex.[6]

Still, believers often support spiritual athletes in the hope that their breakthrough into a sphere of reality where poverty and disease are not known (and therefore cannot exist) might provide entry for them as well. The respect ordinary Hindus show yogis is based on the recognition that renunciation opens possibilities beyond routine human existence. Their mastery signifies the presence of a domain of being, intersecting this one through the bodies of yogis, not ruled by the tyranny of material forces and the tragedy of their inevitable dissolution. In this tacit exchange, miracles become social acts, involving a purposive agent and a receptive audience. But the unified consciousness of a yogi lacks intention. His very disinterest is a sign of his perfected mind; he does not pray or sing or serve gods or humans. For those acts, we turn to the ecstatic embodiment of divine energy in a Hindu saint.

Saint: Miracles of Śri Caitanya

Devotees of the Bengali holy man, Caitanya (1486–1534), regard him as the embodiment of the union of Krishna and his consort Rādhā. Educated in Sanskrit, rhetoric, and logic, Caitanya gave up a promising career as a philosopher to receive initiation in the Vaishnavite tradition (devotion to Vishnu in various forms). When he returned to his home town, he was a changed man. He opened his own school to teach people to recite the names of Krishna, the "great chant" (*mahāmantra*) that is still repeated hundreds of times a day by members of the International Society of Krishna Consciousness (ISKCON): "*Hare Krishna. Hare Krishna. Krishna, Krishna. Hare Hare. Hare Rama. Hare Rama. Rama, Rama. Hare Hare.*" The chanting is a continuous offering of praise which sinks into the mind by numberless repetitions until every thought and action proceed from the intention to glorify and serve Krishna.

The joyous and clamorous singing served the purpose not only of express-ing the devotion of Caitanya's disciples, but also of attracting the attention of others "for Caitanya's movement was highly evangelistic. Caitanya himself dispatched followers to preach from door to door, and he personally toured throughout India to propagate his *sankīrtana* [reciting names of God] move-ment."[7] Caitanya visited pilgrimage sites associated with the life of Krishna and sponsored the building of temples in the locations of Krishna's *līlā*. He eventually took up residence in a center of Krishna worship, and assigned six close disciples, the Goswamis, to develop the institutional forms and philo-sophical foundation for his movement. Caitanya's devotion was ecstatic and unrestrained, frequently bringing him to tears or driving him into extended periods of nearly catatonic concentration. He drowned in a river near Puri while in an ecstatic trance.

Caitanya's devotional excesses led his critics to charge him with madness, but his extreme self-abandonment in adoration of Krishna inspired disciples then and now who believe he was sent into the world to restore truth in the spiritual darkness of the present *kali yuga*. He is called the Golden Avatar because his glowing skin reflected the beauty of Rādhā, whose loving union with Krishna is the model of devotion and the goal of spiritual quest. To awaken people in the shadow of this evil age, however, requires more than mere sight of the avatar. Thus, Caitanya employed not only loud public sing-ing, but also the startling wonder of miracles.

The official account of the life of Caitanya, composed in the generation following his death to represent him as a *saint* (a category that denotes a holy person regarded as an embodiment of deity), fills several volumes and contains many stories of his miracles. Those performed during his youth are replications of Krishna's wonders as a child, underscoring Caitanya's identity as Krishna reborn. Caitanya miraculously appeared in his mother's womb in response to prayers. While still a child, he revealed his true nature to a Brahmin (traditional Hindu teacher) as the new-born Krishna appeared to his own parents as the Supreme Lord. But one story of Krishna's exploits takes a very different turn in the parallel story concerning Caitanya. When his mother scolded him for eating clay, instead of imparting to her a vision of the entire universe in his mouth, Caitanya defended his action on the ground that food was only clay transformed. In response to this precocious expres-sion of non-dualist philosophy, his mother instructed him in the specific uses of different forms of reality. Her teaching exposed the folly of assuming that everything is the same and thus educated her son in the dualist metaphys-ics of Vaishnavite devotion in which the embodiment of Krishna is durably separate from his devotees. Only in such a view of reality is genuine loving service of God possible. The child confessed his mistake and promised henceforth to respect the differences between phenomenal forms. This incident set the stage for Caitanya's career.

As an itinerant holy man, Caitanya performed miracles as a means of persuading others to join in praising Krishna, especially scholars of the non-dualist school of Hindu thought and wandering ascetics who had withdrawn from public life. For example, once Caitanya joined a group of ascetics and literally dazzled them. "After sitting on the ground, Caitanya exhibited His mystic power by manifesting an effulgence as brilliant as the illumination of millions of suns. When the sannyāsīs [ascetics] saw the brilliant illumination of the body of Śrī Caitanya Mahāprabhu, their minds were attracted, and they all immediately gave up their sitting places and stood in respect."[8]

This account was translated by A. C. Bhaktivedanta Swami Prabhupada, founder of ISKCON, who began his commentary on this passage by noting that, since Caitanya is the embodiment of Krishna, the Supreme Yogi, "He can exhibit any mystic power." Bhaktivedanta continued, however, in a cautionary vein. "To draw the attention of common men, sometimes saintly persons . . . and teachers exhibit extraordinary opulences. This is necessary to attract the attention of fools, but a saintly person should not misuse such power for personal sense gratification like false saints who declare themselves to be God." Such reservations constitute a recurrent theme in Hindu tradition. For example, Ramakrishna, a nineteenth-century holy man, told this cautionary story.

> A disciple, having firm faith in the infinite power of his Guru, walked over a river by pronouncing his name. The Guru, seeing this, thought within himself, "Well, is there such a power even in my name? Then I must be very great and powerful, no doubt!" The next day he also tried to walk over the river pronouncing "I, I, I," but no sooner had he stepped into the waters than he sank and was drowned.[9]

The power to perform miracles can be a temptation to pride, yet saints must take the risk. Unlike yogis, who have no motive for working miracles once they achieve transcendent consciousness, saints are in the world precisely to attract attention to truth and righteousness. Thus they perform miracles, but only for the sake of others.

On one occasion the exuberant chanting and drum beating of Caitanya's followers in Mayapur, then under Muslim rule, attracted the attention of the town official, known as the Kazi. He went to their gathering place and broke the large drum, threatening further prosecution if they continued their disruptive devotions. Caitanya responded by organizing a large procession of his followers, each carrying a torch, and led them that night to the official's house. There he engaged in conversation with the Kazi about the Hindu devotional tradition. The official remained unconvinced until Caitanya touched him. At that moment, his disciples believe, the saint communicated truth directly into his mind. Immediately, "The Kazi broke into tears and admitted that he had felt a great spiritual presence. . . . The Kazi experienced a higher ecstasy that cleared all doubts and gave him a religious conviction like never before." Soon, the Muslim official joined in the chanting. "The great spiritual power of the Supreme Lord astonished all as hundreds upon hundreds were converted and joined under the banner of Vaishnava love of God."[10]

The miracle in this case was the subtle imposition of divine influence on the mind of another. Its meaning lies in the confirmation of Caitanya's authority as a religious leader who was capable of liberating others through the quiet intimacy of touch. When arguments about theology are exhausted, the saint communicates truth by means that transcend the mediation of logic and language. As the personal embodiment of supreme reality, Caitanya's physical presence was the irrefutable proof of his preaching. The messenger was the message, the tangible descent of the divine. To be touched by him was to be convinced that God is personal. That claim, however, would have been the exact sticking point for the Muslim.

Under Islamic law, Hindus were classified as "people of the Book," along with Jews and Christians, in recognition of the sacred status of the Vedas and Upanishads. The Muslim reading of these scriptures (and by Caitanya's time Islamic scholars were translating Sanskrit) was that they taught a version of monotheism inasmuch as Brahman is presented as the single, universal, transcendent reality. Because medieval Islamic theology also held that God was utterly beyond human comprehension as the only eternal source of being, Muslims found similar statements about Brahman in the Upanishads acceptable as incomplete, but valid, revelations. Islamic theologians acknowledged that God may have personal characteristics, but they are necessarily hidden from us because the being of God is incomparable. On this basis, most Muslims were suspicious of mystics in their own tradition who claimed to enter into ecstatic personal intimacy with God as their divine lover. The Muslim official who confronted Caitanya would have been just as scandalized by his declarations of knowing God directly. By departing from the nondualist teaching that Supreme Reality is one Caitanya was in danger of losing his status under Islamic law as a person with scriptural support. Thus, the miraculous conversion of the Kazi was not only a victory for Caitanya, it was also a skirmish in the larger conflict between non-dualist philosophy and the personalist theology of devotional practice within Hindu tradition. It was, we might say, a quiet miracle that spoke loudly to those engaged in that polemical battle.

Caitanya also called upon miraculous power over a wild bird to defeat opponents representing Buddhism. According to the story, Caitanya consented to debate Buddhists, just as he had taken on and refuted the representatives of other Indian schools of thought, including adherents of Patanjali's system of yoga. Vaishnavites regarded Buddhism as a particularly repugnant teaching because it denied the enduring reality of both personal deity and individual soul, thus undercutting the metaphysical foundation of devotion to Krishna. In the story Caitanya had no difficulty dismantling their arguments, and they departed to the ridicule of the spectators. To exact revenge, the Buddhists arranged to present Caitanya with contaminated food under the pretense of offering him homage. Before the saint could touch the plate, however, a large bird seized it, flew above the plotters, released the food on them, and dropped the plate on the head of the chief Buddhist teacher. When he fell to the ground unconscious, his disciples thought him dead and implored Caitanya to restore him to life. Caitanya directed them to chant the name of Krishna very loudly in their teacher's ear. As they joined in the chanting, their master awoke and also began to praise the name of Krishna, submitting himself to Caitanya—"and all the people who were gathered there were astonished."

But then, in an even more astounding conclusion to this wondrous performance, Caitanya "suddenly and humorously disappeared from everyone's sight, and it was impossible for anyone to find Him."[11] Like Krishna, Caitanya played hide-and-seek with his devotees to teach them not to take his presence for granted and to increase their desire for unbroken awareness of Krishna. In many traditions the miracle of disappearance serves the function of redirecting the attention of believers to their own responsibilities in a world without the physical presence of the saint. When Jesus ascended into heaven, before he passed out of sight, he charged his disciples with their mission in the world. When the prophet Elijah disappeared into the sky in a flaming chariot, he dropped his cloak and the weight of his prophetic calling on his disciple Elisha. Caitanya disappeared so that his followers could continue chanting without his leadership. Sooner or later, every religious believer—even those who have felt the wonder of the miraculous—discovers the necessity, as the German theologian and martyr under Nazi persecution, Dietrich Bonhoeffer, put it, of living in the world *as if there were no God.*

It was a spiritual condition Caitanya also endured. Among the eight verses he left behind as his only written legacy, two of them contain references to feeling bereft of Krishna's presence. One reads, "O Govinda! Feeling Your separation, I am considering a moment to be like twelve years or more. Tears are flowing from my eyes like torrents of rain, and I am feeling all vacant in the world in Your absence." In another, the last of the series, Caitanya affirmed his fidelity to Krishna, "even if He handles me roughly by His embrace or makes me brokenhearted by not being present before me." [12] Even the one who felt divine power coursing through his own body, bending the natural world to his desires, and who filled every waking hour celebrating his personal relationship with God, had moments of desolation, forsakenness, abandonment.

Caitanya's lament, however, expressed neither despair nor doubt. He fully accepted the sovereignty of Krishna in the remainder of his final verse: "He is completely free to do anything and everything, for He is always my worshipful Lord unconditionally." Perhaps the best way to interpret the melancholy of saints is through the philosophy of *bhakti* (devotion to a specific deity). Just as there must be a distinction between the Supreme Lord and the worshipper in order for a relationship to obtain between them, so there must be an occasional separation to maintain that distinction. If a devotee succeeded in filling the mind with awareness of Krishna, the very success of such devotion would dissolve the sense of difference upon which the relationship depends. Disappearances of the divine being are, therefore, acts of grace that maintain the necessary condition of devotional practice. What Krishna's absence did to strengthen Caitanya's faith was also what Caitanya's disappearance did for his followers. Perhaps this is why believers are rarely discouraged by prayers for miracles that go unanswered.

As long as the saint is in the world, however, one can expect spectacular demonstrations of authority. Such miracles always carry the potential to disrupt established orders. We have already seen that Caitanya's conversion of a Muslim official had the potential for securing political protection for Krishna devotees under Islamic rule. Unlike a yogi who meditates alone in search of spiritual liberation, a saint acts in public to restore right worship and practice and to instruct. Given the conditions of the *kali yuga* in which even religious leaders are corrupt, the saint is something of a gadfly, resisting ritualism and drawing disciples from the margins of society. As a saint, Caitanya challenged the way of both teachers and priests upholding traditional social order and also itinerant ascetics who renounced society by calling everyone, regardless of caste or gender, to join him in the adoration of Krishna as Supreme Lord.

The transformation of individuals through union with supreme reality is the greatest miracle in Hindu tradition and is the final end of all other miracles. The question posed to the reader by countless Hindu miracle stories is not whether the event *really* happened but what path to spiritual freedom the story signifies. The miracles of avatars, yogis, and saints demonstrate the possibility of final liberation by their startling power to reshape the world—and some Hindu teachers also find performing miracles an effective way to awaken religious interest and to demonstrate the liberating effect of Hindu wisdom.

Guru: Miracles of Vision and Healing

Guru, like other categories of religious leadership in India, is a broad and imprecise designation. Some gurus insist that they are not incarnations of deity, but human beings whose insights are accessible by any person of devotion or yogic discipline. But others are viewed by their followers, without objection from the gurus themselves, as manifestations of God. In general, gurus are expected to maintain ascetic detachment, but not itinerancy so that they are available for teaching disciples. One traditional etymology derives the term *guru* from two Sanskrit roots: "*gu* means darkness and *ru* means light; a Guru is someone who can guide a disciple from darkness of ignorance to the bright light of understanding. The Guru, then, acts as mediator between the world of illusion and the ultimate reality."[13] Based on her personal experience and extensive field work, the anthropologist Kirin Naryan describes the guru in these terms:

> A Guru gives people hope: that their lives can change, that suffering has meaning, that spiritual illumination can actually be achieved. Around every Guru I have known . . . tales of miracles are in constant circulation. People are warned in dreams of forthcoming catastrophes; they are healed with an ease that bewilders their doctors; the Guru appears in meditations, benevolent and smiling, to issue blessings and reassurance.[14]

That characterization applies to our subject in this section who is revered as the embodiment of Devi, the Supreme Goddess (a general term in Hinduism referring to a form of dynamic divine energy called *shakti* and personified as female). Her followers fondly call her Amma, Divine Mother. As such, her presence provides a vision of the divine (*darshan*), her focused resolve produces healing, and her energetic love inspires self-giving service.

Mata Amritanandamayi ("Mother of Immortal Bliss") is one of the contemporary Hindu female leaders whom Karen Pechilis, professor of Asian studies, calls "The Graceful Guru."[15] In Sanskrit *guru* indicates both masculine and feminine subjects, and women have been acknowledged as ascetics and teachers throughout Hindu tradition. Most of the women profiled in *The Graceful Guru* generated stories of supernatural powers: visions of deities, healing, mind reading, and materialization of objects. These powers issue from the female guru as an embodiment of *shakti*, feminine divine energy. Identity with a divine being is one point of similarity between gurus and saints. "The guru is both divine and universal, as with the Goddess, and she is an embodied, religiously devoted woman, as with the saints."[16]

Unlike the *bhakti* saints, however, the guru we are considering holds to the non-dualist metaphysics of the Hindu philosopher Śankara (788–820), who taught that Brahman alone is absolutely real, although natural and social orders created by *māyā* (illusion) have provisional authority over human action. One whose insight penetrates to essential reality, however, can overcome *māyā* and reshape its illusion. For the guru who knows that the world of nature and its laws are transient and illusory, the system of ordinary experience presents no obstacle to action. The saint whose devotion to God overflows with love for all creatures, and the guru whose vocation includes instructing others in the knowledge of Brahman, necessarily engage in action in the world. They have both interest and motive in performing wondrous deeds that inspire love or increase understanding. But the guru is in the distinctive position of combining liberating knowledge with the personal authority of an embodiment of deity, evoking devotion that unites the disciple with God.

The followers of Mata Amritanandamayi come to her for healing of body and spirit. She was born in 1953 in Kerala, where she gained a reputation for healing. Even as a teenager she spent time visiting the ill and elderly in her village, offering comfort and hope. Then, as the story is told on her official Web site, "when She began giving darshan several nights a week, a leper named Dattan who was covered in wounds and had been shunned by society sought Amma as his last hope. At the end of every darshan She cared for him like Her own son, even licking his open wounds. Through Her *sankalpa* [resolve], Dattan's wounds healed."

As spectacular as healing the leper's physical state was, commentary on the Web site emphasizes the inspirational effect of the story: "We can still see

Amma caring for those who suffer with Her own hands, as She strokes the paralyzed legs of a devotee, or kisses the swollen brow of a baby with a birth defect. Inspired by Amma's example, thousands have dedicated themselves to serving the poor, the sick, the distressed; in this way, Her hands have become many."[17] One who witnessed her sucking pus from an open lesion on the leper's forehead later became her devoted disciple and authorized biographer. What drew his wondering admiration was as much her heroic exposure to the leper's disease as to Dattan's actual healing.[18]

As a young woman Ammachi identified with Krishna, but later she adopted the persona of the Goddess and often appears before her followers dressed in her regalia. Her authority rests in her own experiences, not in her recognition by any tradition.[19] As a low caste woman who speaks only her regional language, Ammachi is an outsider with the usual disadvantages and benefits of that status. On the one hand, she does not enjoy the sanction of a line of authoritative Hindu teachers. On the other, she is free to develop her teaching without obligation to make it compatible with any established orthodoxy. What counts is whether she can deliver on her self-representation as an embodiment of divine grace and a channel of supernatural healing.

The message of Ammachi is familiar enough. "Her mission, as she defines it, is to alleviate humanity's suffering by restoring selflessness, love and compassion to their rightful place in the modern world."[20] Her method of achieving this ambitious goal is to embrace each of her followers in a comforting gesture of divine love. Maya Warrier, scholar of Indian religion, provides this observation of Ammachi's technique: "At public *darshans* [visions of the divine] devotees queue up in order to receive her embrace. The Mata takes each waiting devotee into her arms, and lavishes her love on them individually. . . . For most devotees the embrace is an intensely emotional experience, and many cry openly in her arms, even as they relish the comforting intimacy of her motherly touch."[21] This love is the encompassing care of the divine Mother in contrast to the erotic attraction some devotees feel for Krishna. Ammachi teaches that there is no distinction between the ultimate Self and the individual; thus, she does not recognize the distance required for *bhakti* adoration. "For Amma, Advaita [non-dualism] is not a mere philosophy, but something to be lived. As such, Amma's every thought, word and deed resound with that greatest of truths: Everything within and without is divine."[22]

Ammachi's embrace does not excite her devotees to ecstasy, but it releases them from their individual burdens and allows them to rest in the eternal Self. Shedding tears in her arms is a signal of release from the cares of this world. As refreshing as hug therapy may be, however, it changes nothing in the material conditions producing the devotee's suffering. To warrant her status as the avatar of Devi, Ammachi offers more than emotional solace. Warrier reports that devotees eagerly tell stories of her miracles: "how she heals the sick and dying, how she solves the financial problems of her devotees, rids alcoholics of their addiction, grants childless couples the boon of children, blesses the jobless with employment, resolves family disputes and settles marital discord."[23] This list demonstrates the wide range of referents in ordinary usage for the term *miracle*. What all the items on the list have in common, however, is that they are viewed as effects of the intentional application of Ammachi's divine power. Bringing someone back from the brink of death may seem to be miraculous in a much stronger sense than reconciling a squabbling husband and wife, but Ammachi's followers celebrate both as demonstrations of her divine power.

In relation to Ammachi, *miracle* designates a personal transformation in the way her devotees perceive and respond to the conditions of their lives. For example, the effect of *darshan* is always conditioned by the receptivity of those who gaze upon the form of the divine; but according to Ammachi's teaching, it is the guru who provides the capacity of a disciple to see God in her. In one recent message to her followers, Ammachi declared, "Just as the radiance of the full moon transforms night into day, the presence of the Guru dispels the darkness within the disciple's heart. The Guru elevates the disciple to the state of supreme bliss by giving him the strength and discrimination to transcend the limitations of the mind."[24] That gift is beyond understanding. "Logic is useful only up to a certain point in understanding the Guru and God. At some point it must be dropped, after which our only means of understanding is faith and surrender."[25] Faced with ultimate mystery, the follower has no choice but to exercise *faith* in its comprehensive meaning as belief, confidence, and loyalty. In that sense faith is not unthinking acceptance, but requires careful interpretation of evidence. In the case of Ammachi's healing power, as is generally true of belief in miracles, the interpretive strategy of faith requires revision of putative facts.

The healing of Dattan the leper set a high bar for displays of Ammachi's love for her followers. That early miracle is referred to in the account of a young man who attended *darshan* daily in the ashram in San Ramon, California. He was a rock musician until Amyotrophic Lateral Sclerosis robbed him of control over his body. According to the account on Ammachi's official Web page, "Like many people, he first came to Mother with dreams of a healing, for there have been cases of people becoming whole by Her grace—

or, as She humbly says, somehow it sometimes happens, due to their strong faith." But after two years, the young man continued to waste away. Despite the obvious love Ammachi feels for him, she has not restored him to health. "Why not? Didn't She suck the pus from Dattan the Leper's wounds until he was healed?" As in this case, so in general, the possibility of miracles intensifies the problem of evil—especially with a precedent of curing debilitating disease already on the record. Why does Ammachi withhold healing from this young man?

The account on the Web page reviews some standard answers. "We know things Mother has said: we need to exhaust our . . . *karma*s. Mahatmas usually let themselves be bound by the laws of the universe; miracles don't breed so much faith as the desire for more miracles. And so forth." But none of these responses is satisfying in light of the young man's agony. The only other explanation is that Ammachi allows him to suffer out of love because she sees in him potential for immense spiritual growth and has carefully calculated the degree of suffering he can endure in fulfilling that potential. While most of us must be gently schooled through lesser trials, Ammachi discerns that he can profit from "the advanced and accelerated curriculum" that leads to final liberation.[26] This pedagogical interpretation of suffering is persuasive under two conditions: that the sufferer's spirit is not crushed by the affliction and that there is an opportunity for the sufferer to enjoy the benefits of the education. The young man seems to meet the first condition by his determination and resiliency, and the Hindu belief in rebirth meets the second condition. So, even in the presence of a guru who withholds miraculous healing, the devotee can interpret his advancing disease as an expression of divine love. This interpretive strategy is employed in other contexts by those whose desire for miracles goes unfulfilled.

Testimonials from followers who have experienced miraculous cures through Ammachi include the story of a Colorado woman whose son was critically injured in a car wreck. The results of an MRI showed brain damage associated with life-long vegetative coma. Through a series of coincidences the mother eventually met Ammachi, who at first declared the son's fate a matter of *karma*. In response to intense appeal, Ammachi made a resolve (*sankalpa*) that the situation would have a favorable outcome. But this was not, in the mother's words, "a stand-up-and-start-talking miracle." The son showed some signs of improvement, but then contracted pneumonia. The mother prayed to Ammachi while visualizing her son receiving *darshan* from the guru. Then, the mother testified, "In a last chance effort, three powerful antibiotics were simultaneously pumped intravenously into our precious child and slowly he began to recover." After months the son did receive *darshan* from Ammachi. The mother concluded, "There is no doubt in my mind that this is a result of our beloved Guru's *sankalpa* manifested in the love and prayers of all our family and friends and in ways we cannot know, but only imagine."

The inevitable question of whether the recovery was due to the antibiotics or Ammachi's will implies the healing must have a single cause. But for a non-dualist view of reality there is only one source of all things, whether called Brahman or, in the generalized sense Ammachi uses the term, God. Since Ammachi is an embodiment of that original reality, healing is consistently attributed to her creative will expressed through the means of material medicine. A recovery that might otherwise be understood as the lucky result of the right chemicals at the right time is open to another meaning: as the gift of the divine mother incarnate in "our beloved Guru." The healing is a sign of divine presence in Ammachi and strengthens the perception of that presence in her appearance. For the mother, with her son's healing ever in her mind, Ammachi will always appear as divine.

Further, to interpret the recovery as caused by the guru's resolve provides the mother a personal focus for her gratitude. Not all miracles in Hindu tradition are seen as divine gifts, but in this case the guru embodies deity in a form that allows the mother to pour out her thanks and relief and receive the reassuring embrace of the Mother in response. Finally, the meaning of the healing is not confined to those immediately benefiting from it. Through retelling the mother's testimony others can enter into her world, share her initial despair, and feel her joy and gratitude for her son's healing through Ammachi's intervention. Her story, once cast as a miracle narrative, becomes available for others to respond to with faith in the midst of their own afflictions. These elements are parts of the psychological process Warrier calls "experience construction" in which devotees interpret every fortuitous event as a miraculous intervention by Ammachi and regard every setback as a test of their loyalty to her.[27] That work of interpretation is a labor of love by which the power of the master emerges from the faith of the disciple.

At the point where the credibility of the miracle worker depends on the credulity of disciples, there arises the opportunity for fraud. It is not our purpose in this book to determine whether any miracle worker is genuine, but we note one way that ordinary Hindus make such judgments: by following the wisdom of folktales about deceptive gurus and their gullible disciples. One guru who employed cautionary stories effectively was Swamiji, the pseudonymous subject of an ethnographic study by Kirin Narayan, who told stories designed to warn his students against uncritical enthusiasm for miracles, thus providing a regulatory mechanism in a religious tradition lacking central authority.[28]

The best known of his tales is the story of the Nose Cutters. As Swamiji retold the yarn, it unwound like this. There was once a great guru who told his disciples he would give them *darshan* of Bhagavān. They spread the word throughout the region and people flocked to the guru. There was, however, one catch. To receive *darshan* a person had to donate 10,000 rupees to the master, but most regarded that a small enough amount to see God. The guru was a handsome man who put on a jeweled crown and held a conch and discus in his hand (symbols of Krishna). He wore golden yellow robes and sat on a throne, giving the appearance of Vishnu. Eager seekers were admitted, one at a time, into a darkened room. A small light was lit and the one who had paid for *darshan* was told, "Look, you can see Bhagavān for just one second. If you look at him any longer than that, you'll be blinded." Then the guru would straighten on his throne, bend his elbows up and down to simulate Vishnu's four arms, and the seeker was led out of the room. Upon rejoining the group outside, he would loudly proclaim he had seen Bhagavān and the others, in turn, followed suit. In this way the guru collected a large amount of money because no one wanted to admit to not receiving a vision after having paid the exorbitant fee.

When the guru died, one of his disciples was apprehended for theft and was punished by having his nose cut off. Immediately, remembering his guru's strategy, he saw his chance to turn the calamity into opportunity and began to dance, proclaiming he could see Bhagavān. First one person, then another, asked him how he had come by his vision and, hearing his story, they agreed to let him cut their noses off. Soon there were hundreds of noseless people, dancing and crying, "I see Bhagavān!" They entered a nearby kingdom and explained to the king that the reason he could not see Bhagavān was because his nose blocked his vision, so if he and his subjects had their noses removed, they would all receive *darshan*. The king ordered his people to gather the next day to have their noses cut off. A wise man in the kingdom objected that the nose is too low on the face to obstruct sight; but if the king insisted on his plan, he wished to be the first to have his nose removed, promising to say truthfully whether he saw Bhagavān as a result. The king agreed, and the next day the leader of the Nose Cutters sliced off the old man's nose and then whispered in his ear, "Look brother, your nose will never come back. The whole world will make fun of you. That's why you should do as we do: say you've seen Bhagavān. Then you will get a lot of reverence and respect." But the old man was too honest to perpetuate the deception. In great pain he declared, "I didn't see anything. These people are just rogues." The king ordered the entire company of Nose Cutters to be whipped, and they quickly confessed they had seen nothing, but each one had followed what the others said.

Swamiji's retelling of the story of the Nose Cutters reflected a general distrust of self-proclaimed gurus, coupled with a suspicion of their ability to work miracles. As a contemporary guru who is aware of traditional cautionary tales, Ammachi Amritanandamayi is more modest in her claims. Nevertheless, her reputed abilities to give *darshan* of the divine and to perform miraculous cures are more problematic than some critics can endure. There is continuing dissent from claims to miracles by thinkers seeking to remain faithful to Hindu tradition.

Dissent: Ancient and Modern Objections to Miracles

In ancient India, two philosophical systems challenged the metaphysical legitimacy and religious value of miracles: the Cārvāka and the Mīmāmsā. As these schools of thought demonstrate, reflective people have always found reason to question whether humans have access to supernatural power. I. C. Sharma, scholar of the history of philosophy in India, described Cārvāka as combining metaphysical materialism, hedonistic ethics, and skepticism regarding all spiritual claims. For Cārvākas the only valid knowledge is derived from direct perception. "There is no heaven, no final liberation, nor any soul in another world."[29] Accepting only the evidence of the senses, they held that human consciousness emerged from the four natural elements and did not have a transcendent basis. "If it is argued that the postulate of God is required to explain the functioning of the causes in the world the Cārvākas retort that there is nothing behind nature, beyond nature, or other than nature."[30] As consistent materialists, they rejected the possibility of miracles, including the wonder of an eternal, ethereal spirit.

The later school of Indian philosophy known as Mīmāmsā was more faithful to Vedic teaching of the soul, even while rejecting belief in miracles, and thus proved more influential in shaping popular moral standards and religious practices. Mīmāmsakas argued that because the Vedas teach that all reality is one, science and religion yield valid understanding of reality from different vantage points: science investigates its manifestations, while religion seeks the vision of its essence. The practical consequence is that science and religion must respect each other's claims and observe the boundaries between their spheres of authority. That separation is not hard to maintain on Hindu grounds since nothing can be deduced from the manifold world about its undifferentiated source, and there is no insight into the immutable Brahman that could yield information about objects in the world. The effect of the Mīmāmsā analysis is to restrict our knowledge of the world to what is possible within structures of space and time.

Thus, the state of consciousness attained by the most adept yogi provides no ground for suspending natural or social order. Even one liberated in this life remains bound by karmic obligations for acts done in former lives. For the yogi who claimed to have attained psychic powers, Mīmāmsakas provided stark alternatives: either he has attained *moksha* (spiritual liberation) and his body should wither away or he is still under karmic obligations and he should get busy fulfilling them through *dharma* (moral virtue and social duty). Under either scenario, there is no room for his displaying "wondrous powers" in defiance of the laws of nature.[31] Theirs was a harsh judgment, but spoken with confidence that they were supported by the Vedas, the highest Hindu authority.

A modern champion of the Vedas also criticized the desire for miracles. Swami Vivekananda (1863–1902) was the eloquent representative of Hindu tradition at the Parliament of World Religions held in Chicago in 1893, who charmed his audiences with a message that affirmed the validity of all religious paths. The title *swami* (from Sanskrit for master or prince) identified Vivekananda as a Hindu teacher with a regal bearing that added to his mystique. He later founded the Vedanta Society to disseminate his teachings in the West. Like the Mīmāmsā system, Vivekananda's philosophy combined respect for Vedic scriptures, emphasis on moral duty, and rejection of miracles. When asked about the crucifixion of Christ, Vivekananda responded that the execution was a "mirage" because Christ was God incarnate and, therefore, could not die. The questioner followed up by suggesting that such a successful illusion could be considered "the greatest miracle of all" and drew this response from the swami: "I look upon miracles as the greatest stumbling-blocks in the way of truth."[32]

Vivekananda equated the desire for miracles with the wish "to get by gift of the gods what ought to be earned by personal effort." He held in contempt those who sought divine favors as engaged in a religion of "shop keeping." Later the swami offered a more sympathetic explanation of why "we are all running after the miraculous and extraordinary" when he called the desire an indication of universal dissatisfaction with human bondage to physical forces. As embodied creatures we cannot escape the inflexible order of the material world, yet "there is that human instinct to rebel against nature's laws." The futile impulse to live free from physical constraint—whether expressed in obsessive technological development or fervent prayers for miracles—is a reflection of our inner longing for spiritual freedom. "As long as we obey the laws we are like machines, and on goes the universe, and we cannot break it." But once we recognize our desire for freedom from gravity, say, as a covert longing to identify with God "as a perfectly free Being," we cannot rest content.[33]

When Vivekananda was challenged to perform a miracle to confirm the truth of his teaching, he declined on these grounds: "In the first place, I am no miracle worker, and in the second place the pure Hindoo religion I profess is not based on miracles . . . There are wonders wrought beyond our five senses, but they are operated by some law . . . Most of the strange things which are done in India and reported in the foreign papers are sleight-of-hand tricks or hypnotic illusions."[34] He did not deny that wonders are possible, but insisted that they occur within lawful order. Extraordinary events follow laws we do not yet understand. He seemed to have in mind what he called "demoniacal powers" exhibited in materializing objects and instantaneous healing. "I have seen fools heal at a glance, by the will, the most horrible diseases. There are powers, truly, but often demoniacal powers."[35] He insisted, "You must not mix up Christ or Buddha with hobgoblins flying through the air and all that sort of nonsense. Sacrilege! Christ coming into a spiritualistic séance to dance! I have seen that pretence in this country. It is not in that way that these manifestations of God come."[36] To Vivekananda Jesus was not a wonder worker, but the bearer of the same universal truth he drew from the Vedas: that humans find divine presence only by looking within, not by seeking miracles without.

That truth, realized in a life of moral purity, was for Vivekananda the essence of the *Bhagavad-Gītā*, as well as the heart of all the world's scriptures, and is "open to all men and women, to all caste and color," beyond distinctions created by ritual regulations. Vivekananda expressed his version of Hindu teaching in simple abstract terms that could be understood and applied by any person of good will. To introduce miracles as the validation of spiritual truth or as the basis of religious authority, he insisted, was wrong-headed because such a move attempted to establish the universal on the particular and make the eternal dependent on the historical. Changes in the physical world, no matter how spectacular, cannot transform the spirit. Thus, the swami stated flatly: "Our religion has nothing to do with them."[37]

Vivekananda was well versed in the *Yoga Sutras* and included a commentary on them in his work called *Rāja-Yoga*. But he did not rationalize the sutras of Patanjali; rather, he began with a direct challenge to Western rationalism: "Immanuel Kant has said, no doubt, that we cannot penetrate beyond the tremendous dead wall called reason. But that we *can* go beyond reason is the very first idea upon which all Indian thought takes its stand."[38] Indeed, Vivekananda asserted that going beyond reason is the way all religions take to a direct understanding of reality. "This going beyond ignorance, and nothing else, is the goal of religion."[39] On this point Kant would agree, but he would draw the skeptical conclusion that the attempt to transcend the phenomenal world and gaze directly on noumenal realities, such as God, is the futile dream of religion that presumes to transgress the limits of reason. For Vivekananda, however, the yogi's consciousness is perfectly conformed to reality beyond the forms or categories by which the mind organizes the field of perception into distinct objects. When we name those objects, we are describing their forms, not their essence; thus, naming as the primary expression of knowledge is only an approximation of the truth. The yogi's mind, by contrast, corresponds exactly to what is real, so that whatever he says about any state of affairs is true. "When this power of truth is established within you . . . whatever you say will be truth. . . . If a man is diseased, and you say to him, 'Be thou cured,' he will be cured immediately."[40]

Such yogic power sounds like the healing "at a glance" Vivekananda earlier declared demoniacal. But the difference lies in the yogi's disciplined practice of meditation that allows him to see and declare the eternally perfect reality that is distorted by the form of a diseased and suffering body. In reality, the man *is* Brahman, undivided and immutable; the yogi speaks what is true and delivers the man from the illusion of sickness. In healing the yogi employs neither demonic nor divine power, simply the illumination of his own concentrated mind. In the same way, Vivekananda explained a yogi's ability to become invisible: "He does not really vanish, but he will not be seen by anyone. . . .You must remember that this can only be done when the yogi has attained to that power of concentration when the form and the thing formed have been separated."[41] The yogi's disappearance is an illusion in that he is still there, but his individuating form has evaporated, dissipated by the yogi's focused concentration on unmanifested Brahman. There is no formed thing left for his audience to see.

Vivekananda proceeded to affirm the possibility of all the *siddhis* (paranormal powers) in the *Yoga Sutras*, and it is surprising to read his unqualified agreement with Patanjali's descriptions of yogic feats. He even accepted the claim that a yogi "can make himself as minute as an atom or as huge as a mountain, as heavy as the earth or as light as air." Further, such a yogi can make his body invulnerable. "In the Vedas it is written for such a man there is no more disease, death, or pain."[42] But Vivekananda underscored Patanjali's teaching that, while the powers are possible to attain, they are not desirable to practice. "The powers which the yogi obtains, however, are obstructions to the attainment of the highest goal, the knowledge of the Pure Self, or freedom. These are to be met on the way, and if the yogi rejects them he attains the highest. If he is tempted to acquire these, his farther progress is barred."[43] Thus, claims to authority by any teacher based on miracles rather than the universality of his teachings are "the greatest stumbling-blocks in the way of truth."

It is important to emphasize that Vivekananda did not object to miracles because he was convinced that Western scientific method provided an exhaustive account of reality—but for profoundly religious reasons. Faithful dissent from belief in miracles is always grounded in new interpretations of themes *within* the tradition. The relative compatibility of those interpretations with modern scientific understanding is a matter of varying interest among the figures we are considering. We turn finally to a political figure of significance in postcolonial India, whose influential restatement of Hindu teaching condemned reliance on miracles.

Sarvepalli Radhakrishnan (1888–1975) was educated in Christian missionary schools, but promoted inclusiveness among religions and formulated his understanding of Hinduism from the version of Vedantism made popular in the West by Swami Vivekananda. After achieving stellar careers at Calcutta University and Oxford University, he filled the post of India's ambassador to the Soviet Union, and served as president of India from 1962 to 1967. Throughout this impressive career, Radhakrishnan remained a reflective scholar, drawing from his study of Indian philosophy to promote ideals of democracy and tolerance.

One brief text among his many writings, based on lectures given at Oxford in 1926, proved influential in communicating to the Western world a view of Hinduism that was free from superstition and magic. He called the book *The Hindu View of Life* and represented the tradition as composed of an unchanging essence contained in evolving forms of beliefs and practices. This distinction is a common modernist device for separating what is regarded as the moral core of a tradition from its outmoded and dispensable aspects. "Above all," he wrote, "what counts is not creed but conduct . . . Religion is not correct belief but righteous living."[44] The implicit premise of this position is that contemporary readers bring ethical insights from a more enlightened viewpoint to the tradition that serve as normative criteria for identifying what is essential and what should now be discarded. For Radhakrishnan, the essence of Hinduism is the identification of the self with the Absolute taught by Śankara, leading him to distinguish sharply between that abstract piety and the concrete religious expectations of most Indian people. "It is true," he sighed, "the thinking Hindu desires to escape from the confusion of the gods into the silence of the Supreme, but the crowd still stands gazing into the heavens."[45] In that posture, he was convinced, his fellow citizens would never join the march of progress.

Radhakrishnan used the non-dualism of Śankara to defend the unity of the spiritual and the natural, while preserving the integrity of nature that precludes intervention in its operation by supernatural agency. "There can be no final breach between the two powers of the human mind, reason and intuition. Beliefs that foster and promote the spiritual life of the soul must be in accordance with the nature and the laws of the world of reality with which it is their aim to bring us into harmony."[46] Further, Radhakrishnan argued that belief in miracles—by encouraging believers to look to the heavens for needed improvements on earth—failed the test of providing impetus to moral action and so must be judged false. Radhakrishnan devoted the second half of the book to explaining *dharma*, moral duty in the broadest sense, as promoting ethical ideals rather than obstructing them. He was aware of the common objections in the West that Hindu allegiance to caste led to fatalism and defeated individual judgment and ambition. Schooled in British ideals of rationality, he acknowledged that some criticisms were justified regarding popular forms of Indian religion; but he was convinced that the deeper teaching of the tradition was metaphysically sound, morally inspiring, and free of miracles.

Opposing the view that *karma* is "sometimes interpreted as implying a denial of human freedom, which is generally regarded as the basis of all ethical values," Radhakrishnan offered a less deterministic view of the effect of *karma* on human action: that its determinative effect is to preserve the past, not to dictate the future. Thus, the "universe is not one in which every detail is decreed . . . There is no such thing as absolute prescience on the part of God, for we are all his fellow-workers. God is not somewhere above us and beyond us, but he is also within us."[47] The divine presence can inspire us to change our moral disposition and move us to heroic action on behalf of others. Humans are free to transform themselves, but no agent, human or divine, can alter the fixed order of nature. "The course of nature is determined not by the passions and prejudices of personal spirits lurking behind it but by the operation of immutable laws. . . . There is the march of necessity everywhere. The universe is lawful to the core."[48] For Radhakrishnan ultimate power sustains the world, but does not change its operation. In the world so conceived, reliance on miracles is bad faith.

Summary

Miracle stories in Hindu tradition are signs of transcendent wisdom, demonstrating the transience and impermanence of the material world and the mutability of moral judgments, social order, and political authority. The stories support the hope that humans are not finally constrained by necessary laws of nature or inflexible demands of *karma*. Through the grace of an avatar or saint, the discipline of a yogi, or the authority of a guru, miracles shatter the illusion that the world and our destinies within it are permanent. The meaning of Hindu stories about moments of cosmic disruption is that each signifies a way to liberation of the self from attachment to this world. Readers willing to enter the narrative world of a miracle story by pursuing the path to liberation traced in it may find the goal of Hindu spirituality, in all its manifold forms, open to them. Faithful dissenters within the tradition, however, insist that belief in miracles undercuts scientific understanding of the natural order, encourages attachment to the material world, detracts from the spiritual authority of religious teaching, and weakens the sense of responsibility for achieving political and cultural advance. Nevertheless, some Hindu believers in miracles insist that they are dramatic proof that even in this darkened age divine energy is still at play in the world, revealing what we cannot see, healing what we cannot cure, and liberating what we cannot set free.

Judaism

Signs of Covenant

One of the most often told miracle stories in the Jewish tradition concerns an argument among rabbis over whether a stove of a certain construction could be ritually impure. Rabbi Eliezer ben Hyrcanus (40–120 C.E.) was certain of his view that the oven was clean, but the others disagreed. According to a later commentator, the incident was called "The Oven of Akhnai" because "they encompassed it with arguments as a snake (*Akna*) and declared it unclean."[1] Here is the story:

Rabbi Eliezer offered all the possible arguments in support of his judgment, and still his colleagues remained unconvinced. "If the *Halakhah* (legal tradition) agrees with me," he declared, "let this carob (locust) tree prove it." Immediately, the tree uprooted and replanted at a distant spot. The other rabbis shook their heads, "No proof may be brought from a carob tree." Eliezer was unfazed. "If I am right," he persisted, "let this stream of water prove it." The stream, at his word, reversed the direction of its flow. "There is no proof in a stream," the others responded. "Very well," said Eliezer, "If the *Halakhah* agrees with me, let the walls of the schoolhouse prove it." At once, the walls began to teeter, but Rabbi Joshua admonished the walls: "What role do you have in settling a dispute about Torah?" Caught between two authorities, the walls did not topple, but neither did they return to their upright position. They stood at an incline. Calling on his final authority, Eliezer said, "If I am right, let Heaven confirm my judgment." Thereupon, a heavenly voice (*Bat Kol*) was heard: "Why do you dispute with Rabbi Eliezer? The *Halakhah* accords with him on every point." But even the echo of divine confirmation was not enough to establish Eliezer's case. Rabbi Joshua quoted from the Bible: "The Torah is not in heaven" (Deuteronomy 30:21). Further, the Law states, "One must incline after the majority" (Exodus 23:2). The matter was settled. Rabbi Eliezer lost the argument and his standing in the community. He was banned from further disputes and only later in his life reinstated as a legal scholar.[2]

This story appears in one of the tractates of the Talmud, the body of Jewish law and commentary on the Torah, and reflects the strong ambivalence in Jewish tradition toward miracles. On the one hand, belief in God's sovereign control of nature and history includes the possibility of his intervening to change the course of either or both. On the other hand, God placed human beings into the world, gave them his Torah or "instruction" for how to live, and charged them with making the best of it through their own intelligence and hard work. On yet another hand—and in Jewish reflection there are at least three hands—the Bible contains stories of divine intervention through prophets and judges that cannot be denied, and there are stories of pious and just masters in the Hasidic tradition who exercise wondrous powers. As a result, the Jewish attitude is skeptical and trusting, idealistic and pragmatic, at the same time. Rabbi Louis Jacobs sums up the position this way: "A Hasidic saying has it that a Hasid who believes that all the miracles said to have been performed by the Hasidic masters actually happened is a fool. But anyone who believes that they could not have happened is an unbeliever. The same can be said of miracles in general."[3]

In our story, Eliezer was an honored rabbi of the generation following the destruction of the temple in Jerusalem (70 C.E.). His piety and insight were legendary, yet not even he was allowed to call upon miraculous control of nature to establish a point of law. The other rabbis insisted that his power could not verify his wisdom; nothing he did to change a tree or a stream could substitute for persuasive argument. In this controversy, the rabbis were not only concerned about asserting the authority of legal scholars over charismatic miracle workers; after all, Eliezer was one of their own. They were also troubled that Eliezer attempted to short-circuit the only process humans have to arrive at truth: prayerful and ferocious argument that continues until one side convinces the other or the dispute extends, unresolved, into succeeding generations of scholars. No leaping tree or backward flowing stream was relevant to that process—and, remarkably, neither was a voice from heaven, called *Bat Kol*, literally "daughter of a voice." *Bat Kol* was the medium of revelation in the period following the last of the biblical prophets, but it was of inferior quality because it was indeterminate in meaning and often indistinguishable from a human voice. So by the time of our story, *Bat Kol* was overruled as an authority in a dispute over *Halakhah* (a term derived from a Hebrew root meaning "to walk" that designates laws governing daily Jewish practice).

The point of Rabbi Joshua's quotation from Deuteronomy, "It is in heaven," is that once God disclosed his immutable will to humans, it became their responsibility to determine what Torah meant in changing historical circumstances. Gershom Scholem (1897–1982), the scholar of Jewish mysticism, placed the story in the larger context of the development of tradition through dialectical interplay between the revealed text (Written Torah) and the rabbis' interpretation over the centuries (Oral Torah). Scholem reads the story as establishing the "authority of commentary over author."[4] According to a later addition to the story, even God conceded that Rabbi Joshua successfully cited Scripture against the heavenly voice. Laughing, the Almighty admitted, "My children have overcome me, my children have overcome me!"[5]

In Jewish tradition, knowledge of God is always mediated, first and foremost through the language of Torah: the echo of God's voice in the present. How that echo resonates in each generation, guiding the lives of the Jewish people through new challenges, depends upon faithful interpretation, arising from debate among reasonable people, whose conclusions will always be provisional, subject to further refinement and application, even reversal. When it comes to how humans are supposed to conduct themselves in the world, there is no final word, not even from heaven.[6] As Scholem put it, "God's word is infinitely interpretable."[7] The very quality that distinguishes divine revelation from human insight is that God's words have no fixed meaning. Accordingly, the cultural critic Michael Walzer reads the story of the oven of Akhnai as an exemplary tale about the never-ending process of moral judgment. Morality, he writes, "is something we have to argue about. The argument implies common possession, but common possession does not imply agreement. There is a tradition, a body of moral knowledge; and there is this group of sages, arguing. There isn't anything else."[8] Whatever miracles may mean in the Jewish tradition, they cannot serve to settle arguments over questions of ethics or theology. Literary critic Susan Handelman notes that revelation is marked by the capacity to generate endless layers of meaning; but "infinite interpretation means many authorities"[9]—a fact that explains why the walls of the schoolhouse froze in mid-totter, unable to decide which rabbinic command to obey. The rabbis themselves were more decisive: they placed Eliezer under a ban.

While Rabbi Eliezer received the news of his excommunication with tears of humility, one authority recorded, "Great was the calamity on that day, for everything at which R. Eliezer cast his eyes was burned up." The effect of his exile was felt even at sea, where one supporter of the ban, Rabbi Gamaliel, found himself about to be drowned by a gigantic wave that he declared to be the judgment of Eliezer. Gamaliel prayed for deliverance while defending his action: "Sovereign of the Universe! Thou knowest full well that I have not acted for my honor, nor for the honor of my paternal house, but for Thine, so that differences may not multiply in Israel."[10] The ocean calmed.

Here we may have the key to understanding why Eliezer's appeal to supernatural intervention led to the severe punishment of exclusion from the community of legal scholars. He called for a special revelation to authorize a particular ruling about Jewish practice. If such an appeal were allowed to stand, a dangerous precedent would be set for introducing innovations in Halakhah, compromising the purity laws that defined Jewish identity and threatening to splinter the community over differences of practice. For the rabbis, the prospect of fragmentation into sects was a daunting threat to their project of unifying the Jewish people under the system of laws. To demonstrate that the heart of Jewish faith was obedience to Torah, not determined by divine caprice or individual charisma, the rabbis excluded miracles and special revelations from the discussion of Jewish law.

Nevertheless, the rabbis' restrictions on miracles did not bind the imagination of the faithful. Popular hope in divine intervention surfaced in the use of amulets, prayers for fertility and healing, and appeals for rescue. They were encouraged by stories of miracles in the Hebrew Bible (called *Tanakh*, an acronym composed of the Hebrew initials for Law, Prophets, and Writings). Yet the fact remained that, even in the Bible, God as a worker of miracles receded from the narrative until, in the crisis facing the Jewish people at the time of Esther during the Persian Empire, God is not even named in the account.[11] Later Jewish reflection attributed his absence not to disinterest on God's part but to the faithlessness of the people when they returned to the land of Israel after their exile in Babylonia. "Why is Esther compared to the morning?" one rabbi asked rhetorically, "To tell you that just as the morning is the end of all the night, so Esther is the end of all miracles."[12] While the rabbis remained skeptical of miracle reports, they could not deny the power of God to intervene in nature and history as stories in the Bible bore dramatic witness.

Lord of History: Exodus and Sinai

The accounts of creation in Genesis 1–3 present us with the miracle of God's creating free creatures whose being and agency were determined by no preexisting conditions and whose freedom was unconstrained. As a result, the biblical narrative after the appearance of Adam and Eve was shaped by tragic choices. While nature offered no resistance to God's purpose, springing into being at the divine word, the human story was marked by rebellion and a lust for power that made divine intervention, on occasion, necessary. Jewish tradition was consistent, however, in reading the stories of miracles on behalf of the children of Israel with critical awareness of the moral ambiguity of even divine acts and the paradoxical claim that divine assistance increases, rather than lessens, human responsibility.

By the end of the first book of the Bible the Israelites were in trouble. Having fled to Egypt to escape famine in Israel, they found themselves, generations later, hopelessly enslaved. Under the iron rule of Pharaoh these descendants of Abraham were without defense and cried out for supernatural deliverance. The story of their release, called *Exodus*, is central in Jewish tradition. The outline of the narrative is familiar to readers of the Bible and has inspired campaigns for justice throughout the centuries. By rescuing the children of Israel from slavery in Egypt and revealing his commandments for moral and religious life at Mount Sinai, God both sealed his covenant with the Jewish people and also disclosed his will that all humans should abide by ideals of justice, peace, and mercy. The event of deliverance at the Red Sea was clearly an act of transcendent power, but so also was the event of revelation at Mount Sinai. Both were miracles, and both were enacted through the human agency of Moses, the first prophet in the Bible and one who spoke directly with God.

The career of Moses was punctuated by miracles, beginning with God's call to him. Moses was born into a poor family during a time when the Egyptian ruler directed that Jewish male infants be killed, lest his subject population become too numerous and rebel against his power. Moses' mother put him in a small ark made of reeds and sent him floating down river to where the Pharaoh's daughter was bathing. The princess rescued the boy, and his sister, waiting nearby, recommended their mother as his wet nurse. So Moses was raised in Pharaoh's palace, unaware of his true identity. As a young man, however, he witnessed an Egyptian overseer beating a Jewish slave. Moved to defend the victim by an impulse born of kinship he had not realized until that moment, Moses killed the attacker.

When Pharaoh sought to kill Moses in retaliation, he fled Egypt to the Sinai Peninsula, where he married a Midianite woman who bore him a son. It was while tending sheep for his father-in-law that Moses received the vision that changed his life. Following his flock on the side of Mount Sinai, Moses saw a bush in the distance, ablaze but not consumed by fire. As he approached the marvel, he heard a voice call his name and demand that he take off his sandals in respect for holy ground. Moses "hid his face, for he was afraid to look at God" (Exodus 3:6). God said he was aware of the suffering of the Israelites and that he was sending Moses to confront Pharaoh and lead the people out of slavery. Moses was reluctant to accept the mission and asked how he should answer if the people asked who had sent him. Then God disclosed his personal name to Moses in the phrase, "I AM WHO I AM." The divine name is signified by four Hebrew consonants that are transliterated as YHWH and rendered by scholars as *Yahweh*.[13] God translated the name for Moses as derived from the verb *hayah* meaning "to be." The mysterious personal name of God evokes controversial speculation in Jewish tradition, but in the immediate context God seemed to give it as an assurance that he would "be there" for Moses and for the Israelites. As God was faithful to his people in the past, so he is now and will be in the future.

The human instrument of divine loyalty to the Israelites was Moses, and his first test was before Pharaoh in a competition with court magicians. The sorcerers threw down their staffs and they turned into serpents. Aaron, Moses' brother and spokesman, duplicated the feat, but his staff-turned-snake swallowed the magicians' serpents. Later tradition interpreted the transformation of Aaron's staff as a miracle, but the magicians' wonder as a trick, accomplished with the help of demonic powers.[14] The rhetorical distinction between miracle and magic, as we noted in chapter 1, is often employed in accounts of contests and functions as a polemical device for explaining how those without divine authorization are capable of performing wonders.

The best known miracles of Moses were acts of judgment he called down on the land of Egypt: the ten plagues. God empowered Moses to turn forces of nature against the Egyptians: the water of the Nile turned to blood, the land was overrun by frogs and flies, the livestock grew sick and died, the people were afflicted with boils, thunder and hail pounded the earth, locusts devoured the remaining crops, and darkness engulfed Egypt. Then, the last and most terrible blow: the firstborn of every creature in the land fell dead. What gave Moses such devastating power? Philo of Alexandria (30 B.C.E.–45 C.E.), who wrote extensively on the life of Moses, commented that "each element obeyed him as its master, changed its natural properties and submitted to his command." For Philo this was "no wonder" because Moses was called the friend of God and "it would follow that he shares also God's possessions, so far as it is serviceable."[15] These miracles of judgment were first and foremost acts of divine power—"these signs of mine," God called them (Exodus 10:1)—of which Moses was the instrument.

Pharaoh finally relented and gave permission for Moses to lead the Israelites out of Egypt. Then, for reasons hidden in the mystery of God's purpose and Pharaoh's motivation, he changed his mind and set out with his army to pursue his former slaves. At the bank of the sea blocking the way to the Sinai Peninsula, the Israelites realized they were trapped. It would seem that two miracles were possible at that point: God could have softened Pharaoh's heart as he had earlier hardened it, making the ruler change his mind yet again and turn back to Egypt, or God could stop the flow of the sea water and create a passageway for the Israelites. God chose the latter miracle and "drove the sea back by a strong east wind all night, and turned the sea into dry land; and the waters were divided"—or "rent asunder" (Exodus 14:21).

Rabbi Hanokh of Alexander (d. 1870) addressed the question why the waters of the Red Sea are said to have been "rent asunder" and not "split apart." To be split, he explained, indicated a small slit but to be rent asunder created a huge opening. Then he noted that the Midrash (exegetical commentary) on the passage teaches that the sea resisted Moses' call to split because it would not go beyond the "pale of nature" at mere human bidding. But when the sea saw the coffin containing the bones of Joseph the people were bearing to the Holy Land, it complied and parted to let them pass. The commentators explain that the sea recognized that Joseph went beyond the pale of nature by resisting the temptation of Potiphar's wife, and so it was willing to follow his example by resisting laws of hydrology.[16] Here is another instance in which the power of the human spirit to exert moral control over physical impulses is compared to the power of a miracle to overcome natural order.

Still, the question of whether the parting of the waters was a natural occurrence rather than a true miracle lurked in the background of Jewish reflection. A skeptic once told Rabbi Israel ben Eleazer (founder of the Hasidic movement whose career we will consider later) that he had calculated the forces of nature requiring the Red Sea to open at the exact hour the children of Israel reached its bank. The rabbi answered, "Don't you know that God created nature? And he created it so, that at the hour the children of Israel passed through the Red Sea, it had to divide. That is the great and famous miracle."[17] Rather than undermining the miraculous character of the event, the description of the precise coordination of physical conditions necessary to produce the effect served, for the rabbi, as proof of God's exquisite control over the interplay of nature and history. This exchange illustrates why, for many believers, the natural account of an event is entirely compatible with its religious interpretation as a miracle. For Jewish understanding the significance of the miraculous rescue from Pharaoh is that it discloses God's special care of the people of Israel and God's general interest in human liberation.

The Exodus also reveals something about the nature of Israel's faith by insisting that seeing is a necessary, if not sufficient, condition for believing. In the annual ritual observance of Exodus, called Passover, the prayer requires those gathered around the Paschal meal to identify with the ancient event by beginning, "When *we* were slaves in Egypt. . . ." To place oneself imaginatively at the bank of the sea, impassable water ahead and implacable enemies behind, is to become an eyewitness to the wonder. The contemporary author of Midrash, Avivah Zornberg, comments, "Sight, the public testimony of the Israelite audience, generates faith and knowledge. . . . The very last words of the Torah tell of 'all the signs and wonders . . . and all the mighty power and all the deeds of great terror which Moses wrought *before the eyes of all Israel*' (Deuteronomy 34:11–12)."[18] The end of the story of crossing the sea also emphasizes the relation between sight and faith: "Israel *saw* the Egyptians dead on the seashore. Israel *saw* the great work that the LORD did against the Egyptians. So, the people *feared* the LORD and *believed* in the LORD and in his servant Moses" (Exodus 14:30–31). Moses instructed the people to walk across the dry sea bed in silence: "The LORD will fight for you, and you have only to keep still" (Exodus 14:14). Zornberg suggests, "Perhaps the emphasis on silence as the people enter the Red Sea is a necessary part of the perception of the miracle."[19] The necessity of silence can be understood in light of the fact that an event can be perceived as a miracle only in the state of wonder, an appreciation of the extraordinary act as such, prior to interpretive commentary or celebrative song. In fact, the latter could be positively misleading.

That observation brings us to another lesson in the miracle at the Red Sea, drawn from the fact that the waters not only parted but also returned in place, drowning Pharaoh and his army. In the moment of wonder a miracle blurs the bright lines of distinction upon which the consistency of rational analysis and moral judgment depends. Miracles are transgressive events that disclose possibilities beyond limits set by reason, nature, and history. As such, miracles often lack clear moral interpretation and so send an ambiguous signal. We have seen that Jewish tradition candidly acknowledges that element of ambiguity and the risk of misreading the significance of a wondrous event. The story of Exodus is a prime example.

After the people of Israel marched through the dry sea bed, God released the wall of water and swept Pharaoh's pursuing forces to their deaths. In celebration of the miraculous escape Miriam, the sister of Moses, led the Israelites in a victory dance. According to rabbinic commentary, the angels pleaded with God to let them join in the festivities. "My children lie drowned in the Red Sea," the Almighty thundered, "and you would sing?" The miracle signified a more complicated reality than a triumphalist reading of the event could comprehend. Emil Fackenheim (1916–2003), noted professor of philosophy, wrote in his meditation on divine presence and catastrophe that this commentary is often quoted in well-meaning sermons on God's universal benevolence. "The real content of the Midrash, however, is otherwise. *Even in the supreme but pre-Messianic moment of His saving presence God cannot save Israelites without killing Egyptians. Thus the infinite joy of the moment . . . is mingled with sorrow . . . God and man in Judaism pay each their price for the stubbornness with which they hold fast to actual—not 'spiritual'—history."*[20] In other words, the Jewish interpretation of any event as a miracle is constrained by the brute facts of history. No matter how much the interpreter labors to draw a spiritual or moral lesson from the story of a divine act, he or she is not allowed to ignore "facts on the ground." If an event is from the hand of the Lord of history, then its meaning cannot evade its effects in history: in this case, Egyptian corpses floating in the Red Sea. While the death of their pursuers was an unavoidable element in their escape, the full meaning of the Exodus as a sign was revealed only at the foot of Mount Sinai.

The diverse commentaries on the parting of the Red Sea agree on one point: that God saved the people of Israel so that they could travel to the southern tip of the Sinai Peninsula and there receive the divine law that would govern their covenantal relationship with God. Exodus and Sinai are intimately related and together constitute the founding of the Jewish community. They are both miraculous events—of divine deliverance and divine revelation—of central importance in Jewish life, referred to often and celebrated in annual rituals of observance.

When they finally reached their destination, God directed Moses to warn the people not to approach the mountain, lest they be struck dead. As the ground surrounding the burning bush was sacred by virtue of the divine presence, so the mountain was transformed into sacred space by God's descent to meet with Moses on the summit. What is sacred is literally "set aside" for divine use, and thus taboo for humans except those specially designated. Only Moses was permitted to approach God and to hear his voice directly. For the people the occasion was terrifying: "there was thunder and lightning, as well as a thick cloud on the mountain, and a blast of a trumpet so loud that all the people who were in the camp trembled" (Exodus 19:16).

What Moses heard on the mountain were God's laws for the Jewish people, beginning with what are commonly called the "Ten Commandments." But Jewish tradition came to include all the other rules Moses received in the

Torah as well. Later commentators identified 613 commandments or *mitzvot* given on Sinai, including laws governing worship, treatment of slaves, property, acts of violence, sexual conduct, financial dealings, annual festivals, and construction of the tabernacle housing the ark containing stone tablets on which the laws were engraved. "When God finished speaking with Moses on Mount Sinai, he gave him the two tablets of the covenant, tablets of stone, written with the finger of God" (Exodus 31:18).

Moses was on the mountain for forty days and, in the meanwhile, the Israelites began to doubt that he had survived the ordeal. They appealed to Aaron to create a statue of a calf cast from their melted gold jewelry, thus violating the second commandment Moses received: "You shall not make for yourself an idol." When Moses returned and saw the people wildly dancing around the golden calf, he was furious. Moses hurled the tablets to the ground, breaking them, smashed the calf to powder, and spread it on water which he compelled the people to drink. Then, in a fiercely retributive act, Moses called upon the men of the tribe of Levi to range through the camp, killing with the sword "a son or brother" and thereby consecrating by blood their own fidelity to Yahweh. Three thousand fell that day. Moses then returned to the cloud-enshrouded mountain, carrying two new tablets, and this time he carved in stone the commandments repeated by the divine voice. When he returned from the presence of the Lord, his face was radiant. Moses "did not know that the skin of his face was shining," but the people were wonderstruck and "they were afraid to come near him" (Exodus 34:29–30).

Jonathan Sacks, Chief Rabbi of the United Kingdom, glosses the story of the two copies of the commandments as two moments of revelation corresponding to "an awakening from above" and "an awakening from below." He explains, "The former is an act initiated by God, the latter, one set in motion by human beings. An awakening from above is the kind of event to which we give the name 'miracle'. . . . A miracle is a moment when the veil behind which God is hidden is lifted and we see a signal of transcendence."[21] Strangely enough, events of supernatural intervention awaken *less* responsibility in those who witness them than awakenings from below. "If an awakening from above is God's gesture of reaching down to humankind, an awakening from below is a human gesture of reaching up toward heaven. . . . The first tablets, made entirely by God, were an awakening from above. The second, hewn by Moses, involved an awakening from below."[22] The point Sacks emphasizes is that the biblical narrative moves steadily in the direction of fewer miracles from above and more demands that humans fulfill the divine will by reaching up from below. This movement continues throughout the tradition and results in a reluctance to affirm miracles if there is any suspicion they might undercut Jewish responsibility to keep the Torah with all one's mind, and soul, and strength.[23]

It is ironic that Sacks draws his Midrash of declining miracles from the revelation at Sinai because Exodus and the giving of the Law mark the beginning of divine intervention in the life of the people of Israel. Inasmuch as the sense of obligation to act toward others with justice and compassion is contrary to the instincts of the human animal, some regard the moral impulse required to obey Torah as a transcendent element in human consciousness. But at the same time, once Torah is given, responsibility for maintaining just social order among themselves and peaceful relations with their neighbors falls on the Israelites themselves. The nature of law is that its subjects must acknowledge its provisions as valid over them and must uphold its demands in their actions or it has no power. Inasmuch as Yahweh established his relation with the Israelites on the basis of law, he made his authority vulnerable to their consent. Despite all the thunder and lightning surrounding God's presence, the deal struck on Sinai was one that required the cooperation of the people standing at the foot of the mountain. It was not until they pledged to accept the revealed laws and to remain faithful to Yahweh alone that the covenant between God and the Jewish people was sealed. Torah was the appropriate link between them: disclosed by divine revelation, but interpreted and upheld by human reason and will. Once Torah descended from heaven, it became the living presence of God among the people, adapting to meet their needs but always demanding unconditional respect as the written symbol of the word of God. Torah is the mediator between God and the people, at one remove from the direct and shattering encounter with the actual voice of God which set atremble the people standing at Sinai.

Zornberg interprets the people's dread at hearing the voice of God as the fear that "fire has invaded their inner being." It is too much for ordinary believers to bear. One Midrash teaches that the divine voice was modulated according to the strength of each individual among the 600,000 standing at the foot of the mountain, so that "it should not cause injury" to the hearers. "The historic effect of their terror is that Moses hears and speaks in their place. Moreover, the effect on future generations is that specific people, prophets, will be chosen to fulfill this role that the people now recognize is beyond their capacity."[24] Henceforth, prophets would endure the inner flame and, when they spoke, the divine fire both illumined and consumed them. Jeremiah found that when he resolved no longer to speak in the name of God, "then within me there is something like a burning fire shut up in my bones; I am weary with holding it in, and I cannot" (Jeremiah 20:9). As those through whom God speaks, prophets are living miracles of revelation.

Prophet: Signs and Wonders

In ancient Israel the prophet is one who speaks on behalf of God, and prophets speak with one voice the primary declaration of Jewish faith: "Hear, O Israel: The LORD is our God, the LORD is one" (Deuteronomy 6:4). Throughout the time of Israel's kings, from Saul to Zedekiah, prophets periodically arose to defend faith in Yahweh against the allurement of other deities and the constant pressure to assimilate to religious practices of Canaanite cultures. The pattern of prophets railing against the apostasy of priests and the injustice of kings recurs throughout Israel's history. On some occasions prophets predicted judgments or blessings to come and their authority was determined by whether or not their visions of future events came true. Not even a successful prediction, however, could authorize a prophet whose message departed from strict allegiance to Yahweh: "those prophets or those who divine by dreams shall be put to death for having spoken treason against the LORD your God" (Deuteronomy 13:5). It is a consistent theme in Jewish tradition that miracles, including preternatural knowledge of the future, cannot establish teaching that contradicts the revelation at Sinai. For the most part, however, prophets in Israel were "forth-tellers," not foretellers; and their message of loyalty to Yahweh was sometimes accompanied by the confirming power of miraculous works.

With Moses, the tradition of prophets as God's mouthpieces (sometimes advocates for the people and sometimes their prosecutors) began. Moses was unusual, however, in that he received God's words directly—"the LORD used to speak to Moses face to face, as one speaks to a friend" (Exodus 33:11)—rather than through dreams and visions as most other prophets.[25] For that reason Moses exercised unique authority, supported by miraculous works. At one point on the long march through the wilderness, the Israelites complained of thirst. God instructed Moses to strike a stone with his staff and a spring of water gushed out for the parched people. But in his zeal Moses hit the rock twice and for that added display of ego God forbade him from entering the Promised Land. It was a harsh penalty, but Yahweh took the second strike as a gesture of pride that made it appear that Moses' strength released the spring from the rock.

It is a clear principle in the tradition that miracles are intended to bring glory to God alone, not to bring attention to the miracle worker. If seeing is the necessary condition for believing, as at Sinai, then Moses obscured the view of God's power behind the display of his own energy. Because the water came as a divine gift, one touch of Moses' staff was all that was required. The added blow Yahweh regarded as an act of unbelief; and he rebuked Moses, "Because you did not trust in me, *to show my holiness before the eyes of the Israelites*, therefore you shall not bring this assembly into the land that I have given them" (Numbers 20:12). The miracle can be perceived as a transcendent event, received with wonder, *seen* as a mighty act of God, only if the human agent fades from view.

The final verses of Deuteronomy recount Moses' death on Mount Nebo, overlooking the land of Canaan, and provide this epitaph for his career: "Never since has there arisen a prophet in Israel like Moses, whom the LORD knew face to face. He was unequaled for all the signs and wonders that the LORD sent him to perform in the land of Egypt, against Pharaoh, and all his servants and his entire land, and for all the mighty deeds and all the terrifying displays of power that Moses performed in the sight of all Israel" (Deuteronomy 34:10–12). Of Moses' death the great medieval Jewish thinker Maimonides (1135–1204) observed, "We learn from the words, 'And Moses the servant of the Lord died there in the land of Moab by the mouth of the Lord,' that his death was a kiss."[26] Although forbidden to enter the land to which he had guided the people for forty years, Moses died in intimate relation with Yahweh, and his last breath was drawn into the mouth of God.

No other prophet enjoyed such closeness to God, although Elijah the Tishbite, who arose as a prophet in Israel during the ninth century B.C.E., also exercised great powers, bringing blessing and judgment. Elijah was the first of the prophets called by God to speak his word to the people of Israel after they were settled in the land promised to Abraham and submitted to the rule of kings. It is significant that the term *prophet* was introduced into the biblical narrative at the time of Saul, who was later anointed as the first king of Israel. Saul was sent to retrieve his father's straying donkeys and sought direction from "a man of God." A later editor injected this helpful note into the text: "(Formerly in Israel, anyone who went to inquire of God would say, 'Come, let us go to the seer'; for the one who is now called a prophet was formerly called a seer.)" (1 Samuel 9:9). The change in terminology at this point signals that there is a connection between kings and prophets that provided dynamic tension in the ensuing history of Israel.

The seer/prophet Saul contacted was Samuel, to whom God had revealed his choice of Saul as first king of Israel. While Samuel duly anointed the young man, he thought it a horrible idea to give in to the people's desire to have a king like other nations because, as he scolded them, "the LORD your God was your king" (1 Samuel 12:12). To emphasize the point he called down thunder and rain to remind them of the divine power available to a prophet. He promised them success as a new nation only if they served Yahweh faithfully; otherwise, Samuel growled in his last words to them, "you shall be swept away, both you and your king." The tone of his message forecast the uneasy relationship between kings and prophets from then on and his exercise of supernatural control over the forces of nature was a sign that prophets could work miracles, while no king of Israel ever performed a wondrous work. With the direct relation between God and the people replaced by the mediation of a human ruler with no access to divine power, it was also necessary to establish an independent voice, authorized by God to confront political (and religious) leaders with the raw unfiltered divine will. That is the vocation of the prophet, and it could be a dangerous calling, as Elijah discovered.

Elijah lived during the disintegration of the kingdom of Israel following the death of Solomon. The kings of Judea (the southern kingdom centered in Jerusalem) and Israel (the northern kingdom ruled from Samaria), with few exceptions, followed Solomon's example of taking foreign wives and creating places of worship for their deities. According to the biblical record, the greatest offender in this matter was Ahab, king of Israel, who married Jezebel, daughter of the Sidonian king, and joined her in the worship of the Canaanite god of storms and procreation, called Baal, and erected a sacred pole in honor of the fertility goddess Asherah. The chronicler summarized his career in these words: "Ahab did more to provoke the anger of the LORD, the God of Israel, than had all the kings of Israel who were before him" (1 Kings 16:33).

It is to this utterly apostate king that Elijah abruptly appeared and warned him that God was sending drought—and then turned on his heel and took refuge in a remote wadi where God sent ravens, morning and night, to deliver him meat and bread. When the wadi dried up, God sent Elijah to Sidon to ask sustenance from a widow. When she brought him some bread from her meager stores, Elijah promised that her jug of oil and jar of meal would not run out of provisions until the drought ended. The miracle sustained them, but one day the widow's son fell ill and died. She accused Elijah of punishing her for some forgotten sin, but the prophet took the boy's lifeless body to his own room, laid him on the bed, and stretched his own body on the child's three times, crying to the Lord to revive him. Soon the boy began to breathe again, and Elijah placed him in his mother's arms. She said, "Now I know that you are a man of God, and the word of the LORD in your mouth is truth" (1 Kings 17:24). The power to restore the boy to life not only confirmed Elijah's authority as a prophet, but also foreshadowed the power of Yahweh to end the three-year drought that Canaanite deities of fertility were powerless to overcome. But first Elijah was called to confront the power of Baal more directly.

We learn in a flashback that Queen Jezebel had waged a campaign against the prophets of God and ordered her forces to kill as many as they found. Elijah was thus rightly fearful of Jezebel, but God directed him to present himself to Ahab and issue a challenge: assemble the four hundred and fifty prophets of Baal and the four hundred prophets of Asherah, "who eat at Jezebel's table," at Mount Carmel, in the sight of all the Israelites, to determine whose deity is more powerful. Elijah set before the people a stark choice: "How long will you go limping with two different opinions? If the LORD is God, follow him; but if Baal, then follow him" (1 Kings 18:21). His question captured the dilemma the people were facing, generations removed from Exodus and Sinai. The glory days of King David were long gone, and the "promised land" was dry and barren. The king of Israel, occupying the office established for the people's direction, worshipped Baal. Who is the true God? To make that decision, as in the days of Moses, the people needed to *see* something. As Karen Armstrong, the prolific British author of works on comparative religion, astutely observed, believers in God have always been pragmatists at heart. Loyalty to any particular deity survives as long as it works to provide benefits, to supply guidance, to make suffering endurable, or to help make sense of one's existence.[27] The desire for demonstration of God's identity is the hidden longing of every believer—a longing fully satisfied in the display of miraculous power, the unmistakable mark of sovereignty over the powers of nature. Elijah's challenge was designed to provide such evidence.

The contest was straightforward enough: set up two altars with the body of a bull on each. "Then you call on the name of your god and I will call on the name of the LORD; the god who answers by fire is indeed God." That was exactly the kind of showdown the indecisive Israelites were looking for and they answered, "Well spoken!" The outcome was never in doubt. The prophets of Baal pleaded to heaven all morning with no result, not even when they joined in the "limping dance" (a ritual movement of bending one knee, then the other, while circling the altar). Elijah mocked them, suggesting that Baal was sleeping or perhaps answering the call of nature. The devotees of Baal increased their efforts, even gashing themselves in ritual enactment of sacrifice, but all to no avail. Around three in the afternoon Elijah began rebuilding the altar to Yahweh that was earlier dismantled, using twelve stones representing the tribes of Israel. He dug a large trench around it, placed the pieces of the bull on the wood piled on the altar, and then drenched everything with water until the ditch was full. He prayed that God would reveal himself to the people and so confirm Elijah's status as his servant.

The answer was immediate, spectacular, and excessive: "Then the fire of the LORD fell and consumed the burnt offering, the wood, the stones, and the dust, and even licked up the water that was in the trench" (1 Kings 18:38). The people of Israel fell on their faces and confessed, in nervous repetition, "The LORD indeed is God; the LORD indeed is God." As happened at Sinai, they saw the power of God and faith followed. Was their believing any less valid because it was conditioned on their seeing? Let us turn the question around: if you had seen what they saw, would you believe that "the Lord is God and Elijah is his prophet"? For any one who holds that seeing is believing, the sight of a miracle would seem to be sufficient warrant for belief. But, as we are arguing in this book, the critical question is *what* belief follows from the sight? How is the event to be interpreted? What is its religious significance?

The aftermath of Elijah's demonstration introduces a note of ambiguity in our reading of this contest because the prophet of the Lord proceeded to order the execution of all four hundred and fifty priests of Baal, rounded up in a dry stream bed. Perhaps the site of their slaughter was an ironic comment on the inability of Baal to bring rain, let alone fire. Elijah exacted a terrible price for their losing the challenge and without a direct command from God to do so. The question of interpretation is what are we to make of the bloodshed? Should we attribute it to Elijah's overwrought zeal? Was it divine retribution sanctioned by the miraculous fire from heaven? Where, in the bloody wadi near Mount Carmel, was the God who mourned for the Egyptians drowned in the Red Sea?

When news of Elijah's defeat and destruction of the prophets of Baal reached Jezebel, she vowed not to rest until Elijah was dead. Elijah fled to "Horeb the mount of God" and spent the night in a cave there. The next day "the word of the Lord came to him," asking why he was this far from the scene of his mission. Elijah was prone to a touch of melodramatic self-pity and protested, "I alone am left, and they are seeking my life, to take it away" (1 Kings 19:10). God commanded him to stand on the mountain and prepare for God's presence to pass by. First came an earthquake, then a fire, and finally "a sound of sheer silence" from which Elijah heard God's voice give him his last commission: to anoint two usurpers as the new kings of Israel and Judah and to designate Elisha son of Shaphat "as prophet in your place."

Elijah found Elisha plowing a field, leading twelve pair of oxen. He threw his mantle over the young man and Elisha pledged to serve him. When the time came for Elijah to leave the earth, he was walking with Elisha and several times sought to leave him behind, but each time Elisha insisted, "As the LORD lives, and as you yourself live, I will not leave you." At several points in their journey, Elisha was approached by members of a "company of prophets" who informed him that God would take Elijah that day. When they approached the Jordan River, Elijah rolled up his mantle, struck the water, and it parted to allow them dry passage to the other side. Then Elijah asked Elisha what he would like, and Elisha asked for "a double share" of Elijah's spirit (2 Kings 2:9). The master acknowledged that was "a hard thing" to supply, but "if you see me as I am being taken from you, it will be granted you." Shortly thereafter, a chariot of fire drawn by horses of fire appeared, "and Elijah ascended in a whirlwind into heaven." Elisha "kept watching" and when Elijah finally disappeared from sight, he rent his clothes in mourning and then picked up Elijah's mantle.

Returning to the Jordan, he cried, "Where is the LORD, the God of Elijah?" and struck the water with the master's mantle. Immediately, the water parted. When the company of prophets in Jericho saw him approaching, they declared, "The spirit of Elijah rests on Elisha!" Then, they made a curious request: to search the nearby valleys in case the spirit of God had caught up Elijah and then dropped him. Elisha gave them permission to look for Elijah's body; but when they returned empty-handed, he said, "Did I not say to you, Do not go?" (2 Kings 2:18). This incident confirmed the miracle of Elijah's ascension in the negative sense of failing to disconfirm it. But such confirmation necessarily leaves room for doubt in those who did not witness the event. Only Elisha "kept watching" with eyes wide open, acting as the witness required for any miracle to be registered as a social event. All others must be content with trusting the witness.

But perhaps there are other direct witnesses, since the tradition teaches that Elijah appears from time to time to play his prophetic role of calling Jews to show greater loyalty to the word of God, to pay more attention to the poor and neglected, and to be less meticulous about details of pious living. In one story a rabbi sent a group of his students on a journey without giving them a destination. When they stopped at an inn for a night, they worried the innkeeper with a multitude of questions about whether the meal was prepared according to strict rules of ritual purity. Finally, a figure dressed in rags sitting behind the stove spoke up: "Listen, you Hasidim. You make a great fuss about what goes into your mouths, but do not pay enough attention to what comes out." Before they could reply, the stranger disappeared, as was Elijah's custom.[28]

Elijah is one of two figures in the Tanakh who was taken directly into heaven without suffering death. The other is Enoch, who "walked with God;

then he was no more, because God took him" (Genesis 5:24). What is notable is that both men, miraculously translated into heaven, figure in later speculation about the end times in Jewish apocalyptic literature written in the period between 200 B.C.E. and 200 C.E. In them Enoch appears as a heavenly figure who reveals divine mysteries, including details of the end of history.[29]

The eschatological (end-time) role of Elijah, however, requires his descent to earth. The last of the Hebrew prophets predicted that Elijah will appear in the last days to prepare Israel for judgment: "Remember the teaching of my servant Moses, the statues and ordinances that I commanded him at Horeb for all Israel. Lo, I will send you the prophet Elijah before the great and terrible day of the LORD comes. He will turn the hearts of parents to their children and the hearts of children to their parents, so that I will not come and strike the land with a curse" (Malachi 4:5–6). Elijah's end-time role is consistent with his calling as a prophet: to recall the people of Israel to their covenantal obligations, as revealed to Moses, including the primary duty of respect and affection within the family. He does not come to announce inevitable catastrophe, the subject of most apocalyptic visions, but to avert divine wrath. Elijah brings hope for a radically different world in which justice, compassion, and peace are lived realities. To believe in the return of Elijah is to believe that only a transcendent event, a miracle, can bring about the transformation of humanity and the healing of the world.

Subsequent events, however, sorely tested Jewish confidence in the corrigibility of human nature, so that many gave up hope in the miracle of redemption and embraced visions of apocalyptic retribution. One such group was the sectarian community at Qumran where the Dead Sea Scrolls were discovered. For them history was a failed project, the covenant a broken pact, and nature an abandoned theater. They despaired of miraculous rescues or healings in their own corrupt age, devoid of divine presence, and steeled themselves to endure its evils to the end; yet they took courage from the prospect of miraculous redemption in a future made radically new by divine action.[30] That is the hidden hope in apocalyptic despair, but for most Jews it was not enough. Their longing for a sense of God's presence in history brought them back to Torah and to those who devoted their lives to its study and practice.

Rabbi: Torah and Miracles

Even after the Romans stormed Jerusalem and destroyed all but one retaining wall of the magnificent temple, Jewish faith in God persisted. The survival of Judaism after the irrevocable loss of the sacrificial system upon which traditional worship had depended for centuries was due in large part to one group of teachers, the Pharisees. They dedicated themselves to the labor of adapting moral and ritual prescriptions of the Law of Moses to changing social and historical conditions. The loss of the temple was the greatest challenge of adaptation they had ever faced, but they responded with astonishing creativity. They shifted the meaning of sacrifice from the literal offering of animals to the symbolic surrender of self-interest through dedicated study and acts of compassion for others. When the most learned of their teachers, Johanan ben Zakkai, was fleeing Jerusalem with the flames of the temple rising behind him, one student cried, "What shall we do now that the place where our sins were atoned is destroyed?" Rabbi Johanan replied, "We have another means of atonement. It is acts of loving-kindness, as it is said, "For I desire mercy and not sacrifice" (Hosea 6:6).[31] By making this strategic move, the Pharisees transferred the focus of Jewish worship from temple to home and synagogue: family and community rituals replaced priestly performance, and study of Torah replaced temple ordinances. In this form of Judaism the trained teacher, or rabbi, was the central leader of the people.

Veneration of wise and powerful teachers gave rise to faith in their capacity to perform miracles on behalf of Jewish communities. When Christian rulers expelled all Jews and Muslims from Spain in 1492, it was the esoteric wisdom of mystic interpretation of the Bible (*Kabbalah*) that provided assurance of God's presence with the people, even in exile. The *zaddikim* ("holy ones") were signs of God's faithful attention to the Jewish people in their scattering (*diaspora*) throughout Europe, Russia, and the Middle East.[32] *Rebbes*, as they were affectionately called, were pure souls through whose prayers God would, on occasion, deliver the Jewish people in times of crisis. The modern Hasidic movement elevated their charismatic leaders to the status of mediators between God and humanity and attributed to them the capacity to exercise miraculous powers.[33]

Shifts in forms of religious leadership from *prophet* to *rabbi* carried momentous changes in Jewish tradition. We will focus on one: the diminishing role of miracles as indicators of divine authority. After the loss of the temple, the Pharisees replaced its rituals as the center of Jewish identity by prayer and good works, both cultivated through concentrated study of Torah to determine how the divine will was to be discerned in each following generation. As we have seen, the majority of early rabbis agreed that miracles were not germane to legal decisions that guided Jewish conduct. Still, the rabbis recognized that miraculous deeds, particularly healings, could signify exemplary piety and divine favor. By the early middle ages, however, even the wonders of Rabbi Eliezer were interpreted by one scholar as a dream sequence, thus denying that the miracles occurred at all.[34] By the late eighteenth century Rabbi Nachman of Bratzlav, himself a reputed miracle worker, flatly declared, "A man should believe in God by virtue of faith rather than miracles."[35]

In this process of devaluing miracles, a key transitional figure is the first-century teacher Hanina ben Dosa. According to a later source, Hanina was the last of the "men of deed," a company of pious men gifted with miraculous powers (like prophets) but not legal scholars (although he was addressed as "rabbi").[36] He was credited with starting and stopping rain, multiplying bread, making vinegar burn like oil, healing a boy of fever, and rescuing a young woman who fell into a well. Biblical scholar Joseph Blenkinsopp comments that these miracles placed "the stamp of divine approval on a life of exemplary observance and piety."[37] Hanina was best known for the occasion when he was rapt in prayer and a poisonous lizard or snake bit him in the foot. Following the tradition that a pious person should never interrupt a prayer, not even if a king should call out a greeting or "if a snake is coiled around his heel," Hanina did not interrupt his prayer. (The requirement is a strenuous test of devout concentration, since ignoring a king could be as fatal as leaving a snake bite unattended.) Hanina survived the deadly strike, and later his students found the venomous creature lying dead at the mouth of its den. They gave voice to what became a proverb: "Woe to the person whom an *arvad* (lizard or snake) has bitten. Woe to the *arvad* that has bitten ben Dosa."

The story, as it appears in the Palestinian Talmud, presented Hanina as a model of piety to be emulated by all Jews after the destruction of the temple in conditions where prayer was the primary defining ritual of Jewish life. In another version of the story Hanina's students asked him whether he felt anything when the snake bit him. He answered, "Let [evil] befall me—as my heart was concentrated on the *tefillah* [prayer]—if I felt [anything]." One commentator linked Hanina's rescue to the psalmist's confidence in God's protection of the faithful: "He fulfills the wishes of those who fear Him; He hears their cries and saves them" (Psalm 145:19). The clear implication is that all Jews who follow the example of masters by engaging in prayer and study can also rely on divine protection.

In the retelling of the story of Hanina and the snake in the Babylonian Talmud, the miracle worker is presented not as a model of focused prayer but as the hero who saves his community from danger. In this version an aggressive *arvad* was striking people and causing them grave injury. They appealed for help to Hanina ben Dosa. He went to the hole of the poison-ous creature and placed his heel over the opening. The *arvad* bit his foot and died. Hanina hoisted its body over his shoulder and brought it into the house of study as an object lesson. "See, my children," he said, "it is not the *arvad* that kills, rather sin kills." They responded, "Woe to the person who met an *arvad*, and woe to the *arvad* that met R. Hanina ben Dosa."

In this form the story fits the genre of miracle narrative familiar in the Hebrew Bible, New Testament, and Hellenistic sources: a problem is identi-fied, the miracle worker responds, the problem is removed. The interpola-tion of the moral lesson disrupts this simple structure by suggesting that the problem is not the threat posed by the *arvad* but the danger of the people's disobedience cutting them off from the Lord of life ("rather sin kills"). To correct that problem does not require a miracle, only a return to loyalty to the Torah which any dedicated rabbi could inspire. It is also significant that the proverb of "Woe" is modified by changing the verb "bitten" to "met" in describing the encounter with an *arvad*. In this moralized version of the story the serpent serves its customary symbolic function in Jewish tradi-tion to represent evil. While overcoming the serpent would be understood in the context as an exercise of divine authority, in this story Hanina does not claim to perform a miracle: the *arvad* bit him and it died. There is no point of discontinuity in the narrative at which one could say, "Aha! Here is where God intervened." Rather, what could be reasonably construed as a natural, howbeit highly unusual, event was invested with the meaning of a miracle by readers who recognized in Hanina a figure of divine authority sent to rescue the community from physical and spiritual danger.

The two versions of the story of Hanina and the *arvad* demonstrate the ambivalence toward miracles in the Jewish tradition, the disposition to sub-ordinate wondrous works to moral teaching. Thus, in the first version Hanina served as a model of piety for others to emulate, thus downplaying his unique powers as a "man of deed"; in the second version, while Hanina played a unique role in saving the community, the miraculous character of the rescue is deemphasized and the moral lesson of the event is highlighted.[38]

Why, then, do stories of miracles recur in rabbinic writings? Elie Wiesel offers an explanation that is consistent with our thesis that belief in miracles, even if one does not experience them, is a symbolic expression that one has not given up hope for a future radically different from the present. "I know," he writes, that miracle stories "may seem shocking, even revolting to the rationalists among us." But we must consider "the immense suffering that Jews were subjected to. Caught in ever-growing despair, what they needed most was a reason to believe. The very possibility of believing was a miracle in itself. That was why *Tzaddikim* performed miracles. To strike the imagination. To inspire awe. To help souls open themselves to faith and hope."[39] As Wiesel knows, better than most, keeping hope alive in conditions of despair requires superhuman courage. At times of great crisis, rabbis were called upon to demonstrate the power of piety through miracles.

There has been no greater tragedy in Jewish history than the Nazi attempt to murder the Jewish population of Europe in the years 1933–1945. That horrific episode of genocide is generally called the *Holocaust* from the Hebrew for *burnt offering*, but many Jews prefer the designation *Shoah* or *catastrophe* to avoid any suggestion that the loss of lives was a redemptive sacrifice. It seemed a time when God had forsaken his people. Rabbi Yekutiel Yehuda Halberstam of Klausenburg, reflecting on living in the hell of Nazi death camps, declared, "The biggest miracle of all is the one that we, the survivors of the Holocaust, after all that we witnessed and lived through, still believe and have faith in the Almighty God, may His name be blessed. This, my friends, is the miracle of miracles, the greatest miracle ever to have taken place."[40] For Rabbi Halberstam the event of transcendent power, impossible on the basis of human strength alone, was the preservation of faith, in God and in humanity, among survivors. As has long been recognized, the Nazis attempted to erase systematically from their prisoners the marks of humanity. Under those conditions, many Jewish survivors believe, any evidence that something of the human spirit remained could not be attributed to natural causes—but only to the divine reality that cannot be touched by demonic cunning or human depravity.

That reality was affirmed in stories of miracles performed by Hasidic rabbis. In one story a group of prisoners in a camp in Ukraine were ordered out of their barracks in the dead of night to gather in a field in which large pits had been dug. Their captors taunted them by promising their lives would be spared only if they could leap across the pits, a task impossible under the best of conditions. Rabbi Israel Spira of Bluzhov stood at the edge of one pit with a friend, a freethinker from a Polish city. The friend counseled that they retain their dignity by refusing the futile leap across the pit already filling with bullet-riddled corpses. The rabbi replied that they should obey the will of God who had placed them before this pit and who had decreed that they be commanded to jump. He then closed his eyes and called out with all his remaining strength, "We are jumping!" When he and his friend opened their eyes, they were on the far side of the pit, spared from execution. The freethinker, astounded to be alive, cried, "There must be a God in heaven.

Tell me, Rebbe, how did you do it?" The rabbi replied that he held on to the ancestral merit of his forefathers, but then, scanning the black heavens above, he asked, "Tell me, my friend, how did *you* reach the other side of the pit?" "I was holding on to you," came the reply.[41] Here generations of pious men conspired to make possible the miraculous deliverance, carrying to safety even the agnostic clinging in desperation to the coattails of Rebbe Israel. The intervention is not attributed to God, but it comes from the transcendent realm where the faithful in heaven, on occasions chosen for reasons hidden from human view, reveal divine mercy.

The meaning of this story for the community of believing survivors who remember and retell it lies in thankful wonder for supernatural deliverance and not in bitter resentment for the hundreds who fell, unsupported, into the pits and were cut down by machine guns. What makes the difference in interpretation? To answer that question would require understanding from what unassailable fortress in the human heart faith holds out against despair. But let me offer one last, I hope instructive, example. A woman named Elaine arrived at Auschwitz determined to remain alive and be reunited with her husband, who was taken away from their village in a separate transport. Despite her good fortune in escaping selection for death by Dr. Mengele several times, one day she was directed into the group headed toward the gas chambers. Instead of meeting death, however, her group was diverted to cattle cars where the young women were crammed together "like vertical boards of lumber." As the train began to lurch forward Elaine looked through a crack between two siding boards and glimpsed, in the bright blue sky, a straight white line. It became for her a veritable life line and she took it as a sign that she would survive. Her discernment proved prophetic because she eventually returned to her village and was reunited with her husband. Thirty years later, she was asked what she thought that white line in the sky really was. She replied, "The line was my source of inspiration, my sign from heaven. Many years later, after liberation, when my children were growing up, I realized that the white line might have been fumes from a passing airplane's exhaust pipe, but does it really matter?"[42] The sight of the white line, perceived as a sign of hope, evoked courage and determination that Elaine received as a divine gift, a miracle.

Master: Hasidic Wonder Workers

In the early eighteenth century, a child was born in a town in the Carpathian Mountains whose birth was said to be a divine gift to the world. He was one of the innocent souls who, when God created Adam, hid in a remote corner of primordial chaos in order to escape the stain of human sin. According to Kabbalah, it is from those pure souls that God chooses one to enter the world, from time to time, to illumine spiritual darkness and recall people to lives of righteousness. The child would become Rabbi Israel ben Eleazer (1698–1760), known as Baal Shem Tov (abbreviated as Besht) or Master of the Good Name. Through the power of the divine name he deciphered mysteries, defeated evil powers, and worked miracles: speaking the language of animals, transporting through the sky, discerning the minds of others, foretelling future events, radiating supernatural light, and raising the dead to life.[43]

Once, absorbed in contemplation of God while climbing a mountain peak, Rabbi Israel was about to walk off a cliff when the nearby mountain moved toward him and he easily stepped onto its peak and continued on his way—whereupon, the mountain returned to its former position. Baal Shem Tov did not command the mountain to uphold his steps; it seemed to act on its own recognition of his spiritual greatness. But in the Jewish understanding of creation inanimate objects do not have volition of their own; they act in accord with the will of God. Read in that light, the story confirms divine protection of the master in recognition of his righteousness. But miracles require an audience to attain their full significance. Rabbi Israel hardly noticed the mountain move, but a band of robbers, not far off, witnessed the miracle and declared the rabbi a holy man, calling upon him to be their judge and to resolve their disputes. He agreed, on the condition that they never again injure a Jew. But one robber, aggrieved over a judgment Baal Shem Tov rendered against him, crept into the room where the master was sleeping to kill him. Before the brigand could strike with his knife, he was beaten by unseen powers and left bleeding on the floor. Aware of his angelic protectors, the master arose and tended to his attacker's wounds. The miracle and its aftermath, then, suggest that the care God shows toward Rabbi Israel is a sign of God's covenant with the people of Israel. The robber broke his promise not to injure a Jew and he suffered the wrath of Israel's guardian angels. Yet the story ends with the compassion of Israel toward one who had thought to be his enemy. The story balances two central values in Judaism: justice and mercy.

Until he reached the age of thirty-six, Baal Shem Tov concealed his wondrous powers, but then God directed him to reveal his true nature. The results were spectacular and attracted a large following. One Wednesday, after gathering a few disciples with him, the Besht announced he was leaving to celebrate the Sabbath in Berlin, over a hundred miles away. The entourage started off in a wagon at a leisurely pace, stopping for dinner that night and spending most of the next day at a tavern, whose owner was dumbfounded by the master's intention to cover the distance requiring a week's ride in one day. Out of curiosity he devised an excuse to ride along. That night, after another lengthy discussion of Torah over dinner, the master harnessed the horse to the wagon, and the tavern keeper soon found himself gliding quietly through the skies, with Rabbi Israel and his disciples again engrossed in conversation about Torah. By sunrise the tavern keeper realized they had re-entered the ordinary world of time and space and the wagon was rolling through the streets of Berlin.

Excited to tell others of this wonder, he encountered a man in wedding clothes, lamenting the death of his bride-to-be that morning. The tavern keeper brought him to Baal Shem Tov, who ordered that the girl be prepared for burial. At the grave site, gazing intently upon the maiden's pallid face, the rabbi's face began to glow with the light of life. Then he grimaced, as if he were exerting tremendous force, and uttered strange words, language from another world. When he began breathing freely again, the bride's face slowly regained color and attendants helped her out of her coffin and into the waiting arms of her joyous husband-to-be. Later, as the rabbi conducted their wedding service, the sound of his voice awakened in the bride the memory of his delivering her soul from the vengeful jealousy of her husband's previous wife. Baal Shem Tov appeared as her advocate before the divine Judge, arguing that the dead have no right on earth. In this world only the living can lay claim to justice or be held to promises or keep covenants.

Baal Shem Tov sought to recognize the divine presence in every creature and to reveal in his actions infinite love for them. His miracles, while relegated by some contemporary Jews to the fanciful category of legend, serve as demonstrations of divine care for the people of Israel. To the extent the Besht healed the bodies and protected the souls of Jews in a time and place where their lives and safety were under threat, to that extent God was keeping his covenant with them. As Kabbalah taught, the divine presence (*Shekinah*) went with the Jews into exile—and the miracles of Baal Shem Tov were a sign of that faithful escort in diaspora. Rabbi Israel's attentive care of poor villagers and unclean tavern owners was meant as a reflection of divine love that excluded no one and a rebuke of the scholars and rabbis who held themselves above the ignorant and non-observant among their own people.

There are miracle stories about many of the Hasidic rabbis in Eastern Europe during the nineteenth century. While most masters share a fundamental ambivalence toward wonder working, including their own supernatural powers, they also agree on the spiritual benefit of transmitting the stories. The great-grandson of the Baal Shem Tov, Rabbi Nachman of Bratzlav in Poland (1772–1811), was a renowned story teller. "Once, it is remembered, he told a tale that lasted for two hours. All who hear it were so rapt in wonder and exaltation that when they came out of the dream of the story, they could remember only fragments of what they had heard."[44] Such is the power of skillfully woven narrative that listeners become detached from ordinary perception, as in a dream so consuming that one awakens in chill sweat, so real is participation in its imagined world. Miracle stories draw listeners into their world of vivid wonders with compelling force that nurtures faith in the unseen world and its incomparable Lord.[45]

One wonder worker was Rabbi Yisakhar Baer of Radoshitz in Poland (d. 1843), widely known for healings and exorcisms (casting out demons from those possessed). So famous were his miracles that he earned the nickname, "little Baal Shem."[46] His career began with a healing. When he arrived for a visit with his venerated teacher, the rabbi met him in tears, wailing that his son was near death and insisting that Yisakhar could make him well. The rabbi was known for his suspicion of miracle workers, but he discerned powers in his student that Yisakhar had not yet discovered. Not knowing what else to do, he rocked the child in his cradle and prayed with as much fervor as he could muster. An hour later the boy was on his way to recovery. When he became teacher of his own school, Rabbi Yisakhar was said not to aspire to reach God in heaven, but to bring God down to earth through working miracles. For him, the purpose of miracles was above all to reveal divine power and mercy, especially to those without formal learning. When he was asked why he did not give up working wonders and concentrate on purifying souls, he responded that his mission in life was "to make the Godhead known to the world."[47] The significance of miracles as revelation, established at Sinai, continued in the Jewish tradition.

In our discussion of the story of the Oven of Akhnai we saw that rabbis in the early centuries of the Common Era were skeptical about miracles, particularly their significance in interpreting the legal code that regulated Jewish life. While they retained a few stories of wonders in the Talmud, they were careful to build "a hedge around the Torah" to protect the text from eccentric interpretations, even if they were validated by miracles. They also wished to retain human responsibility for interpreting the relevance of Torah in each succeeding generation and upholding its demanding ethical code. In this respect, their ambivalence toward miracles is the spirit that centuries later moved Baruch de Spinoza to ban miracles altogether from his modern view of the universe, while retaining a passionate "intellectual love for God."

Dissent: Modern Objections to Miracles

Jewish critics of supernaturalism constrained claims to transcendent power or knowledge within rational limits and emphasized ethical criticism of the Bible. The move from miracle to morality continued in the early twentieth century in the Reconstructionist movement, but faced its ultimate challenge in the Holocaust. God's apparent indifference to the murder of six million Jews convinced many that hope in miracles was delusional. Post-Holocaust thinkers abandoned belief in miracles because they could not sustain faith in a supernatural actor who could watch horrendous evil while sitting on his hands, so to speak. Yet even in the face of faithful dissent and a history of failed expectations, belief in God and his power to intervene in history persists in the Jewish community, expressed in liturgical prayers.[48]

Baruch de Spinoza (1632–1677) lived during the golden age of the Dutch Republic. In the tolerant and prosperous circumstances of Holland at that time, the large community of Jews joined in astounding advances of science, art, political liberty, and commercial enterprise. The young Spinoza received a rigorous education in Jewish tradition. He was a precocious student, mastering Hebrew and memorizing large swaths of the Bible. But his intellectual passion was aroused more by new ideas than by old certainties. Spinoza was particularly interested in the skeptical method of inquiry of René Descartes. When he applied the Cartesian method of questioning to the religious claims of his tradition, he soon concluded that little in the Bible could be defended on rational grounds.

Spinoza's radical critique of traditional supernaturalism as superstition prompted the leaders of the Jewish community to conduct a formal examination of his views. They concluded that he was guilty of "abominable heresies" and "monstrous deeds" and pronounced him "excommunicated and expelled from the people of Israel."[49] Perhaps the severity of his punishment reflected the awareness by Jewish elders that their security in Amsterdam depended on their quietly minding their own business, commercial and theological. After all, Christians were also threatened by attacks on the truthfulness of their Old Testament. Further, the clear implication of Spinoza's critique of biblical authority was to undermine the theocratic authority that certain Christian philosophers were attempting to establish elsewhere in Europe. From the beginning, Spinoza posed a threat by advocating a modern revolution against the divine right of established religious and political authorities in the name of individual rights and democratic polity. Neither Jewish nor Christian powers could allow his challenge to stand.

Spinoza's theological project raised two questions: whether God is transcendent over the world or immanent within nature, and whether genuine piety requires the humble constriction of human initiative under traditional laws or the bold flourishing of human reason and imagination without external constraints. Spinoza's faithful dissent from Jewish tradition was aimed at defending the latter alternatives. In his *Theological-Political Treatise*, published over a decade after his excommunication, he set out his critique of biblical authority. The superstitious multitude, Spinoza argued, ascribed equal authority to all portions of the Bible, while he extracted from the biblical writings the "Word of God," by which he meant the divine revelation of timeless moral truth, "namely, to obey God with all one's mind by practicing justice and charity."[50] For Spinoza, accounts of miracles did not qualify as the "Word of God," but reflected a form of misplaced piety. The common people, he wrote, "revere the power of God when they envisage the power of nature as if it were subdued by God." Spinoza believed this dualism between God and Nature began with the ancient Hebrews who distinguished their single, invisible deity from the gods worshipped by pagans in the form of natural forces. Spinoza found the motive for this theological innovation far from innocent: "People have always been so drawn to this idea that to this day they have not ceased to invent miracles, in order to foment the belief that they are dearer to God than others. . . . What will the common people not arrogate to themselves in their foolishness!"[51]

Against such folly Spinoza argued for a seamless unity of God and Nature. Because God knows the world to be precisely as he determined it to be, all natural events are expressions of the immutable divine will. It follows that there can be no deviation from the operation of natural laws any more than there could be an instance of God changing "the necessity and perfection of the Divine nature." For Spinoza a miracle would be a symptom of divine dissociation, an internal contradiction in which God would violate his covenant to maintain the world he made in its "fixed and immutable order." Far from proving God's benevolent interest in human welfare, as most religious people believed, a miracle for Spinoza would be an indictment of God's character. It is no wonder he rejected miracles with as much vehemence as his abstract vocabulary allowed.

He also believed that he could make the case against miracles by appealing directly to passages of Scripture that assert "that nature's course is fixed and unchangeable." Drawing from Ecclesiastes, in which Solomon wearily declared that there is nothing new under the sun, Spinoza denied the possibility of genuine novelty in the course of natural events: "miracles were natural events and therefore must be explained so as not to seem 'new' . . . or in conflict with nature."[52] A miracle is a strange happening waiting for an explanation to make it familiar, even ordinary. In the meanwhile, wonder is an emotional place holder for the cognitive understanding that reason will eventually and inevitably discover. Spinoza was a paradigmatic Enlightenment thinker, both in his breath-taking confidence in human reason as an infallible explanatory resource and his brave resignation to a universe indifferent to human interests.

Spinoza was unusual among modern thinkers in retaining his love of God while accepting the hard fact that God would not reciprocate his interest with any personal gesture. The God who *is* Nature exists in supreme indifference to human need. In its practical effects, Spinoza's theology required adult believers willing to assume responsibility for seeking justice and charity for their own sake without promises of supernatural intervention now or reward beyond the grave. In short, Spinoza offered theism without supernaturalism, ethics without transcendence, and love of God without emotion. To worship Spinoza's God is consistently and exclusively to pursue moral virtue, unaided by supernatural assistance. For Spinoza, the claim to miraculous power by religious leaders was a dishonest attempt to control uneducated believers, while the popular desire for miracles was the result of scientific ignorance and religious immaturity. Spinoza's critique proceeded from a profoundly Jewish viewpoint: belief in miracles stands in tension with the moral imperative of justice and the rational desire for reliable order in nature. It is a viewpoint that also found expression in the Reconstructionist version of Judaism.

Mordecai Kaplan (1881–1983) founded Reconstructionist Judaism on the premise that Judaism is more than a religion and constitutes an evolving civilization, a cultural system that includes literature, art, music, science, and politics, as well as ritual practice. He called on Jews to accept the modern scientific account of the natural order and abandon belief in supernatural intervention in favor of his religious naturalism. On the specific question of miracles Kaplan acknowledged that "natural sciences like physics and chemistry cannot disprove the possibility of miracles, though they may assert their improbability." But he followed the critical argument of Hume that "the objective study of history has established the fact that the records of miracles are unreliable, and that the stories about them are merely the product of the popular imagination." Further, he argued, "The traditional conception of God is challenged by history, anthropology and psychology; these prove that beliefs similar to those found in the Bible about God arise among all peoples at a certain stage of mental and social development."[53] Again, like Hume, Kaplan believed that advanced civilizations, in whose company he sought to situate modern Judaism, would eventually outgrow such fanciful notions.

Kaplan went so far as to deny supernatural intervention in the Bible's account of the founding of the people of Israel. The traditional claim that Israel had a supernatural origin in the Exodus "can be treated as nothing more than a poetic idealization of the Jewish people," designed to bolster their status as specially chosen by God. Kaplan supported the rejection of Israel's election also on moral grounds: "From an ethical standpoint, it is deemed inadvisable, to say the least, to keep alive ideas of race or national superiority, inasmuch as they are known to exercise a divisive influence, generating suspicion and hatred."[54] He was an ardent Zionist and promoted the state of Israel, but he did not defend the Jewish right to land in Palestine on the basis of divine election. Rather, he argued that Jewish civilization was a concrete reality that required a geopolitical location for the development of its institutions.

Kaplan's reconstruction of Jewish thinking entailed collapsing the traditional dichotomy between natural and supernatural: "The so-called laws of nature represent the manner of God's immanent functioning. The element of creativity, which is not accounted for by the so-called laws of nature, and which points to the organic character of the universe or its life as a whole, gives us a clue to God's transcendent functioning. God is not an identifiable being who stands outside the universe. God is the life of the universe, immanent insofar as each part acts upon every other, and transcendent insofar as the whole acts upon each part."[55] Kaplan believed his conception of God would inspire modern Jews to pursue traditional values—justice, mercy, and peace—that enhance the world as a whole. The evidence that the human spirit is not determined by blind material forces is our capacity to rise above the demands of natural order by answering brutality with compassion and nurturing hope that the world can be different than it is. The catalog of horrors created by authoritarian regimes—war, persecution, genocide—were not inevitable. The problem is that supernaturalism requires loyalty to a fictional being and its abstract ideals for which humans are moved to kill each other. Kaplan insisted that the ennobling values symbolized by his reconstructed idea of God could motivate humans to surpass selfish interests and pretensions of absolute authority.

Kaplan's strenuous effort to discredit supernaturalism has as its flip side the affirmation of an element of transcendence in the human spirit that makes its very resiliency a kind of miracle. But that resiliency was tested almost beyond belief in the greatest catastrophe in Jewish history. The program implemented by Adolph Hitler as leader of the German government to destroy every Jew within his control was an unprecedented horror, an exercise in genocide that employed the latest advances in technology to commit mass murder. The killing was relentless and merciless, with no restraint of compassion or sympathy on the part of the murderers. If ever a people had the right to feel "God-forsaken," it was the Jews in the grip of the Third Reich. While some retained and even deepened their faith in God during the monstrous atrocities, for many Jews to live after the Holocaust is to inhabit a world from which God is absent.

Richard Rubenstein is an ordained rabbi in the Conservative branch of Judaism, but his radical revision of Jewish theology worked out in the shadow of the Holocaust places him on the margin of his tradition. He extended Kaplan's critique of supernaturalism to the point of atheism. Rubenstein cannot accept the optimism in Reconstructionist Judaism about God as the ultimate source of values and about humanity as the progressive bearer of those values. Considering the evils perpetrated in the first half of the twentieth century, Rubenstein concludes, "Man's image of himself and of God was permanently impaired by what took place."[56] In a long career of teaching and writing, Rubenstein created a post-Holocaust vision of Judaism, stripped not only of supernatural elements but also of belief in divine transcendence. He offers a systematic interpretation of the tragic ambivalence that Elie Wiesel expressed in his memoir of the death camps. At the point he first saw human beings burned alive, Wiesel swore, "Never shall I forget those moments which murdered my God and my soul and turned my dreams to dust. Never shall I forget these things, even if I am condemned to live as long as God Himself. Never."[57] Wiesel made it his vocation as a Holocaust survivor to bear witness to the unspeakable carnage in order to keep alive the memory of the dead and to insure that God never forgets that he allowed the murders to take place. Rubenstein devoted his career to reinterpreting Jewish identity so that Jews can begin to forget God and the fantasy of divine intervention in human affairs.

Rubenstein, giving voice to faithful dissent, sees no contradiction between maintaining Jewish culture, even religious rituals, and joining in the postmodern declaration of the death of God or, in less dramatic and more biblical terms, the withdrawal of God from the stage of history. By throwing responsibility for maintaining the integrity and continuity of Jewish identity on the members of the community themselves, without the illusion of divine support, Rubenstein plays the role of Walzer's "connected critic," one "who earns his authority, or fails to do so, by arguing with his fellows—who, angrily and insistently, sometimes at considerable personal risk (he can be a hero too), objects, protests, and remonstrates."[58] As other connected critics, Rubenstein calls on the tradition even as he reinterprets it.

For example, Rubenstein criticizes the body of legendary stories as failing the test of historical credibility, but he explains their enduring significance in psychological terms. These stories, many of which we have seen were generated at times of crisis for the Jewish community, Rubenstein credits with the power to sustain hope and to provide "the gift of meaning" to the people's struggle to survive in hostile conditions. They do so, not by constructing elaborately detailed models of conduct—as legal scholars created through *Halakhah*—but by exemplary stories. Only such stories have the power to sustain hope for a better future. Rubenstein, of course, does not believe the stories are a reliable basis for believing the future state of the world will be more just or peaceful than the past and present, but he recognizes that the stories inspire many to continue their efforts to pursue a better future. On the other hand, Rubenstein agrees with Kaplan that not even stories in the Bible should be read as providing the Jews with divine authority, fulfilling a supernatural vocation as instruments of divine will. That view amounts to "a savage denial of the meaningful character of genuine human encounter, which can only exist when human beings are present to one another, not as ideological marionettes acting out superordinate roles."[59] The primary problem with supernaturalism, in all its forms, is that it encourages people to hide their natural dispositions grounded in a common humanity behind masks put on to play roles in an imagined divine drama.

What Rubenstein implies is perhaps the most devastating criticism of any worldview that includes belief in miracles or direct supernatural action in history. The criticism is twofold. First, the possibility of miraculous works compromises believers' full acceptance of responsibility for defeating evil and enacting justice. Second, belief that God is the ultimate agent in history, directing and acting in a drama of his own composition, reduces humans to supporting actors, no longer moved by natural human dispositions but by a divinely authored (and authorized) script. In the final analysis, Rubenstein concludes, "the most adequate theological description of our times is to be found in the assertion that we live in the time of the death of God," that is, a time when God no longer figures in our explanatory accounts or our redemptive projects.[60]

Summary

Miracle stories in Jewish tradition express confidence in God as the original creator of the world, revealer of moral law, and champion of justice in human history. Biblical stories of Exodus and Sinai are interpreted as miracles performed on behalf of those with whom God entered into covenant. In the subsequent history of Israel, God worked miracles through prophets, rabbis, and masters to recall the Jewish community to their responsibility for restoring the world to justice through obedience to Torah. Miracles served the purpose of confirming the authority of divine revelation, defeating the persecutors of the Jewish people, and demonstrating God's faithfulness to his covenant with Israel in the most extreme circumstances. Divine interventions, however, are rare and often ambiguous in their effect and interpretation. Claims to perform miracles and prayers for personal miracles are strictly regulated lest people come to depend upon divine assistance and neglect their duty under the covenant. For many Jews the traditional ambivalence toward miracles has deepened since the Shoah, while their determination to remain faithful to Jewish identity by pursuing justice, mercy, and peace in an imperfect world has increased. As some might put it, if it pleases God to work a miracle once in a while, who would complain? Just don't count on it.

Buddhism

Signs of Transcendent Wisdom

We begin this chapter with a miracle of the Buddha, an act of lev-itation and transformation.[1] According to one version, the event occurred on his return to his homeland to share his teaching with his father, King Śuddhodana, and the elders of his clan, the Śākyas. But they denounced him for becoming a wandering mendicant and demanded that he return to his royal duties. He countered by condemning them for their ignorance. The elders turned to leave when, in a final effort to win them over, Buddha per-formed the "miracle of the pairs."

> Knowing that nothing short of a spectacular display of supernormal power would suffice to soften the proud hearts of the Śākyas, [Buddha] ascended into the air while flames of fire issued upward from his body and torrents of water poured down. Then the flames went downward while the water went up toward the sky. Next, fire came from the right side of his body, and water from the left. Then the fire and water changed sides. After twenty-two variations of pairs had been exhibited, Śākyamuni [sage of the Śākya clan] exercised his supernormal powers to create the illusion of a jeweled promenade in the sky along which he walked. Coming down from the sky, Buddha told the people the story of his existence . . . which preceded his birth. . . . And the king and all the nobles realized they beheld, not just a man, nor a mere god or god's messenger, but a Buddha Supreme.[2]

Several elements of this story arouse wonder: Buddha's rising from the ground, his issuing fire and water from his body, his strolling in mid-air on a walkway made of jewels, and his retelling of his past lives. In another ver-sion we find an added miracle: the water that flowed from his body cured a woman of blindness. The scales over her eyes "were pierced through the vir-tue of the Buddha. Her sight became clear and faultless as before."[3]

We recall from chapter 2 that in the Indian context knowledge of previous existences is as much a cause for wonder as levitation because both are listed among the "marvelous powers" or *siddhis* described in the *Yoga Sutras*. Thus, one purpose of this story is to establish that Buddha was a master of yogic technique. Patanjali listed many powers the yogi attains through practice of *samyama* or "the discipline of gaining complete control over the object of contemplation."[4] These powers include the knowledge of previous life-states; knowledge of other minds; power to become invisible; as well as the power to levitate and translocate at will.

In the story before us, Buddha demonstrated more than the capacity to suspend gravity. The miracle of the pairs was possible because Buddha attained the highest level of integrated consciousness possible, allowing him total control of the elements of the material world: earth, fire, air, and water. He rose above the earth, occupying space in the air, and manipulated the movement of fire and water at will. Further, he rearranged the direction and movement of the elements as he brought them forth from his own body. Buddha's mind reached the state of undifferentiated consciousness, the primal source. That ultimate achievement of meditation transformed his body into the matrix of a physical order in which he was able to levitate.

As astounding as Buddha's display of yogic mastery was, however, it was not until he returned to earth and resumed his role as teacher that his authority was recognized. The levitation drew attention and aroused wonder, stopping the retreating elders in their tracks; but it provided no instruction of its own. The distinctive Buddhist cast to this story is evident in the ending. It was Buddha's knowledge of his past lives—available only to one whose ego was obliterated—that convinced his skeptical audience he was Buddha Supreme. It is consistent with this emphasis that his feat served to open the eyes of a blind woman: a symbol of the divine gift of illuminating knowledge.

Miracles in Buddhism signify the authority of spiritual attainment, but their primary purpose is pedagogical. They are performed for the sake of teaching the witnesses what the Buddha discovered: that everything, including the world of nature with its seemingly inflexible order, is impermanent. Therefore, we should not expect to find lasting satisfaction by clinging to anything in the world; everything arises and passes away in a process of mutual dependence, leaving nothing behind. How better to illustrate that truth than to show that the natural elements, bound to each other in paired opposition, could as easily reverse their pattern of relationship as maintain it? There is no immutable substance to *nature*, any more than there is to a *chariot* when it has been dismantled into its parts; and what is true of the *world* is true of the *self*. The miracle of the pairs is an object lesson in the transient character of each of the italicized words in the preceding sentence.

Another account of the miracle of the pairs is told in the context of a challenge to Buddha's authority later in his career. Knowing that Buddha forbade his monks to display yogic powers in public, his opponents hoped that he would refuse to perform a miracle so that they could claim he lacked the ability to do so. But on the appointed day Buddha rose into the air before them and fire and water issued from his body. His challengers were forced to accept his superior power and insight. The main theme of this version is Buddha's triumph over rival teachers rather than persuasion of his clan members. Using miracles to establish the truth of his teaching was not characteristic of Buddha, but under certain political conditions Buddhists have found this miracle a significant resource. For example, it is celebrated in a Tibetan ritual which represents the "marvel of the pairs" as "an appropriate symbol for the overcoming of evil forces, and of Buddhism's past victory over Bon," the indigenous Tibetan religion.[5] The story takes on contemporary political significance as it is retold in the context of Tibetan resistance to Chinese rule. We will note *how* different a miracle story can *mean* in changed historical conditions.

The primary sources of miracle stories about Buddha are regarded by Buddhists as sacred texts. But it is a modern mistake to assume that religious readers always interpret sacred texts in a literal way. For many Buddhists sacred texts are not so much read as contemplated. The question for faithful readers of a miracle story is not "Did that *really* happen?" but "What does that *mean*?" That is, the story presents moral or spiritual instruction, not scientific or historical information. Many Buddhists have little doubt that miracles can happen as the effect of disciplined meditation. As Robert Brown notes, miracles are "expected" in a world constructed according to Buddhist principles.[6] What mind has given in the forms of body, emotion, time, and space, mind can take away or reconstruct in other forms. The miracles of Buddhist masters may astound or enlighten, depending upon the spiritual condition of the witnesses, but finally, miracles represent merely the temporary re-ordering of transient elements that have no enduring significance. Miracles in Buddhism are effects of knowing the world to be not the fixed construction of a deity, but the impermanent construal of illusion and so subject to modification by a fully realized mind. The only question is how learning from a miracle story promotes the moral virtue or spiritual insight that is the ultimate goal of religious life. Thus, many Buddhists cherish stories of Buddha's miracles as disclosing the meaning of his wisdom in their troubled historical circumstances.

Buddha: Miracles of the Enlightened One

Buddhists, like members of other religions, wove into the history of the founder of their tradition stories of miracles: supernatural features of his conception and birth, signs of his destiny, and wondrous manifestations of his enlightened mind. Popular tales about Siddhartha Gautama (560–480 B.C.E.) are retold at celebrations of his birthday and other ritual occasions. Just as Jews recall the crossing of the Red Sea on Passover and Christians retell stories of Christmas and Easter, so Buddhists learn stories of Buddha's miraculous birth and career and transmit them to their children. In Buddhist tradition the question is, how do the stories represent Buddha's nature and character?[7] Do Buddha's supernormal powers belong to him alone, or could they be exercised by anyone who followed his way of meditation and practice? Are his miracles demonstrations of his virtue and concentration, or are they symbols of supernatural assistance his followers may rely upon in their search for liberation? While these questions are important for comparative study, we must keep in mind that they imply a distinction between natural and supernatural that is not found in Buddha's teaching and is at odds with his conviction that there is only one reality, other worlds being creations of our minds without enduring substance of their own.

Nevertheless, Buddhist tradition later divided over the question whether Buddha was a divine being who exercised supernormal powers in graciously assisting others to reach the "other shore" representing freedom from suffering. Mahāyāna ("Great Vehicle") and Vajrayāna ("Diamond or Thunderbolt") branches of Buddhism emphasize such beliefs, while the more traditional Theravada ("Way of the Elders") school insists that Buddha was an exemplary human and that others must exert their own efforts, either as monks or as supportive laypeople, to reach liberation. The split in Buddhist tradition reflects Buddha's ambivalence about miracles. Despite his performance of wondrous acts, he relegated miracles to a minor role in spiritual practice and prohibited members of his monastic community (*sangha*) from indulging in wonder working. Further, his central metaphysical premise that nothing in the world carries enduring significance discourages Buddhists from assigning religious meaning to any historical event, whether caused by natural or transcendent power. Nevertheless, the capacity to surpass limits of the material world is one of the effects of concentrated meditation and, when that capacity is exercised with compassion, miracles follow, as they did in the life of Buddha.

According to Buddhist tradition, the conception of Siddhartha Gautama was miraculous. His mother dreamed that she was visited in the night by a white elephant and discovered that she was pregnant. In one early depiction of the event the elephant's trunk is poised over her womb, and in one text it was Buddha, intervening from another world, who chose his own mother by the power of his mind.[8] He also determined the time of his birth, "splitting open" his mother's womb while she rested under a flowering tree, yet without causing her pain or illness. As soon as he was born, he stood and declared, "I am born for supreme knowledge, for the welfare of the world. Therefore, this is my last birth." The text adds, with understatement, "He had not been born in the natural way." In one tradition, at the time of Buddha's birth "he was washed by fragrant rain that sprang forth from the mouth of a dragon." During celebrations of Buddha's birthday (on the eighth day of the fourth lunar month in most Buddhist countries), in ritual re-enactment of that auspicious sign, his images are bathed in scented water or warm tea.[9] As do the infancy narratives of Jesus and Muhammad, these stories reflect devotional piety so strong that it extended retroactively into the early life of Buddha powers and insights it took Siddhartha Gautama a lifetime to attain.

Siddhartha Gautama was born in luxury, a prince of the Śākya clan in northern India in the foothills of the Himalayas. Shortly after his birth, wise men foretold that he would become either a great emperor or an enlightened teacher. His father, determined that his son would follow in his royal footsteps, built him three apartments within the palace, each "furnished with the delights proper for every season."[10] Siddhartha chose the most beautiful maiden in the kingdom for his wife; and, in his twenty-ninth year, she was expecting their first child. Then, on a rare excursion outside the palace, Siddhartha encountered what have come to be known as the Four Passing Sights: an old man, a victim of disease, a corpse, and an ascetic monk. According to one account of his life, these sights were miraculously arranged by the gods; even the ascetic was a disguised divine being who told Siddhartha he had abandoned all to seek liberation in "that happy indestructible abode" where the terror of birth and death vanish. Having accomplished his task of awakening Siddhartha's memory of what he had learned in his many past lives, the ascetic rose "like a bird to heaven," leaving the young prince astonished. He was set on his path by supernatural events.[11]

The shock of these sights drove Siddhartha to leave his wife without looking at his new-born son and begin his journey to find the way to be free from life's miseries. Siddhartha began his spiritual quest under the instruction of ascetic Hindu gurus. After six years of harsh self-denial, nearly starving, he concluded that not even the most extreme discipline could bring enlightenment. He realized that asceticism is self-defeating because either one becomes acutely aware of the body's sensations as the pain of the exercise increases or one dies without ever achieving the goal. Thus, he concluded, "The mind's self-possession is only obtained when the senses are perfectly satisfied."[12] All things, even overcoming physical desire, should be pursued in moderation. Thus, Buddha's practice is known as the "middle way."

After taking food, Siddhartha splashed cold stream water on his face and was awakened to a naive realism: the world is not entirely good to be sure, but neither is it unqualifiedly evil. The ascetic's cynicism and pain cloud his vision of the actual world as a mixture of good and evil, light and darkness, cold and warmth. No amount of self-inflicted agonies or nausea can change the world any more than delusions of everlasting happiness can. Then, sitting with fierce determination under the Bodhi ("enlightenment") tree, Siddhartha came to see that the problem is not the world or the body: but the desiring mind which attaches enduring importance to the world and the body. The best way to quiet desire is to avoid the extremes which excite it by neither desiring the world nor being repulsed by it. Thus, Buddha offered a way to liberation which stilled desire by extinguishing that which desires, rather than degrading what is desired.

One sutra (scripture) calls the insight that came to Siddhartha "transcendent." "All Buddhas, of the past, present, or future, bound to irrefutable Transcendent Wisdom, reach completely full understanding and the highest awakening."[13] At that point, "he knew all as it really was."[14] His awakening was not a revelation in the sense of disclosure of truth from a deity. What Buddha realized was truth concerning his own being, insight into the nature of existence that arose from reflection on lessons learned in thousands of past lifetimes. "He the holy one . . . pondering by his own efforts attained at last perfect knowledge. Then bursting the shell of ignorance. . . . He became the perfectly wise . . . the *Tathāgata* ["one who has gone"], the one who has attained the knowledge of all forms, the Lord of all science."[15] It would be presumptuous to attempt to explain what Siddhartha understood as he became Buddha since his *ideas*—as the Greek root of the word (*eiden*, to see) suggests—were *images*, not concepts, and were directly *seen* rather than known through discursive thought. Thus, Buddhist tradition cautions that one can master every philosophical concept in Buddha's teaching and still not see what he saw. His vision was immediate and, unlike our sight, involved no separation between seeing subject and seen object. Buddha saw with transparent immediacy the nature of being.

Buddha's enlightenment proceeded through stages of meditative trance he learned during his training as an ascetic. The final stage of trance included magic powers, divine hearing and vision, knowledge of the minds of others, and memory of former lives. Buddha exercised miraculous powers throughout his career, but the account of his enlightenment, in the first-century B.C.E. work called *Acts of Buddha*, does not mention wonders. This text describes the highest point of Buddha's insight as the "knowledge of all forms." We have some reflection in later scriptures on what that knowledge entailed. The *Heart Sutra* teaches, "Form is emptiness, emptiness is form. Form is not other than emptiness, and emptiness is not other than form."[16] At the very least, we may conclude from this statement that no configuration of natural elements is permanent. But if that is all Buddha's knowledge consisted of, then he did not advance beyond observation of the transience of material things. What makes his enlightenment "transcendent wisdom" is that he perceived the emptiness of immaterial realities as well: consciousness, soul, and mind. At the very points other religious leaders located the transcendent dimension of human existence, Buddha discovered what the Mahāyāna tradition calls emptiness (*śūnyatā*).

Was Buddha's enlightenment, then, a transcendent event in the sense we are using that phrase to describe a miracle, or was it an achievement of insight that, in principle, anyone who develops the power of concentrated meditation could attain? To answer the question we must consider what *transcendent* means in Buddhist tradition. In the *Heart Sutra* the adjective is applied to wisdom, not to act or event. The truth Buddha discovered was not a riddle to be solved by mental gymnastics and it was not a mystery beyond human comprehension, but a basic fact that came clear to him when he stilled his mind. What does that mean? One answer is that he succeeded in maintaining conscious awareness without the focus of a specific perspective. His quiescent mind did not construct a filter for his perception; thus, Buddha saw things *as they really are* without narrowing or directing his vision through the lens of preconception and prejudice. In this sense, he achieved what Western philosophers since Kant have declared impossible: knowledge of things-in-themselves. In Kant's language, Buddha had direct intuition of noumenal reality. The decisive difference from Kant is that Buddha saw emptiness there as well. Postulates of an immortal soul or divine moral legislator were not logical necessities for Buddha, as they were for Kant. Rather, such notions are speculative distractions from meeting the challenge of reaching insight into the nature of reality, a challenge that can be met only when the mind is still, free from the busyness of shaping perceptions and constructing concepts.

In this sense, Buddha's enlightenment was not an immanent possibility since the human mind is incessantly active in ordinary cognition. Thus, if Buddha attained wisdom beyond the reach of human means of knowing, then his awareness was a *transcendent event*. Further, Buddhist tradition assigns great *religious significance* to the event—and it was an achievement so rare and astonishing that it continues to evoke *wonder* and exert a *transformative effect* on those who hear or read about it. On the basis of our definition of miracle, we conclude that Buddha's enlightenment was miraculous, even if not supernatural.

Buddha's confidence in the perfect wisdom he had attained and his vow to guide others in the way to liberation propelled him into a lifetime of teaching (*dharma*), the heart of which he summarized as Four Noble Truths:

1. All life is suffering.
2. The cause of suffering is desire.
3. Suffering can be overcome by eliminating desire.
4. Desire can be overcome by following the Eightfold Path.

Buddha taught that suffering is present throughout the whole of one's history and in the whole of one's being; the only way to overcome it is to follow a way of life that subordinates self to wider reality. That way is the Eightfold Path, a progressive series of steps toward enlightenment consisting of right knowledge (the Four Noble Truths), thought, speech, behavior, livelihood, effort, mindfulness, and concentration. The first followers of Buddha formed a small community (*sangha*) based on Three Vows: "I take refuge in the Buddha. I take refuge in the Dharma. I take refuge in the Sangha." These sources of guidance continue to be of primary importance to Buddhists worldwide. Buddha's example demonstrated that any person willing to adhere to his path of morality and wisdom could also attain *Nirvāna* (*Nibbāna* in Pali) or enlightenment, but to reach liberation one must expend dedicated effort. In his last recorded words, Buddha emphasized that the impermanence of existence charged the spiritual quest with urgency: "And now, monks, I declare to you—all conditioned things are of a nature to decay—strive on untiringly."[17]

Buddhist teaching about reality and individual selves (human and divine) is complex, but to appreciate the metaphysical principles upon which Buddhist views of miracles are based, we must make an effort to understand three terms: *Nirvāna, śūnyatā,* and *anatta.* The word *Nirvāna* derives from the Sanskrit verb "to be extinguished," as when a fire dies when deprived of oxygen.[18] What is blown out in that state of unconditioned consciousness is the boundary of the illusory self, as when one draws a circle in sand, then erases the line. What remains can be described as nothing or everything, but not as unreal or no-thing. Nirvāna is the awareness of the impermanence of all distinctions between self and other, loss and gain, birth and death, and of the emptiness at the core of everything we perceive as real. According to Mahāyāna scripture, awareness of "the emptiness of every existence" brings to the one who abides in meditation "great joy," as well as "transcendent powers."[19] Knowledge in this case truly is power because insight into the nonsubstantiality of things signifies that every arrangement of beings is temporary and subject to modification. That is the metaphysical condition for the occurrence of miracles: the mutability of natural order.

Buddhists draw the radical conclusion that emptiness alone is truly real. Thus, one cannot unite with ultimate reality for it, as well as oneself, is empty of enduring substance. For that reason Buddha rejected Vedic teaching about union with Brahman, as well as the desire in *bhakti* tradition for ecstatic communion with a beloved god or goddess. Because in Nirvāna all things are equally empty there is no basis for the relationship of deity and devotee. The *Diamond Sutra* records Buddha's words on this subject: "As many beings as there are in the universe of beings . . . all these I must lead to Nirvāna. . . . And yet, although innumerable beings have thus been led to Nirvāna, no being at all has been led to Nirvāna. And why?" Buddha's answer is that in the mind of an enlightened being there is no place for notions of being or self.[20] For such a person, rebirth ends because the one who reaches Nirvāna eliminates entirely needs and desires; no remnant of ego persists to bear the effects of karma and no trace of ordinary consciousness persists to entertain ideas of self or other. Such a one realizes the truth of "no-soul" or *anatta.*

In the career of Buddha, the wisdom of emptiness attained in Nirvāna and compassion for creatures suffering under the illusion of their own permanence combined to produce, from time to time, miracles as signs of his teaching and demonstrations of his enlightened mind. For example, according to the *Acts of Buddha,* after attaining enlightenment, Buddha "mounted on a throne, up in the air to the height of seven palm-trees." Thus suspended in space, he instructed myriad heavenly beings on the way to perfect knowledge: "everything is achieved by meritorious works, therefore as long as existence lasts acquire merit."[21] Here a central element in Mahāyāna teaching was given the sanction of Buddha's authority symbolized by his ascension.

In another story Buddha used the psychic power of levitation to avert a war over water rights. Buddha heard of a dispute between kinsmen from two branches of his family who lived on opposite sides of the Rohini River. Each spring they joined together to dam the river and shared the water to irrigate their fields. This summer, however, brought a severe drought and each side threatened to divert all the water for their own use. The conflict escalated to the point that both sides gathered their armies at the river's banks. "The Buddha, surveying the world with his supernormal powers, saw his relatives on both sides of the river coming out to meet in battle and he decided to stop them. All alone, he went to them by going through the sky" and appeared levitating over the middle of the river.[22] He addressed each side, asking them to compare the relatively small value of water to the great worth of human lives and then challenged them: "Great Kings, why do you act in this way? Were I not here today you would have started a river of blood flowing. You live in enmity and hatred. I live without hatred."[23] Astonished by his wondrous appearance and abashed by his teaching, the two sides made peace. The transcendent wisdom of Buddha was signified by the appearance of his body in the mediating position, suspended over the disputed water, and was articulated in his words that call both sides to "go beyond" their economic interests and embrace a higher ideal.

On another occasion Buddha was received with great joy by the king of Kapila. In response, Buddha rose into the air "and made manifest in his one person a form comprehending the universe," appearing in turn as fire, sun, moon, stars, various animals, celestial beings, and deities. It was a display reminiscent of Krishna's revelation to Arjuna, and the author of the text interpreted this miracle in a similar way, as disclosing Buddha's nature as the single universal source of all being: "whatever is conspicuous in the universe the holy one created it all, becoming the universal one." Consistent with the Buddhist view of miracles as pedagogical, the story continues, "When the king had thus been instructed, the lord of saints went to the Satya heaven, and then from the sky, seated on his own throne, he proclaimed the twelve-fold Law."[24]

In this story Buddha demonstrated his yogic attainments. In his authoritative introduction to Buddhist tradition, Peter Harvey, scholar of Pali, the language of northern India, points out that "the results of [psychic] powers are not seen as supernatural miracles, but as the supernormal products of the great inner power of certain meditations."[25] We have seen that *supernatural* is not a term properly applied to *siddhis*, but inasmuch as the powers suspend natural laws they certainly qualify as *transcendent*. That designation is consistent with a text in the Pali Canon in which Buddha cited "super-normal powers" as evidence of a concentrated mind. Among the powers of an advanced monk are these: "being one, he becomes many—being many, he becomes one; he appears and disappears; he passes through fences, walls and mountains unhindered as if through air; he sinks into the ground and emerges from it as if it were water; he walks on the water without breaking the surface as if on land; he flies cross-legged through the sky like a bird with wings."[26] These wondrous abilities are the standard attainments of a yogi in meditative trance. According to the Pali Canon, it is clear Buddha expected his disciples to acquire miraculous powers along the way to Nirvāna.[27] But it is equally clear that he did not expect them to remain at that stage of spiritual development and become entranced by their own wondrous deeds.

We conclude this section of the miracles of Buddha with a story about a miracle that did not occur: the story of Kisagotami and the mustard seed. Buddhist scriptures written in Pali are organized in three sections, called the Three Baskets; one of them known as *sutta* contains discourses by Buddha and others. The best-known version of the tale of Kisagotami appears in the commentary on a section of the *Sutta Pitaka* called *Therīgāthā* (*Verses of Elder Nuns*). Kisagotami gave birth to a son who died in the midst of childish play. "Because of this, sorrow-to-the-point-of-madness arose in her" and she wandered the city, pleading with people to provide her medicine that would restore the boy to life. Finally, a wise man directed her to seek help from Buddha. The woman approached Buddha, carrying her dead son in her arms and begging for medicine. Buddha agreed to grant her wish on the condition that she bring him a mustard seed from a household in the village which had never lost a member to death. Her futile search reconciled Kisagotami to the truth that death is universal and life is impermanent for everyone. She buried the body of her son and returned to Buddha for permission to join the community of nuns. The story concludes, "It was not long before, through the doing of deeds with careful attention, she caused her insight to grow . . . and she became an [enlightened woman]."[28] The story illustrates the saying attributed to Buddha: "'These sons belong to me, and this wealth belongs to me,' with such thoughts a fool is tormented. He himself does not belong to himself; how much less sons and wealth?"[29]

This occasion was ripe for the performance of miraculous healing, and Buddha does not deny his capacity to bring Kisagotami's dead son to life. But this time he fulfilled his pedagogical aim by *not* working a miracle. Miracles evoke wonder, a state of awareness prior to analysis and evaluation, and Buddha's goal was to engage Kisagotami's mind in understanding the truth of impermanence. A miracle of resuscitation would have prevented her from grasping the point that suffering does not cease until the desire for permanence is abandoned.

In another version of this story the heroine is named Patacara and she underwent not one tragic loss but a series of disasters that outpaced the torments of Job. On the way to her parents' home to give birth to her second child, her husband died of snake bite. She delivered the child and then was forced to protect her children from a raging storm with her own body. The next day, an eagle carried off her newborn and her older child drowned in the swollen river along the way. When she reached her parents' home, she learned they and her brother had died in a fire caused by lightning from the previous night's storm. She went insane and wandered half-naked until she came upon Buddha. His teaching restored her senses and she became ordained as a nun. She summarized what she had learned in this verse: "With family killed, despised by all, my husband dead, I reached the Deathless."[30]

The point of both stories is that miraculous intervention to prevent deaths, even of the innocent, is not necessarily a benefit. We cannot overcome death and our fear of it by prolonging life under the inescapable condition of impermanence. The only realm where death has no power is Nirvāna, deathless because there is no rebirth. Miracles may be useful to confirm authority and provide visual images as teaching aids, but apart from the wider context of Buddha's teaching, wondrous works can be more hindrance than help in spiritual development. It is that conviction that led Buddha to forbid his monks to display psychic powers in public.

In the *Vinaya Pitaka* (*The Book of Discipline*) Buddha set out the code governing the lives of monks, including the four "rules of defeat." Any monk who violated one of them forfeited his membership in the Sangha. The first three are not surprising: no sexual intercourse, no theft, and no murder. The fourth is unusual in that it does not proscribe a type of action, but a kind of misrepresentation: "false proclamation of superhuman faculties."[31] Thus, monks may not declare mastery of wondrous powers or greater understanding of Buddha's teaching than they possess. Why are these four acts the most serious offenses? The first three are clearly instances of desire and hatred, two of the dispositions that cause suffering. The third disposition to overcome is ignorance; and it may be that claiming power to work miracles to advance one's own interest is the supreme instance of ignorance: failure to realize the emptiness of ego.

Many commentators regard the fourth rule as evidence Buddha disapproved of all miracle working. But what is the transgression here: exercising paranormal powers or lying about doing so? Did Buddha intend to forbid monks to perform miracles or to condemn the pride and falsehood entailed in exaggerating one's attainments? When Buddha was told of a monk who used telepathy to locate two kidnapped children and was praised for his wondrous act, Buddha replied, "Monks, there is no offence for one who possesses psychic power in the sphere of psychic power." On another occasion he excused a monk who used supernormal perception to predict future events on the ground that he spoke the truth; therefore, Buddha declared, "there is no offence."[32] Because lying about one's spiritual progress defeats the purpose of joining others to examine oneself unsparingly and to seek release from self-interest, it is fitting that it result in expulsion from the monastic community (particularly if the monk's purpose in boasting about his powers was to impress a young woman—always a concern in monastic rules!).

As with every law, there is a story behind the fourth rule of defeat; and the intent of the prohibition may become clearer as we examine the occasion that led to its promulgation. One sutra specifies where and when Buddha announced each rule for monastic conduct, but the reference for the fourth one is expressed in general terms: "This moral precept was prescribed by the Blessed One, with regard to the monk Abhimānika and the many village dwelling monks, in Śrāvastī . . . in the sixth year after perfect enlightenment." Charles Prebish, scholar of Buddhist monasticism, suggests that the offender's name is symbolic and might be translated "a self-conceited monk."[33] Following that clue we might consider the story of one prideful monk who displayed superhuman powers in a village, and received a sharp rebuke from Buddha, as emblematic of the occasion for Buddha's proscription of displaying miraculous powers.

In this story a village merchant devised a test to determine whether there were any "perfected ones" among the monks in the nearby monastery. He placed a sandalwood bowl, intricately carved, on the top of a tall bamboo pole and challenged anyone to bring it down by the use of psychic power. Followers of other teachers, including a Jain, were unsuccessful. But one of Buddha's chief disciples, called Mogallāna the Great, addressed another monk, "The venerable Pindola Bhāradvāja is a perfected one as well as of psychic power. Go along, fetch down this bowl; this bowl is for you." Thus encouraged, or enticed, Pindola rose into the air, seized the bowl, and circled the village three times. The people praised "master Pindola" in loud voices and formed a procession behind him as he returned to the monastery. When Buddha heard the commotion following this wonder, he admonished the monk in these words: "It is not proper, Bhāradvāja, it is not becoming, it is not fitting, it is not worthy of a religious man, it is not allowable, it is not to be done! . . . Even as a vulgar woman exhibits herself undressed to the common people for the sake of a miserable pittance, so did you exhibit to the common people . . . a wonder of psychic power, for the sake of a miserable bowl!" Turning to the other monks, Buddha turned the rebuke into a general prohibition: "Whoever exhibits [psychic powers] is guilty of wrongdoing."[34] Buddha ordered the bowl destroyed.

One bystander, named Kevatta, apparently did not hear Buddha's instruction to his monks and implored Buddha to allow a monk to come to his town and "display a miracle of psychic power from his superior human state" so that the people of his village "would to an even greater extent have faith in the Blessed One."[35] Buddha vehemently refused, saying, "I despise, loathe, abhor, and reject miracles of magic power and divination! My disciples and I gain adherents only by the miracle of instruction." Robert Allen Mitchell condensed into these two dramatic sentences Buddha's response to Kevatta which later tradition expanded to an entire sutra. Read in the context of the *Kevatta Sutta*, Buddha's restriction of yogic powers is more qualified inasmuch as he included them in his explanation of the "miracle of instruction." Buddha distinguished three types of miracles: *psychic power*, including levitation, disappearance, and ascent to divine realms; *telepathy* or mind reading; and *instruction* that persuades laymen to take up the ascetic way of monks. Because the first two types of miracles could be mistaken for the effects of magic charms, Buddha declared that he felt "horrified, humiliated, and disgusted" by them. The miracle of instruction, on the other hand, transformed a householder into a monk "consummate in virtue," dedicated to celibacy, non-injury, abstinence from luxury and frivolity, independence from political and religious authorities, and concentrated meditation.

At the fourth and highest stage of meditation the monk attains wondrous powers, including the capacity to create other bodies by his mind and to exercise control over forces of nature. As a skilled potter can fashion from clay whatever vessel he chooses, "in the same way—with his mind thus concentrated, purified, and bright, unblemished, free from defects, pliant, malleable, steady, and attained to imperturbability—the monk directs and inclines [his body] to the modes of paranormal powers. . . . He exercises influence with his body even as far as the Brahma worlds." Then Buddha added, "This, too, is called the miracle of instruction." The point is not that supernatural powers are invalid, but that their meaning is disclosed only in the context of Buddha's teaching. If they are perceived outside that context, as inevitably happens when they are displayed in the public square before uninitiated householders, the powers cannot be seen as evidence of great insight but only as magic tricks. Many stories of wonders in Buddhist tradition underscore the statement in the *Lotus Sutra* that miracles are skillful means of instruction.[36]

For Buddha the greatest miracle was the detachment of the human mind from judgments and distinctions that lead to alienation from others. The stories of his wondrous deeds, then, are retold to instruct listeners and readers in the way of wisdom. The *Lotus Sutra* recounts an occasion when Buddha "manifested his great transcendent powers" by sticking out his "wide and long tongue which reached upwards to the Brahma World. He emitted innumberable and immeasureable colored rays of light from all his pores and universally illuminated the worlds in the ten directions."[37] This extravagant image combines two familiar metaphors of teaching and learning: oral projection from the mouth and light radiating across the entire field of knowledge. It represents Buddha's wisdom as transcendent.

After the death of the Buddha, his monks were assailed by doubts and began to debate what they should believe and how they should conduct themselves. Every religious community seeks to sustain the insights of its founder; but with the authoritative living example gone, the followers often disagree on how best to preserve and interpret the founder's wisdom. For early Buddhists among the most contentious questions were whether Buddha was a human example or a divine savior and whether humans reach liberation through their own efforts or through supernatural assistance. Many found the latter alternatives more appealing and began to imagine beings, both heavenly and historical, who could help them gain liberation. These saviors are called Bodhisattvas.

Bodhisattva: Miracles of Wisdom and Compassion

Bodhisattva ("enlightened being" or "Buddha-to-be") is a category of religious leadership indicating one who is determined to become a Buddha in order to enable all sentient beings to reach liberation. A Bodhisattva combines the virtues of *wisdom* and *compassion*. After vowing to renounce worldly interests and to serve others, a Bodhisattva cultivates spiritual perfections, culminating in his entrance into the world to lead others in the way of release from suffering—and to provide them with saving effects of virtue they may lack.[38] But there is a problem with understanding the Bodhisattva as a savior in this way.

One traditional image of a Bodhisattva is a person who travels through wilderness to finally arrive at a walled enclosure. Climbing the wall he looks over to see paradise. Instead of leaping into bliss, however, he climbs back down and vows to remain outside to guide others on the path. The problem with this appealing analogy is to explain why anyone would turn down the opportunity to enter paradise, a metaphor for Nirvāna, after spending a lifetime trying to achieve it. In one early Mahāyāna sutra Buddha implies the resolution of the seeming contradiction by describing one quality of a genuine Bodhisattva in these words: "he gives gifts in order to mature beings, and yet he has no expectation of any fruition of the act of giving for himself."[39] Buddha cleared up the problem of motivation implied in the analogy by teaching that the intention to act compassionately toward others, out of solidarity grounded in the wisdom that self and others are alike empty, constitutes the state of selflessness that *is* liberation. As a result, the compassion of a Bodhisattva is pure, free from pity and condescension because it is offered by a selfless being to those who are also "non-self."

Popular enthusiasm for miracle-working Bodhisattvas flourished in the Mahāyāna tradition, which began some time between 150 B.C.E. and 100 C.E. In the course of two millennia since then, the number of Bodhisattvas and the celestial kingdoms they occupy have multiplied as ordinary believers— whether suffering from disease, poverty, or political persecution—sought an ever-growing company of heavenly saviors to rescue them. The austere demands of Buddha's Four Noble Truths, made even more rigorous and exclusive in the Theravada tradition, were more than most people could bear alone, especially in India where thousands of gods and goddesses were available to assist faithful Hindus. Further, as Buddhism moved into China, Tibet, and Japan, it encountered crowded directories of deities upon whom people called for help through prayer, offerings, sacrifice, and ascetic discipline. It was perhaps inevitable that versions of Buddhism would emerge capable of accommodating the desire for supernatural intervention. From the pantheon of Bodhisattvas we will consider two: *Avalokiteśvara*, whom Buddha praised for his miracles of deliverance; and *Maitreya*, the future successor of Buddha who will bring Dharma to the entire world.

The twenty-fifth chapter of the *Lotus Sutra* is devoted to the Bodhisattva Avalokiteśvara, whose name means "He Who Observes the Sounds of the World," particularly the cries of beings in distress who call upon his name. The two roots of his name are *to look* and *lord*, so his sovereign observing is visual as well as auditory. Thus, Avalokiteśvara is associated with light and illumination.[40] The promises of miraculous deliverance in this chapter are numerous and specific. If an enemy pushes you into fire and you "contemplate the power of Avalokiteśvara, the fire-pit will change into a pond." If someone pushes you off a mountain cliff, "you will stay suspended in the air like the sun." When anyone contemplates the power of Avalokiteśvara, that person will be saved from murderous robbers, delivered from prison and the executioner's sword, made immune to poisons, rescued from wild beasts, protected from natural disasters, saved from suffering, and made victorious in battle.[41] It is an impressive list of benefits, and early on a body of writing emerged, testifying to the efficacy of the Bodhisattva's interventions.

In translations of the *Lotus Sutra* from Sanskrit to Chinese, Avalokiteśvara's name was rendered Guanshiyin from the Chinese character for *radiance*. During the third to seventh centuries China was convulsed by foreign invaders, catastrophic floods causing famine and plague, and destructive internal struggles for political control. In the cataclysmic conditions Buddhist writers speculated about the end of the world, and the cult of devotion to Guanshiyin grew as the *Lotus Sutra*, with its promise of deliverance from dire circumstances, circulated widely. In this context, there also developed a set of miracle stories, recording the Bodhisattva's wondrous powers and thereby demonstrating the superiority of the Buddhist savior over local deities and, by extension, the greater wisdom of Buddhism over Taoist teachings. Assimilation of Avalokiteśvara into Chinese devotion was part of the broader process of adapting Buddhism to Chinese culture, culminating in stories of the wondrous deeds of Guanshiyin.[42]

In the miracle tales the Bodhisattva used transcendent power to deliver victims of political oppression. One woman, who was wrongly imprisoned, sought refuge in reciting the *Guanshiyin Sutra* (chapter 25 of the *Lotus Sutra*) continuously for ten days. She then had a vision of the Bodhisattva who told her to "just get up." When she did, her shackles fell off and she suddenly found herself back in her own home. In another story a man was captured by northern invaders and held in their camp. His mother prayed to Guanshiyin for his release, concentrating her mind on the Bodhisattva before seven lit lamps. After a year the son was able to escape and began walking south. At night, when he lost his way, seven points of firelight appeared to direct him. Following those lights he arrived home to find his mother prostrated before an image of Guanshiyin. They realized his escape and guidance were "due to the Buddha's power." In a third story, the promise in the *Lotus Sutra* that Avalokiteśvara will save those facing execution was fulfilled. Two men about to be killed began chanting the name of Guanshiyin "with perfect sincerity." When the time of execution came, their names had been mysteriously expunged from the list of victims. The crowd was astounded by this turn of events and, in the ensuing commotion, the two men fled to safety.

In a final story, devotion to Guanshiyin resulted in the birth of a son to a Taoist elder. Desperate for an heir, the elder turned to a Buddhist monk who advised him to "respectfully and with perfect mind recite the *Guanshiyin Sutra*. You may then hope for success." The elder gave up following the Tao (or "Way" taught by Lao Tzu) and within a few days he had a vision in a dream that his wife was pregnant. She subsequently gave birth to a boy. This story both confirmed claims for the Bodhisattva's power in the *Lotus Sutra* and also demonstrated the greater efficacy and wisdom of the Buddhist Way over the Chinese Tao.

Another account of the intervention of the Bodhisattva, known in Japan as Kuan Yin, is found in the record of an earthquake in Tokyo in 1922. As buildings collapsed and fires broke out, thousands of desperate people gathered at a temple dedicated to her, chanting her name and calling upon the Bodhisattva to save them. "Miraculously, every time the towering flames tried to burn towards the temple, another gust of wind would blow the flames back. . . . Many people also witnessed the physical manifestation of Kannon [Kuan Yin] in the typical Japanese form, riding on the head of a dragon. Many thousands were saved during that catastrophic day."[43] The narrator of the tale, Tan Peng Yau, comments that "most individuals normally don't reveal such interventions out of humility and other reasons pertaining to personal privacy." While the reticence of Japanese devotees may reflect a cultural meme of modesty that prevents them from claiming to be special recipients of divine favor, our narrator also insists that one should not practice Buddhism in order to benefit from miracles.

Rather than petitioning the Bodhisattva for favors, one should pray the mantra of six syllables associated with her: *Om Mani Padme Hum*. The mantra begins and ends with sacred words. *Om* indicates direct awareness of universal truth, while *Hum* signifies the embodiment of wisdom in a compassionate human life. *Mani* means *jewel* and refers to the wish-granting gem the Bodhisattva holds in her hands as a symbol of the benefits she offers. *Padme* means *lotus* and recalls the origin of the Bodhisattva in the flower that takes root in the muck at the bottom of a pond but eventually unfolds in a pure white flower that floats on the water: a Buddhist image of the process of attaining Nirvāna. The mantra defies translation, but Tan Peng Yau renders it into English this way: "Avalokiteśvara, who possesses the body and wisdom of the Buddhas, behold us!" Thus interpreted, the mantra is not a request *to see* the compassion of the Bodhisattva displayed in a miraculous event, but a plea *to be seen*, that is, to be acknowledged by the divine being as one of the sentient, and therefore suffering, beings a Bodhisattva vows to save. Whether that salvation includes visible acts of divine mercy is left to the disposition of the Bodhisattva's compassion but requires the best efforts of the petitioner: "Praying is not an occasion for bribery or laziness. *We need to start helping ourselves before the Buddhas can assist us in any way.*"

Whether that assistance constitutes a miraculous event or a pedagogical aid to grasping Buddha's wisdom is a dispute about interpretation our next story demonstrates. According to this tale, the people of Korea commissioned Chinese artisans to fashion a wooden statue of Avalokiteśvara. When the splendid image was completed, it was carried to the beach of the harbor where it was to be loaded on to a boat bound for Korea. To the stevedores' amazement, the statue became so heavy it could not be moved. When the two nations agreed that the image would remain in China, the statue returned to normal weight and was enshrined in a nearby temple. For Chinese devotees of Avalokiteśvara this event was a miracle, signifying that the Bodhisattva had a special interest in bringing benefits to them and would not allow his image to be carried away.

For Zen interpreters, however, this incident raised the question: "In the sutra we read that Avalokiteśvara is the possessor of miraculous powers, and in all the lands of the ten quarters there is not a place where he does not manifest himself. Then why is it this holy statue refused to go to Korea?" One modern teacher answered that the Chinese did not want to part with such a fine image, so "superstition and mass psychology" combined to create the impression that the statue could not be moved. Another suggested that the story should motivate Koreans to create their own image or, at a deeper level of spiritual insight, that the empty ship returning to Korea should prompt a Buddhist there to "open his eyes. . . . Is he not a true Avalokiteśvara?"[44] The meaning of the miracle, once again, depends on the interpretive framework the witness or reader brings to the story and on the cultural context in which it occurs.

In Tibet, Avalokiteśvara is known as Chenrezig (Noble Sovereign) and his cult became popular in the eleventh and twelfth centuries. In Tibetan tradition his entrance into the world was a miracle: Amitabha Buddha was moved by compassion for all beings and emitted from his right eye a beam of white light that took the form of a young man. Realizing the necessity of a corresponding deity in the form of a young woman, Amitabha issued a green beam from his left eye, giving rise to Tārā. The young man appeared on earth in a lotus, afloat on a lake near the palace of a king and chanting, "Poor beings! Poor beings!" The king took him to be his long-desired son; but Chenrezig was intent on fulfilling his Bodhisattva vow, intensified by his oath to break into a thousand pieces if he failed to keep his promise to save all sentient beings. But after eons of faithful service to others, Chenrezig realized that the number of those remaining in ignorance could not be counted and he decided to abandon the task and remain content in Nirvāna. Immediately, his body exploded into a thousand pieces, causing him great suffering. Amitabha Buddha then reconstituted Chenrezig's body, giving him eleven faces and a thousand arms and eyes so that he could better fulfill his renewed vow.[45]

Amitabha also gave him the six-syllable mantra (*Om Mani Padme Hum*) with the power to liberate beings from rebirth. According to one Tibetan teacher, reciting the mantra transforms one's ordinary mind into the wisdom of Buddha and guarantees that in the next lifetime one will "achieve the irreversible stage of the Bodhisattva and finally attain Enlightenment."[46] One example of the miraculous power of the mantra is in the story of an eleventh-century master, Gelogma Palmo. Born into a royal family, she contracted leprosy and was cast into a forest. There she was led by a vision to the practice of devotion to Chenrezig. After many years of reciting the mantra before his image, she was healed of leprosy and became an enlightened nun with a large circle of disciples.[47] This story confirms the efficacy of meditation on this Bodhisattva and inspires devotees to hope for his intervention. But faith in supernatural help can also be undermined by tragedy and oppression, as in Tibet.

Tradition holds that Buddha charged Avalokiteśvara to bring his teachings to Tibet, thus grounding the national identity of Tibetans in a manifestation of the Bodhisattva. Further, since the fifteenth century Chenrezig has been directly involved in the religious and political leadership of Tibet in the form of the Dalai Lama, who served as ruler of Tibet until Chinese occupation forced the current Dalai Lama to flee the country in 1959 and take up residence in northern India. As an incarnation of Chenrezig, the birth of every Dalai Lama is an event of transcendent power with great religious significance—in short, a miracle. Not surprisingly, such power also carries political authority, so that Tibetans continue to resist Chinese rule in the belief that the Dalai Lama is their rightful sovereign.

That hopeful faith faces severe challenge as Tibet falls under Chinese hegemony. Current suppression of Tibetan religious practices, coupled with past destruction of Buddhist monasteries and assassination of monks, create the precise conditions from which Avalokiteśvara promised in the final chapter of the *Lotus Sutra* to deliver his devotees. Whether his failure to rescue the people of Tibet will lead to their loss of devotion to him is a question for the future. In the meantime, it seems that the Bodhisattva who vowed to protect them abandoned Tibet to obliteration through assimilation by China. Thus, the Dalai Lama seems to be preparing Tibetans for a future without supernatural intervention, one in which Chenrezig's past miracles are symbolic of the transforming effect of Buddhist teaching rather than stories of deliverance the Tibetan people can expect to have replicated in their present situation.

The current Dalai Lama expressed doubts about the efficacy of his mediating attempt to gain regional autonomy for Tibet within the People's Republic of China; he admitted that negotiations over many years have yielded "no concrete result at all."[48] He even declared that the next incarnation of the Dalai Lama will not occur in Tibet if present conditions persist, but in a land where political freedom would allow his current campaign to continue.[49] Insisting that Tibetans pursue their national integrity by non-violent resistance and offering sympathy to Chinese families who lost members in the violence of revolt and repression, the Dalai Lama follows his vocation of embodying compassion. The power of the Bodhisattva which he is believed to embody, however, is restricted to the moral authority and persuasive influence of unjust suffering: a power effectively wielded by Mahatma Gandhi and Martin Luther King, Jr., to bring about social and political change. So far, however, these resources have proven impotent against Chinese military force. It would appear that, for the Dalai Lama, Chenrezig is not a forceful agent in history but a symbol of the wisdom of skillful means of peaceful resistance by a minority people and the compassion toward enemies that fulfills Buddha's teaching that "hatred ceases by love." If a miracle were to occur, it would be the success of those means in persuading the Chinese to act with respect for the cultural and religious traditions of Tibetans.

In the traditions we are considering, miracle stories are about power, but more importantly they are about authority: the right to exercise power. The meaning of a miracle is never limited to its display of sheer power because brute force is not intelligible in itself. The exercise of transcendent power evokes wonder as an initial response, but blank astonishment cannot yield meaning. To understand a miracle requires interpretive effort, and interpretation proceeds as a creative act of translating what is wondrous into what can be known and communicated. For Mahāyāna Buddhists the wondrous works of Bodhisattvas signify that believers are not entirely on their own in this world of suffering and injustice and that the virtue of compassion is not a theoretical ideal but a practical power in history. Faith in the power of compassion to transform political conditions requires risk and suffering, as others who have followed that path discovered. On the rare occasions the power is effective, however, the result is more than surprising. When humans respond to the suffering of others—suffering they may have caused—by setting aside self-interest and national ambition to realize an ideal possibility, believers discern a transcendent event. Faith in Avalokiteśvara reflects the conviction that his promises of deliverance will be fulfilled, if not in miracles of intervention, then through the astonishing capacity of compassion to transmute enemies into friends—and if not in this world, then in the next.

All Buddhists cherish texts that foretell the coming of the successor of Śakyamuni Buddha, a Bodhisattva named Maitreya (Sanskrit for *kindness* or *friendliness*), who now waits in heaven for his final incarnation. According to one text, Buddha taught that Maitreya will appear in the far distant future when people live for 80,000 years and the memory of Buddha's teachings will have faded and even his relics burned to ashes. He will "teach the Dhamma . . . in the spirit and in the letter, and proclaim, just as I do now, the holy life in its fullness and purity."[50] In one version of Buddhist teaching about the end of history, moral and material conditions "gradually improve as the advent of the next Buddha approaches."[51] In one nineteenth-century Thai text Maitreya predicted a glorious future age immediately preceding his coming. When wars cease and people act generously toward one another, practicing virtues of patience, kindness, and joy, then Maitreya "will take living beings miraculously up to the city of *nibbāna*." In this utopia people will "no longer abuse their authority and oppress others," wives and husbands will be faithful to each other, wealth will never fail, and all debilitating diseases will be cured. At that shining moment, when humans fully develop their potential for moral and physical perfection, then the Bodhisattva will appear to take them to the final destination which they cannot reach on their own: the unconditioned bliss of Nirvāna.

This brief consideration of two prominent Bodhisattvas demonstrates that their miracles are signs of transcendent wisdom and universal compassion. While different powers are ascribed to these heavenly beings in various cultural contexts, and historical conditions often shape whether the stories of their miracles are interpreted literally or symbolically, Buddhists find in the miracle stories of Bodhisattvas a ground of confidence that divine compassion will meet every human need, whether in the form of wisdom or power—or both, as in Tibetan Buddhism.

Lama: Miracles and Mysticism

According to tradition, Buddhism came to Tibet in the seventh century when King Srong-btsan unified warring noble families into a powerful state. True to his policy of integration, the king took two wives, one from China and one from Nepal, who brought Buddhist images with them. Later accounts represent the king as an incarnation of Avalokiteśvara and his wives as incarnations of Tārā, venerated as a heavenly benefactor in her own right. It was a century later, however, before the form of Tibetan Buddhism which continues today, called Vajrayāna, arrived in the teachings of a master from India named Padmasambhava. Close to Mahāyāna in its veneration of Bodhisattvas, Vajrayāna offered a more direct way to liberation by combining meditation with esoteric rituals and magical power. The name *Vajrayāna* suggests a flash of lightning revealing the adamantine wisdom of the Buddha (diamond-like in firmness and clarity). Unlike other forms of Buddhism, the Thunderbolt Vehicle values supernormal attainments as a means, rather than a hindrance, to ultimate insight.

Further, in Tibet the tradition of the Buddha is understood as progressive so that later practices are exempt from earlier proscriptions of wondrous powers.[52] Padmasambhava was particularly adept at ritual techniques of exorcism (casting out of demons). As he proceeded throughout Tibet, he confronted and defeated local demons defending their territory. Without exception they yielded to the great wonder worker and vowed to protect Buddhist Dharma. Padmasambhava's victory over native Tibetan spirits associated with the indigenous religion called *Bon*, and his enlisting them in the advance of his teaching, were symbols of the power of Buddhism to assimilate local deities and rituals as it moved into new cultural contexts.[53]

Padmasambhava is credited with establishing the first Buddhist monastery in Tibet and writing and translating important texts. He also figures in rituals celebrating the victory of Buddhism over opposition by Bon priests. One school venerated him as an appearance of Avalokiteśvara. Elsewhere he is honored as one of the eighty-four *mahāsiddhas*, masters of miraculous powers who were active through the eleventh century. The biographies of these masters represent their wondrous deeds in an esoteric form of writing, called in Sanskrit "twilight language," indicating that its words convey truth that lies in the dimly lit world of shadows between literal and mystical meaning. For one Tibetan teacher, Lama Anagarika Govinda, the language signals that miraculous powers are expressions of mystical advance. "In the symbolic language of the *Siddhas* experiences of meditation are transformed into external events, inner attainments into visible miracles and similes into factual, quasi-historical events."[54]

According to Govinda, what is true of stories of their miracles also applies to accounts of their sexual practices. He recognizes that *Siddhas* shocked complacent monks by their erotic images of mystic states, but insists they never indulged in sexual intercourse. Yet some *siddhas* did act in intentional violation of conventional morality and monastic discipline by drinking alcohol and consorting with low-caste women. Their scandalous behavior demonstrated their freedom from social expectations and traditional authority, and was part of their meditative practices which sought to realize the unity of reality obscured by distinctions made in moral judgments and by the separation of men and women required by celibacy. One *siddha* sang, "Just as salt dissolves in water, in the same way dissolves the mind of him who takes his own wife."[55] Sexual and spiritual union served as the means of realizing the unity of consciousness that is Nirvāna. As eccentric as his methods were, this same master reached the insight that is the final goal of all Buddhist meditation: "Mind is the seed of everything, from which sprouts both existence and *nirvāna*. Pay obeisance to it, for, like the wish-fulfilling gem, it gives you the fruit that you desire." Tantric practice, then, is as effective in modifying the world as appeals to Avalokiteśvara, who holds in his hand the jewel that dispenses favors. The point is that stories of miracles and of sexual exploits have in common symbolic reference to the transcendent wisdom reached by breaking through conventional natural and social orders.

In the eleventh century, Buddhism was established as the dominant religion of Tibet with strong royal patronage; and a close alliance between palace and monastery continued throughout most of the history of Tibet, with monks often designating rulers as incarnations of Bodhisattvas and kings supplying food and goods to monks. Buddhism also incorporated elements of Bon into its worldview, including belief in divine powers present in nature, exorcism, the magic power of texts, and means of appealing for special favors from gods and goddesses. This was also the time an Indian *siddha*, named Nāropa, reintroduced meditative practices leading to yogic powers. The most famous of the masters of these techniques was Milarepa (1052–1135), who was said to have endured the bitter winter cold in his Himalayan hermitage, clad only in a thin cotton robe, by generating internal heat through the practice of the Yoga of Inner Fire.[56] The practice of this power continues among Tibetan monks who soak themselves in icy water and enter meditative trances while steam rises from their robes. It is also the discipline that generates luminescent auras that surround masters. Lama Govinda acknowledges, "When the mind has become luminous, the body too must partake in this luminous nature." He cites a European who reported seeing an Indian saint's body turn into a luminous form before his astonished eyes.[57]

For Tibetan Buddhism the world is filled with transcendent powers, benevolent and hostile, and a spiritual master, called *Lama*, controls them, even as he directs the disposition of his physical body, by the resolution of his mind. To illustrate that capacity we will consider one story of levitation and translocation by a Tibetan master.

A student named Jñānasūtra traveled to China to study with the master Shrīsimha twenty years, training in meditation and esoteric disciplines. But Shrīsimha would not entrust him with his most profound teachings until the disciple was specially empowered. One day the master was invited by a king in a distant province. Rising into the sky, the teacher flew there, riding a white lion, sitting in a silk tent under three layers of parasols, and held up by six powerful young attendants. He was gone for six days. On the morning of the seventh day, Jñānasūtra heard a loud noise in the sky. He looked up to see the master, seated in the air, as a mass of light. Jñānasūtra realized the mortal body of the master had dissolved. As he offered prayers, the book of the master's teachings fell into his hand.[58]

This story is set in the remote past of Tibetan Buddhism. The narrative is rich in details that anchor it in its specific cultural tradition; and it assumes the multi-layered view of reality developed in Buddhist metaphysics, in turn derived from the multiple worlds of ancient India. On the surface, however, the story seems to present a fairly straightforward account of the transmission of teaching from master to disciple: a rite of passage assuring continuity of authority that is common to many religious traditions. But is that all that the miracle means?

The master's flight seems to be a show of power both *in* the world and *over* it, perhaps intended to impress the emperor. Shrīsimha arrived in the domain of an earthly king with a heavenly retinue. His flight across an expanse of space that was divided on the ground by political, ethnic, and linguistic differences confirmed his freedom from such distinctions and their limitations. On this reading the story is about politics, setting the religious leader in the clouds above the king on his throne and establishing the authority of the wisdom the master left behind. Further, because the setting of the story is in China, present-day readers may interpret it as an assertion of the independent authority of Tibet's religious tradition over against China's political control. In this reading, through the lens of postcolonial criticism, the story has to do with the distribution and maintenance of political power.

What transpired between the ascetic master and the provincial ruler we are not told, but when the master returned he had attained an exalted spiritual state in which his material body dissolved, leaving behind only the corpus (body) of his teachings in written form. That element of the story cannot be reduced to political symbolism. Shrīsimha possessed no earthly power; he had no subjects because he was free from subjection and subjectivity. His mind was "fully realized" and his flight in defiance of gravity demonstrated that fact. Any attempt to disclose the meaning of this story that obscures its function as marking the master's religious attainment, his transcendent wisdom, misses something critical. For that understanding we must place it in the context of Buddhist religious teachings.

According to Buddhist metaphysical premises, enlightened beings appear in three bodies: *Transformation-body*, as earthly teachers, manifest in flesh and blood; *Enjoyment-body*, as miracle workers, manifest in forms and powers relative to their virtues, capable of creating and living in ideal worlds; and *Dharma-body*, as Buddhas, manifest as infinite and universal knowledge, usually in the form of radiant light perceptible only to other Buddhas. With this teaching in mind, we understand that the disciple first saw the master in Enjoyment-body, performing the feat of levitation. When the master later appeared as "a mass of light," he had transformed into Dharma-body. But it would only be possible for Jñānasūtra to see him in that form if the disciple were also a Buddha.[59] Any lesser developed being would have been blinded by the sight. On this reading, the point of the story shifts from the authority of the text the master left behind to the status of his disciple as an enlightened being worthy to receive the text.

The written testament, however, seems more like a souvenir, a reminder that the master in his Transformation-body was essentially an embodiment of teaching. In the story the master literally appeared in successive stages of spiritual development: a living illustration of the three-body doctrine. The master manifested the power to inhabit in his Enjoyment-body the layer of reality his consciousness had attained. Further, the event was possible only in a world already transformed by the mind of the disciple in such a way that he could discern the Dharma-body of his master, thus becoming his equal. Or was it the manifestation of the master's Dharma-body that transformed the mind of his student? Was the miracle one of the master's manifestation or the disciple's perception? Since the vision required both a revelatory object and a receptive observer, and neither condition was given in nature, it constituted a transcendent event. Like other miracles in Buddhist tradition, this one is pedagogical: the master's transformation was a sign of the esoteric wisdom of the three bodies of a Buddha. Compared to the direct sight of the embodied teaching, the words in the teacher's manual were indistinct traces, subject to loss and misunderstanding. For the one instructed by a miracle, however, there can be no mistake or doubt or failure to realize the transcendent wisdom that in turn empowers further miracles.

According to the founder of esoteric Buddhism in Japan, a monk called Kūkai (774–835), similar revelatory vision is available to all who follow his meditative practice. For Kūkai, the Dharma-body is "a corpus of transcendent qualities shared by all buddhas"; and Kūkai promised, "you will obtain Buddha's body as boundless as the entire universe and as empty space, the body which is none other than the wisdom of the essential nature of the universe." In this way, not only will it be possible to attain enlightenment "with miraculous, inconceivable speed," but also the body of the adept will "soon be endowed with the five miraculous powers. Continue your practice, and then without abandoning this body of yours, you will enter the ranks of buddhas."[60] Kūkai interpreted the Dharma-body as a symbol of the wisdom and virtues that mark the presence of enlightened beings. For him the ending of the story, in which the master's body dissolves in light, leaving behind his book, would be entirely appropriate as a parable of the supremacy of teaching over teacher. But there is a hint in the story of a more basic insight.

Could the meaning of the miracle be that the master, an individual of lofty attainments, is finally empty? At the moment of his highest realization he disappears. All that remains is his version of the truth, but it is inadequately cast into language and destined to decay. Our story, then, ostensibly told to confirm the authority of the master and his teaching, serves to underscore the impermanence of both. This fundamental belief that nothing has enduring reality may be the final word about this miracle—and perhaps all miracles in Buddhist tradition. For Buddhist critics of belief in miracles the irony of this conclusion is that a primary element of Buddha's transcendent wisdom reduces miracles to insignificance.

Dissent: Ancient and Modern Objections to Miracles

Faithful opposition to the hope for miracles arose early in Buddhist tradition. In the Theravadan school, miracles are one of the attainments of an *arhat* ("perfected one"), but only a few are capable of the monastic discipline required to reach that goal. Lay Buddhists should seek to acquire merit for the next rebirth by supporting monks in their quest. On this view there would be no purpose for exercising miraculous powers since laypeople cannot gain insight from them and, more importantly, Buddha's code of monastic conduct discouraged such displays. Most Mahāyānists, however, practice ritual means of appealing for miracles. A.G.S. Kariyawasam, a contemporary teacher from Sri Lanka where Theravadan influence has been strong since the second century B.C.E., asserts that Mahāyāna reliance on "the saving grace of bodhisattvas" betrays the Buddha's emphasis on individual effort. He explains the attraction of heavenly figures like Avalokiteśvara as "the natural result of the intrinsic human nature which seeks for external protection and consolation either in a male or a female divinity."[61] His criticism reflects the suspicion that Mahāyānists offer "short-cuts" to Nirvāna based on the illusion of deities, although he couches the objection in modern psychological terms of infantile dependence.

Theravadan teaching also includes the category *Bodhisattva*, but applies it only to a being who, having met detailed qualifications including physical wholeness and moral perfection, decides to be born as a human being at a particular time and place (somewhere in northern India) and of a mother who will not live more than a week after the birth (so that she cannot conceive another child). Kariyawasam recognizes that Mahāyāna doctrine developed as a reaction to the arid intellectualism of the typical Theravadan monk who had become "a fossilized antique living in a world of his own." Yet, in his judgment, Mahāyāna belief in Bodhisattvas as divine saviors swung the pendulum too far in the opposite direction. Bodhisattvas, he argues, are treated in the Pali Canon as merely "larval forms" of the Buddha, thus "a rare type of man appearing at a certain stage in time and space," extraordinary models and not divine saviors. A Bodhisattva is one who knows how to live among people without sharing their delusions and vices, including belief in miracles to improve the conditions of their lives.

At least one school of Mahāyāna Buddhism, Zen, agrees that miracle stories are at best teaching aids and at worst distractions from the urgent task of reaching ultimate insight. That miracles are possible follows from Zen confidence in the power of mind to surpass the illusion of material reality—and there are accounts of Zen masters exercising the psychic powers of yogis—but Zen practitioners are more concerned about realizing the emptiness of the phenomenal world than reconstructing it. Zen practice is famously spare and rigorous, offering two forms of meditation: emptying the mind and "just sitting" (*zazen*) with blank consciousness (Soto) or focusing the mind on a mysterious riddle, called a koan, until rational thought is exhausted (Rinzai) and one enters the state of non-dualist consciousness called in Japanese *satori*. While Zen teaches that *satori* comes in an instant, like the freezing of water, the process of gaining insight into one's Buddha-nature develops in stages of clarity. It can take years of disciplined meditation to achieve, and both the process and the goal are highly individual. There is no one pattern of insight or action by which everyone reaches *satori*; neither is there a single prayer or sutra that serves as the vehicle for everyone. Thus, it is futile to imitate someone else's demonstration or expression of *satori* because each person must discover the truth and the means to enact it for himself or herself (Zen is open to both men and women). One may be guided by scriptures, teachers, and the example of Buddha; but the final insight is irreducibly singular.

For that reason, Zen rejects supernatural assistance and regards miraculous power over laws of nature as inferior to control over one's own body and mind. In one story, a priest of a Mahāyāna sect interrupted a lecture by the Zen master Bankei with this challenge: "The founder of our sect had such miraculous powers that he held a brush in his hand on one bank of the river, his attendant held up a paper on the other bank, and the teacher wrote the holy name of Amida [a name of Buddha] through the air. Can you do such a wonderful thing?" Bankei replied, "Perhaps your fox can perform that trick, but that is not the manner of Zen. My miracle is that when I feel hungry I eat, and when I feel thirsty I drink."[62] What is striking about this exchange is that the Zen master did not defeat his opponent by performing a greater miracle but by reinterpreting what powers qualify as miraculous. Causing the name of Buddha to appear at a distance was a remarkable act of devotion, and it evoked admiration for the miracle-worker and praise of the divine being who promised to bring all who placed their faith in him to a glorious paradise after death. Those effects, however, do not evoke the depth of wonder stirred by the freedom of the Zen master who follows no schedule constructed by personal habit or social expectation: he eats when he feels like it and sleeps when he is tired. Living as simply as possible demonstrates the insight that emptiness is the truth of all things—self, society, nature, gods—and the true miracle, the exercise of transcendent power, is to live apart from the impermanent structures that govern the lives of others.

The story is both constructive and polemical. It serves not only to express a central Zen teaching, but also to emphasize the superiority of Zen insight over the dependence on divine beings in other Mahāyāna schools. Denial of miracles is consistent with the famous Zen saying, "If you meet a Buddha on the way, slay him!" Zen masters issue robust dissent from reliance on intervention by deities or human beings, no matter how exalted their spiritual accomplishments. Zen teachers objected particularly to the elevation of Buddha to divine status, thus vitiating his achievement as an exemplary human. In one story the eccentric Zen master Tosui left the monastery to live among beggars and supported himself by making vinegar. When one of the beggars gave him an image of Buddha, he hung it on the wall of his hut with this sign: "Mr. Amida Buddha: This little room is quite narrow, I can let you remain as a transient. But don't think I am asking you to help me to be reborn in your paradise."[63]

Thus, objections to belief in miracles can be found in the earliest stratum of Buddhist tradition preserved in the Theravada school and in one of the most widespread forms of the Mahāyāna school. In both cases, dissent is grounded in the suspicion that reliance on supernatural assistance undercuts the personal discipline required to follow Buddha's path.

Modern objections to miracles in Buddhism take two forms: philosophical and political. The first involves an attempt to interpret Buddhism as a form of perennial philosophy, teaching universal truths grounded in reason and compatible with scientific accounts of reality. Advocates of this version excised references to supernormal powers from their biographies of Buddha and representations of his teaching in accord with standards of historical criticism developed by Western scholars. The project of rendering Buddhism into a philosophical system was initiated in the nineteenth century by the co-founders of the Theosophical Society, Helena Blavatsky and Henry Steele Olcott. They arrived in Ceylon (now Sri Lanka) in 1880 and took the vows of lay Buddhists. Olcott appealed to the intellectual elite on the ground that his interpretation, later called "Protestant Buddhism" because of its critical posture toward traditional authority, was more faithful to Buddha's teaching because it excluded "superstitious" belief in supernatural beings.[64] Buddhist scholars were attracted to this reading of Buddhism as an expression of universal wisdom, expurgated of legendary elements and fully equal in its rationality to modern Western religious thought.

One Sri Lankan monk, Walpola Rahula (1907–1997), followed this line in his popular book, *What the Buddha Taught*, by representing Buddhism as teaching "the Truth" accessible to all thoughtful people and in a way that respected freedom of thought and tolerance of other religions. He even claimed, against historical evidence, that Buddhism spread across Asia without a single example of coercion or violence. Behind this idealized picture of Buddhist tradition as reasonable and peaceful was the modern Western view, mediated through Olcott's liberal Protestant ideas, that religion should promote moral development and reconcile its claims with the scientific account of reality. The modernist version of Buddhism also sought to avoid the charge, advanced by David Hume, that belief in supernatural beings carries with it a disposition to arrogate supreme authority to particular religions. Since deities represent absolute power, the argument went, there is no higher court to adjudicate conflicts that arise between their devotees and, as history shows, wars follow. (This objection could be applied to Buddhism only by mistakenly assuming that gods and goddesses in Asian religions function the way God does in monotheistic religions; but Hindu and Buddhists deities have limited power and are subject to karmic law.) The hope of modernist Buddhists was that Buddhism shorn of the transcendent, presented more as philosophy than religion, would teach Western cultures how to live in harmony with nature and with one another without reliance on supernatural direction. It was an appealing prospect, and Rahula made every effort to promote it.

Writing during the Cold War, Rahula was bravely optimistic about the efficacy of his version of Buddhism: "What the individual thinks and does is what the nation or the state thinks and does. . . . If hatred can be appeased by love and kindness on the individual scale, surely it can be realized on the national and international scale too. Even in the case of a single person, to meet hatred with kindness one must have tremendous courage, boldness, faith and confidence in moral force. May it not be even more so with regard to international affairs?"[65] Ironically, in Sri Lanka the attempt to revise Buddhism led to strife: "the ideological movement to create a modern, purified Buddhism has been implicated in the political movement to 'purify' Sri Lanka of Tamil influence, a movement that has fed the cycle of ethnic violence."[66] If removing the supernatural from Buddhism required purging elements that recalled its origin in India, where intervening gods and goddesses abound, the corresponding political move was removing Hindus from Sri Lanka. The desire for purity always works against the ideal of tolerance; in this case philosophical economy justified ethnic cleansing. The moral of the story may be that belief in supernatural beings is *not* the root cause of conflict in the world after all. The problem lies at a deeper level of human disposition than the longing for divine favor.

Another faithful dissenter to belief in miracles, the Japanese scholar Daisetz Teitaro Suzuki (1870–1966), was exceptional in his gift for translating Zen Buddhist teaching into American idiom. Suzuki's influence was greatest during the 1950s when Americans were not ready to embrace monastic discipline, but were eager for the earthy humor and dizzying paradoxes of Zen.[67] Suzuki also prepared the way for Asian teachers who popularized Buddhism in the 1960s, a time of cultural upheaval in Europe and the United States marked by demands for self-realization and immediate political and social transformation. In that context, Suzuki's version of Zen as the way to sudden enlightenment through individual effort by stripping away formalities and abandoning reliance on authorities found a receptive audience. Zen provided a way of embracing "spirituality" while jettisoning "religion." It was an irresistible combination for many, who welcomed Zen meditation as a liberating alternative to the restrictive morality, repetitive ritual, and exclusive claims of Christianity.

Accordingly, like other modern thinkers, Suzuki dispensed with references to the supernatural. He argued that Zen Buddhism differed from Indian Buddhism by rejection of the miraculous, specifically the "deification" of Buddha. In the transition from India to China in the sixth century, he claimed, Buddhism moved from an intellectual climate of extravagant imagination to one of spare practicality. While texts from India are replete with eye-popping miracles, unimaginably expansive companies of celestial beings, and incomprehensible durations of time, the Chinese prefer terse and direct expression. "The superabundance of Indian imagination issued in supernaturalism and wonderful symbolism, and the Chinese sense of practicalness and its love for the solid everyday facts of life, resulted in Zen Buddhism."[68] For Suzuki, however, the difference was not between naiveté and realism. Indian Buddhists were fully aware that their language was symbolic: "the introduction of supernaturalism into the Mahayana literature of Buddhism was to demonstrate the intellectual impossibility of comprehending spiritual facts."[69] That is, stories of miracles were symbols of truths beyond the grasp of reason, transcendent wisdom.

For Suzuki Indians expressed that incomprehensibility in imaginative visions of the supernatural, while the Chinese did so by means of paradoxical statements, abrupt gestures, and silence. In both cases, the intention was to communicate the conviction that ultimate insight is "always characterized by irrationality, inexplicability, and incommunicability." Attempts to understand it end in frustration because explanation is a form of intellectual autopsy that reduces living reality to its dissected parts. "When [satori] is explained at all, either in words or gestures, its content more or less undergoes a mutilation." Setting aside the cultural stereotypes Suzuki used, his parallel between Indian miracle stories and Chinese paradoxes is instructive. Both employ symbolic language to point to referents beyond the field of ordinary knowledge; and both are instances of "performative language," designed to bring about a transformation in the reader's or hearer's consciousness.

That transformation is so momentous that even Suzuki cannot refrain from using the language of miracle to describe it. "Whatever this is, the world for those who have gained a satori is no more the old world as it used to be. . . . Logically stated, all its opposites and contradictions are united and harmonized into a consistent organic whole. *This is a mystery and a miracle,* but according to the Zen masters such is being performed every day."[70] We return to a point of analysis that recurs in this study: a transformation of consciousness that is *transcendent,* that is, inexplicable in terms of physical forces and laws of nature, is no less a miracle than a human body levitating over a river. The state of mind that is the goal of Zen meditation is achieved either through intentional modification of chemical processes in the brain (as some researchers suggest) or it is a genuine breakthrough to insight that is not otherwise possible for the human mind. Satori belongs to the same class of experience as Buddha's enlightenment: transcendent but not supernatural. As such, it fits under our definition of miracle.

Suzuki would have resisted that conclusion by arguing that his focus on internal change is the heart of Buddha's original teaching and talk of miracles belongs to its culturally conditioned expressions. "The claim of the Zen followers that they are transmitting the essence of Buddhism is based on their belief that Zen takes hold of the enlivening spirit of the Buddha, stripped of all its historical and doctrinal garments."[71] This distinction is typical of modernist reinterpretations in which it is also described as separating the kernel of the tradition from the husk or the spirit from the letter. The distinction implies that the present interpreter knows the normative version of the tradition and can use that standard (canon) to judge all other versions. Suzuki, as a self-described "progressive modern Buddhist," believed he interpreted miracle stories in the way the Buddha originally told them: as allegories of the ineffability of spiritual insight, skillful means of instruction along the path to transcendent wisdom. Suzuki employed a literary interpretation of miracles as pedagogical narratives, expressing Buddha's wisdom. Our last example of faithful dissent from miracles is political and relies on an appeal to Buddha's compassion.

Thich Nhat Hanh is a Vietnamese monk best known for his protest against the war in Vietnam and his consequent leadership in the movement of "engaged Buddhism." Barred from his home country in 1966, he has lived and worked in France since 1982. He frequently lectures in the United States promoting his views that Buddhism encourages its followers not to withdraw from the world but to seek social justice and political liberty with dedication, skillful means, and "mindfulness," by which Nhat Hanh means "keeping one's consciousness alive to the present reality." The power of mindfulness to focus attention on the here and now, to collect scattered thoughts and distracted emotions into a single integrated moment of awareness, is what he regards as miraculous. "People usually consider walking on water or in thin air a miracle," he writes, "But I think the real miracle . . . is to walk on earth." In his long letter to a staff member of the School of Youth for Social Service in South Vietnam in 1974, published under the title *The Miracle of Mindfulness*, Nhat Hanh counseled the younger monk to follow the method of counting his breaths and taking every ordinary activity as an occasion for meditation. He astutely observed, "It is only in an active and demanding situation that mindfulness really becomes a challenge!"[72] Given the superhuman effort required to maintain tranquil concentration in the midst of the destruction and displacement of war, it is not surprising that Nhat Hanh used the term *miracle* to describe mindfulness in the historical circumstances.

Through meditation one comes to realize directly, without conceptual mediation, the truth of Buddha's teachings—particularly the doctrine of co-origination and interdependence. For Nhat Hanh the practical consequence of such meditation is personal release from suffering, fear, and dread, and recognition of one's essential unity with other persons. That recognition gives rise to the determination to promote the liberation of others, in both the spiritual and political senses of the term. One who reduces this direct insight to a philosophical system will remain content with a sense of intellectual satisfaction, but will miss entirely the responsibility for helping others here and now, in this world. The test of spiritual progress is moral sensitivity: "When your mind is liberated your heart floods with compassion."[73]

Compassion, for Nhat Hanh, is interpreted through the ideal of the Bodhisattva: active service on behalf of others to the point of self-sacrifice. To promote such service he coined the phrase "engaged Buddhism," making its first directive to reject all claims to absolute truth, "even Buddhist ones." Mindfulness should make one open to the viewpoints of others, as well as sensitive to their suffering. Nhat Hanh also emphasizes the necessity of being open to the wonder of everyday life: "Be in touch with what is wondrous, refreshing, and healing both inside and around you. Plant seeds of joy, peace, and understanding in yourself in order to facilitate the work of transformation in the depths of your consciousness."[74] Because that transformation can turn the natural tendency to preserve one's life into "the courage to speak out about situations of injustice, even when doing so may threaten your own safety," it is a miracle. But what Nhat Hanh means by *miracle* is literally a world away from belief in the possibility of supernatural assistance. In the contemporary situation, shaped by centuries of anger, fear, and ignorance, we must summon the resources of our minds to relieve the suffering of all beings and seek opportunities for reconciliation. While Nhat Hanh directs that Buddhist communities should not align with particular political parties, he counsels that any religious community "should take a clear stand against oppression and injustice and should strive to change the situation without engaging in partisan conflicts." As difficult as that precept may be to follow in actual "partisan conflicts" (we think of Tibet), what is clear is that any favorable outcome depends on human wisdom and skillful means. Reliance on miraculous appearances of divine saviors would not be an expression of either Buddhist virtue.

For Nhat Hanh interpretation of Buddhism in the twenty-first century entails re-visioning its categories through the lens of compassionate service. Let us consider, for example, his understanding of the doctrine of three bodies of Buddha, a teaching we earlier used to interpret the vision of a levitating master. Nhat Hanh translates the three bodies as three states of consciousness cultivated through meditation. He interprets Transformation-body as the historical manifestation of Dharma in human form. Like the other two, this body also is "deep within you; it is only a matter of discovery. . . . Allow yourself to be struck by the beams of light emanated by the Buddha and to be transformed. . . . The Buddha depends on us to live mindfully, to enjoy the practice, and to transform ourselves, so we can share the body of the Dharma with many other living beings."[75] Again, what in the tradition is objective becomes subjective and metaphysical claims are restated as moral imperatives. Nhat Hanh relocates miracles from the world of nature where they are anomalies to the domain of consciousness where, presumably, they are less offensive and more effective in inspiring political action on behalf of others.

Through his reinterpretation Nhat Han retrieves one of the most esoteric elements of Buddhist tradition and enlists it in the service of the virtue of compassion. He applies the category *miracle* to the wondrous transformation of consciousness that inspires "engaged Buddhists" to embody the Bodhisattva ideal, with no expectation of help from an actual celestial being. Buddha taught, "Him I call indeed a Brahman who, after casting off bondage to men, has risen above bondage to the gods, and is free from all and every bondage."[76] For some Buddhists the final liberation is freedom from all dependence, even reliance on divine beings.

Summary

In Buddhist tradition, miracle stories are signs of transcendent wisdom, serving the pedagogical purpose of demonstrating the truth of Buddha's primary teaching: that everything, including the order of nature and the identity of self, is a temporary aggregation of characteristics combined through a process of mutual dependence. As Buddha demonstrated in his miracles, even the order of primary elements is impermanent and subject to rearrangement by a mind that has realized the ontological emptiness at the heart of being. Buddha severely restricted, but did not absolutely prohibit, the exercise of miraculous powers on the ground that they would mislead rather than enlighten uninstructed observers, thus negatively enforcing the educational role of miracles. Bodhisattvas emulate Buddha's example by performing miracles that assist their disciples in gaining wisdom, but also draw on transcendent power to exercise compassion in acts of healing and rescue. Later masters replicated Buddha's miracles to teach qualified disciples by skillful means and also to engage in polemical contests with philosophical opponents. Zen Buddhists oppose belief in miracles because in their judgment it encourages indolent reliance on supernatural beings rather than rigorous discipline that leads to the discovery of Buddha nature. For "engaged Buddhists" answering Buddha's call to transform the world requires manifesting the Dharma body of wisdom and compassion through one's own actions.

Christianity

Signs of Divine Presence

The most familiar miracle stories in the New Testament are the accounts of Jesus of Nazareth walking on the waves of the Sea of Galilee. The story is so thoroughly assimilated into Western culture that the phrase "to walk on water" commonly indicates ability and virtue beyond the range of ordinary people. For most Christians, the popular understanding is appropriate because they believe Jesus was unique among humans as the embodiment (*incarnation*) of God, sent into the world to die as the atoning sacrifice for the sins of humanity and, through his resurrection from the dead, to bring eternal life to all who have faith in him. Christians believe that Jesus is the supreme expression in human form of divine love, as the well-known verse in the Gospel of John puts it, "For God so loved the world that he gave his only Son, so that everyone who believes in him may not perish but may have eternal life" (3:16). Thus the miracles Jesus performed, and the wonders wrought in his name since, are events of transcendent power that signify the nature of God as love (1 John 4:16). As divine love includes compassion, forgiveness, and justice, miracles in Christian tradition are signs of God's presence in history supporting moral ideals and delivering the distressed from oppression, disease, and death. Even miracles that require the imposition of sheer force—as in casting out demons (*exorcism*) or subduing natural forces—are understood as expressions of divine compassion for those suffering or threatened. The meaning of the initial miracle of Christianity, God entering the world as a human being, set the standard for understanding all subsequent wonders in Christian tradition. Miracles are events of power that signify the divine presence in history—as this story and its variations illustrate:

After feeding a crowd of five thousand people with two fish and a few loaves of bread, Jesus went off by himself to pray and sent his disciples ahead to cross the Sea of Galilee in a small boat. As night fell, a storm arose, and the disciples were hard-pressed to make headway against the wind and the waves. They had been rowing for hours, into the early morning, when they saw Jesus walking on the sea. He intended to pass them by, but they cried out in fear, thinking that he was a ghost. Immediately, Jesus turned to them and said, "Do not be afraid. It is I." Then he entered the boat, and the wind calmed. The disciples were utterly astounded and filled with wonder.[1]

When Jesus approached his disciples on the Lake of Galilee, Mark records that his appearance evoked terror and incomprehension in them. The disciples were then stunned by the unearthly power that allowed him to restore calm to waters as unruly and vacant of care as those that covered the primeval void. To compound their confusion, according to Mark, "He intended to pass them by." But if his goal was not to rescue his followers, what was he doing out there in the rain in the dead of night? For Mark there was mystery in Jesus's presence on the lake that could not be fully explained. Even after the wind died down and Jesus entered the boat with them, they remained "utterly astounded." What meaning could they discern in this display of supernatural power?

In religious symbolism water often represents chaos, the unformed counterpart to cosmos that is always poised to batter the fragile edges of world order like the erosive lapping of waves. The opposition of the restless waters to the creator's formation of the world suggests intentional resistance, and for mythic imagination the ocean depths were the abode of dragons or demons. Some Christian exegetes thus interpreted Jesus's power over the storm as a victory over demonic power represented by the deadly frenzy of wind and waves. This way of reading the story is consistent with Mark's emphasis on Jesus's confrontation and defeat of enemies—demonic and human—throughout his Gospel. The miracle of walking on water, then, reveals Jesus as the presence of the divine creator, calming forces of nature that threaten to destroy human life.

But the meaning of the act of calming the Sea of Galilee may be extended to signify Jesus's authority over earthly rulers as well, those whose pride and greed threatened moral order. In an earlier account of Jesus's stilling a storm, he was already in the boat asleep when the tempest arose. His terrified disciples implored him to save them. "He woke up and rebuked the wind, and said to the sea, 'Peace! Be still!' Then the wind ceased, and there was a dead calm" (Mark 4:39). In this story Jesus commanded the natural elements in the same way that he "rebuked" a demon and demanded that it depart in his exorcism of a possessed boy (Mark 9:25). The parallel between Jesus's power over destructive natural forces and demonic spirits is enforced by Mark, who follows the miracle of calming the sea with the story of Jesus arriving on the far shore and entering the region of ten Hellenistic cities (called Decapolis) where he encountered a man possessed by demons. When Jesus called for his name, the man responded, "My name is Legion; for we are many" (Mark 5:9). The demons begged Jesus to allow them to enter a herd of pigs. He granted them permission, and the herd ran into the sea and drowned. In the meanwhile the possessed man was released from the cacophony of voices in his head and was restored to his "right mind" (Mark 5:15).

Biblical scholar Simon Samuel interprets this narrative sequence as a covert sign of resistance to Roman imperial power: Jesus "takes the twelve across the sea despite the dangers posed by the storm and the wave (4.35–41) and manifests his power in subduing 'Legion' in Decapolis (5.1–2) as though he is the new Caesar who can cross the stormy sea and conquer the enemy."[2] Few of Mark's readers would have missed the reference to the pitiless and seemingly invincible Roman legions, marching several thousand strong in terrifying battle array. When the demonic legion entered the swine, rushed over a cliff, and drowned in the sea, those readers would have cheered. For them the story was a coded representation of their hope that the soldiers who sacked the temple in Jerusalem and enforced oppressive Roman occupation might also be driven into the primal depths of the Mediterranean and suffocated by divine justice as surely as Pharaoh's army was drowned in the Red Sea.[3] Samuel's postcolonial reading extends Jesus's authority into the political conflicts facing Mark's readers and, by extension, Christians under oppressive regimes today. Samuel locates the meaning of the miracle story in its rhetorical effect of subverting totalitarian power by imagining it to be as uncaring as a storm and as destructive as mental fragmentation. The full meaning of the miracle, then, is that divine compassion and justice can overcome all enemies of human flourishing, whether storms, illness, or tyranny.

In the Gospel of Matthew, the story of Jesus's walking on water was recast so that the moral significance of his display of supernatural power was clearer to his disciples and to later readers. Matthew revised the story by dropping the note that Jesus "intended to pass them by" and adding a section about the disciple Peter joining Jesus on the sea. Peter no more than stepped onto the roiling waves when he became afraid and began to sink. Jesus upheld him by the hand, saying to him, "You of little faith, why did you doubt?" (Matthew 14:31). In Matthew's version Peter served as the model of someone who is saved by Jesus's power, now made familiar rather than daunting by its use in rescuing his threatened disciples. As in Mark, when Jesus joined them in the boat, the storm subsided. But in Matthew the disciples were not left in bafflement; they worshiped Jesus, recognizing him as the Son of God. Matthew humanized Jesus's power over the storm by giving it a moral purpose—a purpose that readers could share. For Matthew the power of the Creator is not merely superior force over demonic resistance as in Mark, but the presence that sustains and nurtures others.

Jesus's miracles revealed him to be the exemplar of divine love and champion of those oppressed by illness, injustice, and death. In the narrative world of Christian miracle stories the desperately sick are restored to health, imperial powers are exposed as impotent, and the dead are raised to life. There may be several interpretations of a single story, like Jesus's walking on water, but taken together they invite readers to enact in their everyday lives the primary themes of the Christian gospel: love, faith, justice, and hope. Further, miracle stories reflect Christian commitment to the principle of incarnation and thus the reality of divine presence in historical events. What the biblical scholar Howard Clark Kee said of the author of the Gospel of Mark applies to the convictions of many Christians: "He was not content with the notion that God's purpose for creation was disclosed through the words of Jesus; he wanted to demonstrate that the revelation came through a public person performing public acts in interaction with the civil and religious authorities of his time."[4] While Jesus's recorded words are revered by Christians, most worship him as the living Word, the revealed presence of God in history.

In witness to Jesus as God incarnate, saints in the medieval period and healers in the modern world replicated his miracles. Roman Catholic saints saw visions and bore marks of Christ's crucifixion on their bodies. These miracles replicated Jesus's visions at his baptism and transfiguration, and his redemptive suffering. Some charismatic Protestants perform healings in the manner of Jesus. In these varied instances we can trace a common theme: miracles are signs of divine love that evoke compassion for others and hope of deliverance from suffering and, finally, the defeat of death. For Christians the meaning of miracles as signs of divine love is established in the stories of Jesus's healings, provisions, and resurrection.

Christ: Miracles of Jesus of Nazareth

All four of the Gospels of the New Testament include stories of Jesus's miracles, events of transcendent power that evoked wonder in the witnesses and carried religious significance for those who heard or read about them. While preaching in the city of Jerusalem, Peter appealed to the crowd's knowledge of Jesus's miracles as the basis of his divine authority: "Jesus of Nazareth, a man attested to you by God with deeds of power, wonders, and signs that God did through him among you, as you yourselves know" (Acts 2:22). Also, unlike divine interventions in the Hebrew Bible, miracles do not gradually disappear from the pages of the New Testament. On the contrary, Revelation, the last book of the Christian Bible in canonical and chronological order, offers a panorama of divine actions of judgment on the world. Further, Jesus promised his disciples that "the one who believes in me will also do the works that I do and, in fact, will do greater works than these" (John 14:12). Finally, the writer most represented in the New Testament, the self-designated apostle called Paul, asserted that it was the miracle of being raised from the dead that revealed Jesus's divine nature. While Christ was "descended from David according to the flesh," he "was declared to be Son of God with power according to the spirit of holiness by resurrection from the dead" (Romans 1:3–4).

In popular Christian imagination, however, Jesus was divine from the very beginning. While the earliest account of Jesus's life, the Gospel of Mark, began with his adult career, the Gospels of Matthew and Luke revised Mark's account by adding infancy narratives that, taken together, comprise the well-known stories re-enacted in Christmas pageants. The Gospel of Matthew emphasized that Jesus was conceived through the Holy Spirit—that is, he was of divine origin—and his birth marked the beginning of a new age (for that reason the Christian calendar begins with Christmas, not Easter). Matthew highlighted divine conception, not virgin birth. In his account Mary was the silent recipient of new life startlingly stirring in her womb, while an angel reassured Joseph with these words, "Do not be afraid to take Mary as your wife, for the child conceived in her is from the Holy Spirit." Then the angel disclosed the child's divinely chosen name, "You are to name him Jesus, for he will save his people from their sins" (Matthew 1:21). Jesus's destiny was not to be a world-conqueror like Krishna or a supreme teacher like Buddha or a law giver like Moses, but a savior. Given that Jewish atonement for sin required the sacrifice of unblemished animals in temple ritual, the name *Jesus* (from Hebrew meaning "he saves") expressed Christian hope of gaining salvation through his suffering and death.

For Matthew, Jesus's miraculous conception and birth fulfilled prophecy from the Hebrew Bible, specifically the reference in Isaiah 7:14 to the birth of a child to a young woman in the reign of Ahaz, who was king of Judah seven hundred years earlier.[5] According to Isaiah, the birth of the child was to signal the beginning of the end of intimidation of the kingdom of Judah (in southern Israel) by the alliance of Syria with the kingdom of northern Israel. Isaiah promised the Judeans that, if they trusted God and did not turn to other nations for protection, they would be delivered from danger within two years. The child was to be a living calendar to measure the time of the testing of their faith. His name *Emmanuel*, meaning "God is with us," was a reminder of Judah's only hope. By applying Isaiah 7:14 to the birth of Jesus, Matthew expressed his faith as a Christian that God will be with those who accept Jesus as the divine Messiah, just as God was with the faithful of Judah long ago.

In Matthew an angel announced the birth of Jesus to Joseph, but in the Gospel of Luke the archangel Gabriel addressed Mary directly, explaining that "the power of the Most High will overshadow you; therefore the child to be born will be holy; he will be called Son of God" (Luke 1:35). The language is euphemistic and avoids any hint of divine impregnation of the sort recounted in Greek myths. The emphasis is on Mary's hearing and submitting: "Here am I, the servant of the Lord; let it be with me according to your word." Readers familiar with the opening chapter of Genesis where the entire creation sprang into existence in response to the divine word would recognize the power of the angel's words to create the reality they announced. Mary responded with a speech called the *Magnificat* (from its Latin translation): "My soul magnifies the Lord . . . from now on all generations will call me blessed." She declared God's name holy and praised his mercy "for those who fear him." But then her tone changed dramatically as she marveled, in specific detail, at what God had done: "He has brought down the powerful from their thrones, and lifted up the lowly; he has filled the hungry with good things, and sent the rich away empty" (Luke 1:32–33).

Suddenly, the humble virgin was aflame with the vision of the kingdom of God, where injustice will be dethroned, the hungry will sit down to a banquet, and the rich will lose the power of their hoarded wealth. The presence of the Messiah, already leaping in her womb, was good news for the poor and the powerless. In his mother's vision Jesus would deliver them from soul-crushing deprivation, universally felt at the most elemental level as insistent, dispiriting hunger. Mary understood her son's name in the terms Gabriel announced it: "you will name him Jesus. He will be great, and will be called the Son of the Most High, and the Lord God will give to him the throne of his ancestor David. He will reign over the house of Jacob forever, and of his kingdom there will be no end" (Luke 1:31–33). In Luke there is no mention of Jesus's saving his people from sin by becoming a sacrificial lamb, but of his re-establishing the glory of the reign of King David when the power of Israel reached its greatest height. The miracle of Jesus's entrance into the world was a display of divine power that raised Mary's humble piety into political fervor because it was a sign of God's sovereign presence in history, directing events toward the messianic age of peace and justice. In comparing the accounts of Jesus's birth in Matthew and Luke, we encounter themes that characterize the meaning of miracles in general in Christian tradition: Jesus entered the world as the compassionate savior who gave his life to save others from their sins and Jesus's birth was a sign of the coming rule of God, delivering the poor and oppressed from injustice. The miracles of Jesus's conception and birth demonstrate the presence and power of divine love in history.

The story of Jesus's miraculous birth is a narrative expression of Christian belief in incarnation (God "becoming flesh") as interpreted by Athanasius (296–373), bishop of Alexandria and defender of Christian orthodoxy at the Council of Nicea (325). Athanasius argued that Christ, as the immortal Word of God, was no more subject to the corruptibility of material things than were the eternal ideal forms of Plato. As those ideals inform our minds and allow us to recognize the essence of individual objects, so the divine Word became human in an ideal body and conquered death through the resurrection of that incorruptible body. Athanasius taught that the sinless perfection of Jesus was preserved by his miraculous conception and birth: "He took *our* body, and not only so, but He took it directly from a spotless, stainless virgin, without the agency of human father—a pure body, untainted by intercourse with man."[6] By informing that pure body with the immortal Word of God, Christ bestowed the possibility of eternal life on all humanity. Setting aside the ascetic denigration of sexuality, Athanasius's Platonic interpretation of Jesus's birth implies that every person henceforth has the capacity for holiness and is deserving of compassion and justice. Inasmuch as the incarnation re-formed human nature, it restored the reflection of divine image, including immortality. In this reading, the story of Jesus's miraculous birth signifies divine energy, bursting boundaries between divine and human, life and death, in an event of transgressive power and unbounded generosity.

In the Gospel stories, the miracles Jesus performed also signify power and love surpassing human measure, including the miracle that attracted his first disciples. One day, on the shore of a lake, Jesus was pressed by the crowds he consistently attracted, so he boarded a boat belonging to Peter and directed him to put out from shore and lower his nets. Peter sighed in frustration, "Master, we have worked all night long but have caught nothing. Yet if you say so, I will let down the nets" (Luke 5:5). To his astonishment the nets immediately filled with so many fish they were in danger of splitting. Peter called to his partners, James and John, and they filled both boats to the point of sinking. Luke recorded that they were all "amazed," filled with wonder. Peter alone offered an interpretive response to the excessive display of divine power and benevolence: "Go away from me, Lord, for I am a sinful man." His confession recalled a parallel incident in the Hebrew Bible when the prophet Isaiah confronted the dreadful presence of Yahweh in the temple in Jerusalem: "I am an unclean man in the midst of an unclean people" (Isaiah 6:5). The translation of wonder into moral terms, rendering awe as guilt, is a persistent tendency in religious texts; but repentance is not the response this text seeks to evoke in the implied reader.

The extravagance of the miracle, producing a quantity of fish that surpassed the capacity of the nets to contain them, reflected the parable Jesus told about the farmer whose seed fell on good ground and yielded "thirty and sixty and a hundred-fold" (Mark 4:8). Both the miracle story, with its bursting nets, and the parable, with its asymmetrical mathematical progression, signify the astonishing fecundity of nature charged by divine presence. As a sign, the miracle of the fish was overwhelming, violent, enormous—a supply beyond all reasonable need. The event demonstrated that transcendent power has no gentle or subtle means of entry into our world. Even when exercised in benevolence, divine intervention is a disruptive intrusion that is literally surreal, an excess of creative energy. Thus, the original shock of the wonder produced fear in the disciples, so that Jesus's first words to them were, "Do not be afraid." The same combination of fear and assurance occurs in stories of Jesus's healings, undeniable acts of compassion that are also unsettling displays of transcendent power.

Stories of Jesus's healing are found throughout the New Testament Gospels.[7] The accounts are vivid, expressing wrenching need and generally instantaneous healing. The maladies include blindness, paralysis, leprosy, deafness, and many unspecified illnesses. Jesus's methods of healing varied from case to case. Sometimes he touched the person on the affected area or he pronounced a word; on one occasion he concocted a potion from dust and his own spit that he applied on the eyes of a blind man. Some who approached him believed in his divine power, others knew him only as a charismatic wonder worker, and one man confessed himself an honest agnostic desperate for his son to be healed: "I believe; help my unbelief." At times Jesus acted as if he were a magician; and opponents charged he was possessed by demons, the common indictment of those performing magic.[8] In the three cases where Jesus raised a dead person to life, family members supplied the faith that made the miracle possible. Accordingly, when unbelieving skeptics challenged him to provide a "sign from heaven" to satisfy their test of his authority, Jesus refused (Matthew 16:1–4).

What is of primary importance in the healing stories is the claim that the rule of God is near or "in your midst" (Luke 11:20). The healings signified God's intention to restore the creation to its original health or wholeness. Thus, Jesus's healings often included his declaration of forgiveness of sins, making his patients whole in both the physical and moral senses. While there were many healers and exorcists in Palestine at the time of Jesus, the question for Christian tradition is not whether Jesus's healings were unique but whether they signified the greater miracle of the establishment of the rule of the transcendent God on earth. When accused of using the power of Satan to perform exorcisms, Jesus said, "If it is by the finger of God that I cast out the demons, then the kingdom of God has come to you" (Luke 11:20). Jesus's healings signaled the presence of God's rule as marked by compassion and justice.

The American theologian Harvey Cox finds both themes in the interrelated story of two healings—one of a woman with chronic internal bleeding and the other of the comatose daughter of a leader in the synagogue (Mark 5:21–43). The woman with the "flow of blood" touched Jesus's robe as he was on his way to the home of the sick child, pressed on all sides by a great crowd. Jesus immediately sensed "that power had gone forth from him" and asked who touched him. The woman, whose bleeding was staunched the moment she made contact with Jesus's garment, stepped forward. Jesus said to her, "Daughter, your faith has made you well; go in peace, and be healed of your disease." For Cox, Jesus responds with what the Second Vatican Council would later call "the preferential option for the poor": "Jesus not only treats her 'preferentially,' he even refers to her as his daughter. Still, it should be noted that the other daughter, the scion of privilege lying at death's door in the synagogue ruler's ample house, is not neglected either. Jesus heals her, too. But only after he has healed his own 'daughter,' the intruder from the dust."[9] Cox is impressed that those who were sick left Jesus's presence healed, no matter what their social or economic status.

New Testament scholar Mary Rose D'Angelo emphasizes that Jesus's gift of healing was exercised in these two cases only in cooperation with initiating belief. "In Mark's world, Jesus' power required faith. In the narrative, faith is manifested by a 'demand.'"[10] Such faith is not expressed in servile, desperate pleading for help but in forceful pushing through the crowd, whether on one's own behalf or for the sake of another, to release Jesus's divine power:

"the teller/narrator invites the hearers to identify with the one making the demand."[11] The text implies the response it seeks to evoke: to enter into the narrative world of the miracle story by exercising faith in the continuing possibility of divine healing. Without that collaboration, the healer is powerless, as was the case in Jesus's hometown: "And he could do no deed of power there, except that he laid his hands on a few sick people and cured them. And he was amazed at their unbelief" (Mark 6:5–6). Jesus's healings, then, did not provide unambiguous proof of his divine authority or of the truth of his message. Witnesses to his miracles, along with contemporary readers, must make their own decisions, laden with risk, about whether to believe that his healings can be replicated in their own lives.

For the Gospel of John, miracles of Jesus were "signs" performed to evoke faith in him as divine. John began his story with the claim that Jesus is the human form of the eternal Word (in Greek *logos*) of God. "And the Word became flesh and lived among us, and we have seen his glory, the glory as of the Father's only Son, full of grace and truth" (John 1:14). The purpose of Christ's descent from heaven into this world was to bring to humans the true knowledge of God. The first one to recognize the truth was a Jewish leader named Nicodemus, who said to Jesus, "Rabbi, we know that you are a teacher who has come from God; for no one can do these signs that you do apart from the presence of God" (John 3:2). Nicodemus identified Jesus's miracles as signs of the divine presence, a linkage that shaped the rest of John's narrative. John selected only seven of Jesus's miracles to record, although he assured his readers at the end of his Gospel that "there are also many other things that Jesus did; if every one of them were written down, I suppose that the world itself could not contain the books that would be written" (John 21:25). But he is clear about his principle of selection: "Now Jesus did many other signs in the presence of his disciples, which are not written in this book. But these are written so that you may come to believe that Jesus is the Messiah, the Son of God, and that through believing you may have life in his name" (John 20:30–31).

The most dramatic sign of Jesus's divine authority in John is the raising of Lazarus of Bethany from the dead. Lazarus was a beloved friend of Jesus; and his sisters, Mary and Martha, provided hospitality for Jesus during his visits to Jerusalem. When the sisters sent news that Lazarus was near death, Jesus chose to delay before setting out for Bethany. By the time he arrived, Lazarus had been dead for four days. His sisters, surrounded by mourners, declared that if Jesus had been present, their brother would not have died. Jesus's response to their tears of lament was curiously unsettled: "he was greatly disturbed in spirit and deeply moved" (John 11:33); he began to weep with them. Given Jesus's deliberate staging of this event by waiting until he was certain Lazarus was dead, it seems odd that he would be overcome with emotion at the point of the most impressive display of his divine power. While many commentators attribute Jesus's sorrow to his deep human sympathy, perhaps the story reveals profound anxiety evoked by the undeniable reality of death, in face of which not even Jesus could take for granted the miracle he had come to perform. Poised at the opening of the burial cave, Jesus "looked upward" to thank God for hearing him, then shouted into the darkness, "Lazarus, come out!" The revived friend stumbled into the light and Jesus commanded his shroud be removed.

In John's account Jesus provided the meaning of the miracle of resuscitating Lazarus in his words to Martha: "I am the resurrection and the life. Those who believe in me, even though they die, will live, and everyone who lives and believes in me will never die." Martha responded, "Yes, Lord, I believe that you are the Messiah, the Son of God, the one coming into the world" (John 11:25, 27). In this confession, Martha became the ideal for the implied reader of John's Gospel: belief in Jesus as Messiah and Son of God was precisely the purpose for John's selection of miracle stories. As the eternal Word of God, Jesus the Christ entered the world to show divine mercy to those under the power of suffering and death and to reclaim in the name of compassion the rightful rule of the Creator over the power of life. For John the miracle of the raising of Lazarus was the final sign of Jesus the wonder worker. It would be surpassed only by the event of transcendent power that would raise Jesus himself from the grave and impel him into the heavens to be reunited with the God he called Father.

The resurrection of Christ is the confirming miracle of the Christian tradition, included in the profession of faith most widely shared by Christians known as the *Apostles' Creed*. The second article of the creed professes faith in Jesus Christ, "who was conceived by the Holy Spirit, born of the Virgin Mary, suffered under Pontius Pilate, was crucified, dead and buried. He descended into hell. The third day he rose again from the dead; He ascended into heaven, and sits at the right hand of God the Father Almighty. From there he shall come to judge the quick and the dead." While the creed contains no reference to Jesus's teachings or miracles, the wonders of his resurrection from the dead and ascension into heaven are prominent. Inasmuch as this creed is honored in practically all branches of Christian tradition, belief in some interpretation of the story of the resurrection of Jesus is universal among Christians.

St. Paul staked Christian identity on belief in Christ's resurrection: "If Christ has not been raised, your faith is futile and you are still in your sins. Then those also who have died in Christ have perished" (1 Corinthians 15:17–18). While Jesus's healings were signs of his divine authority to declare the rule of God over disease, natural forces, and demonic powers, his resurrection was the demonstration of his victory over the ultimate enemy, death. For Paul, the meaning of the miracle is that it established the ground of Christian hope that all believers will also be raised to new life in bodies that will endure forever. "But each in his order," Paul taught, "Christ the first fruits, then at his coming those who belong to Christ." Paul tied the hope of resurrection to the belief in Christ's return: "Then comes the end, when he hands over the kingdom to God the Father, after he has destroyed every ruler and every authority and power. . . . The last enemy to be destroyed is death" (1 Corinthians 15:24–26). The relation between the two events is understandable. Where is the comfort in anticipating an end of the world which is also the end of the self? Paul asserted, "We will not all die, but we will all be changed" (I Corinthians 15:51). How? For Paul there will be a difference in substance between one's mortal body and one's resurrection body, but not in identity. Resurrected persons will be identifiable as the same characters in order to be subjects of moral judgment, which may be why Paul called the resurrected body a "spiritual body" (1 Corinthians 15:44) indicating a form of embodiment reflecting the spiritual identity of the one raised.

Perhaps that explains how Paul recognized the risen Christ when he appeared to him. Paul never met Jesus of Nazareth, but he claimed that it was Christ who called him to preach the gospel. Paul understood the event as revelation, a miracle of divine disclosure, that gave him the same authority that Christ's post-resurrection appearances granted the original apostles (Galatians 1:12, 15). Yet neither Paul's letters nor the Gospels contain any physical description of Christ, only accounts of his virtue, wisdom, and power constituting a portrait of his spiritual identity. To recognize the risen Christ would require more than acquaintance with the restored body of Jesus; it would take a miraculous gift of insight into his divine perfection. Thus, when Christ appeared to two of his disciples, they were unaware of his identity until "their eyes were opened, and they recognized him" (Luke 24:31). The meaning of the story seems to be that the capacity to perceive the presence of the resurrected Jesus *as Christ* required a miracle of disclosure. We are not told what the disciples saw, and Paul does not describe the resurrected body of Jesus. Nevertheless, the vision impressed upon Paul's mind and will a vivid image of Christ that served as the template for the rest of his life: crucified and risen Savior.

In his missionary career Paul performed "the signs of a true apostle . . .signs and wonders and mighty works," but regarded his miracles as lesser proof of his identity with Christ than his weakness (2 Corinthians 12:1–14).[12] For Paul the consistency with which he imitated Christ in his suffering was the measure of his faith and the basis of his hope for resurrection: "I want to know Christ and the power of his resurrection and the sharing of his sufferings by becoming like him in his death, if somehow I may attain the resurrection from the dead" (Philippians 3:10–11). Paul's image of Christ as crucified and risen Savior came to dominate Christian theology. Among the early martyrs Paul's statement—"I carry the marks of Jesus branded on my body" (Galatians 6:17)—became the standard of their identification with Christ.

Whatever the circumstances of their executions, early martyrs were venerated by Christians as following the example of Jesus in submitting to unjust persecution, suffering terrible deaths, ascending into heaven, and subsequently appearing to their followers. Paul's teaching of the delay of the resurrection until the end of history did not survive the early Christian conviction that those who lived righteous lives and died martyr's deaths were not "asleep in Christ," but fully awake and active in answering prayers. Catholic and Orthodox Christians continue to believe that saints are capable of working miracles from heaven.[13]

Saint: Miracles of "Holy Ones" in Catholic Tradition

In the New Testament the term *saint* or "holy one" applies to all Christians. The English word derives from the Latin *sanctus* from the verb "to consecrate" and refers to one who is dedicated to the service of the Lord. Extending the idea of consecration, one New Testament writer taught Christians that God chose them "to be a holy priesthood, to offer spiritual sacrifices acceptable to God through Jesus Christ" (1 Peter 2:5). Every Christian, then, is a saint in the sense of being called to a life of self-sacrificial holiness; but early in Christian tradition certain individuals were recognized as possessing virtue and divine favor beyond that of ordinary believers. Their lives served as inspiring examples of nearly perfect imitation of Christ, and it was believed that they were received directly into heaven at death from where they continued to assist Christians on earth through miraculous interventions. The annals of Christian history are replete with the stories of saints and their miracles, beginning with Mary, the mother of Jesus, and continuing to the present day. We will consider a few examples in some detail as these stories of the wondrous deeds of saints reflect the core meaning of miracles in

Christian tradition: signs of divine presence in history expressing the ideals of compassion and justice.

Francis of Assisi (1181–1226) is one of the most popular saints in Roman Catholic tradition, admired for his simple way of life and revered for his gifts of communicating with animals, healing the sick, and bearing the wounds of Christ in his body. He is venerated today as the patron saint of Italy and Pope John Paul II declared him the patron of all who care for the natural environment. He was canonized as a saint two years after his death by Pope Gregory IX. For incontrovertible proof that Francis deserved sainthood, Gregory cited his confidence in reports of Francis's miracles, as well as his personal observation. "Therefore, since the wondrous events of his glorious life are quite well known to Us . . . and since We are fully convinced by reliable witnesses of the many brilliant miracles, We and the flock entrusted to Us, by the mercy of God, are confident of being assisted at his intercession and of having in Heaven a patron whose friendship We enjoyed on earth." For Gregory, the miracles confirmed that Francis entered heaven directly on the strength of his superlative virtue and, as a result, "With the consultation and approval of our Brothers (*i.e. the cardinals*), We have decreed that he be enrolled in the catalogue of saints worthy of veneration."[14]

What wonders did Francis perform to qualify for such honor? Gregory commissioned Thomas of Celano, an early member of the Franciscan Order, to write the earliest biography of Francis, which was published in 1230 under the title *The First Life of Saint Francis*, followed later by *The Second Life of St. Francis*. Thomas drew from stories provided by members of the order Francis founded. Their memories, embellished in light of his canonization, yielded a rich treasury of miracle narratives, including the story of how Francis was called from the active life of a soldier into the service of God. Walking past the deteriorating church of St. Damian one day, Francis felt compelled to enter. Prostrating himself before the altar, Francis heard a voice coming from the moving lips of the crucifix. "Francis," the voice called, "Go and repair my house, which, as you see, is completely destroyed." Unsettled by this wonder, Francis proceeded on his way to complete a business transaction. Burdened by the money he received in profit, he returned to the church and left it there. Eventually, Francis worked to repair the church while he ministered to lepers in the town and gathered followers.[15] The miracle of the talking cross was not directly witnessed by anyone other than Francis, but it impelled him into a career of public demonstration of sanctity.

What struck his companions with astonishment was Francis's rapport with animals. In one incident he spotted a gathering of birds and ran to address them in these words: "My brothers the birds, you should love your creator deeply and praise him always. He has given you feathers to wear, wings to fly with, and whatever else you need. He has made you noble among his creatures and given you a dwelling in the pure air. You neither sow nor reap, yet he nevertheless protects and governs you without any anxiety on your part." Francis's companions reported that the birds responded with gestures of receptivity, "stretching their necks, extending their wings, opening their mouths, and gazing at him." Francis then walked among them, touching their heads in blessing, made the sign of the cross over them, dismissed them, and they flew off. The meaning of the miracle of speaking the language of birds may be seen as the extension of divine compassion, through the person of the saint, to all creatures. None is excluded from God's care, as Jesus taught, "Look at the birds of the air; they neither sow nor reap nor gather into barns, and yet your heavenly Father feeds them" (Matthew 6:26). Compassion is a central and recurrent theme of miracles in Christian tradition, but it is usually demonstrated by mercy shown to human beings. In Francis's communion with animals, down to the level of worms and insects, he not only exercised divine knowledge but also invested care of non-human creatures with religious significance.

The most widely read anthology of Francis's miracles is *The Little Flowers of St. Francis of Assisi*, written for the stated purpose of restoring stories of wonders that had been excised from official biographies. As such, *Little Flowers* is an exercise in hagiography (writing about holy people to demonstrate their saintly qualities) and thus more an expression of faith than a record of history. "All authors of hagiographic texts 'write faith' in the sense that they construct and reconstruct saints' lives and miracles for believers."[16] In that respect hagiographers follow the example of the writer of the Gospel of John in selecting and shaping miracle stories in order to promote belief in their subjects as mediators of divine presence. But by the mid-sixteenth century the Roman Catholic Church felt compelled to insist on greater attention to historical credibility in recounting the lives of saints.

The standards of hagiography set at the Council of Trent (1545–1563) were summed up by a late sixteenth-century Jesuit this way: "The lives of the saints . . . are not to be mere historical biographies, since the purpose of the life of the saint is to edify."[17] The dual purpose of hagiography required deft balance of piety and historicity to achieve, but it was essential in the broader framework of defending Roman Catholic veneration of saints against accusations by Protestant reformers that the records of saints' miracles were exaggerated fictions and constituted no proof of their sanctity or intercessory power. The dilemma facing the bishops at Trent was how to affirm miracles performed by saints during their lives as evidence of their holiness, while maintaining credible standards of historicity in their biographies. Their solution was to insist that "the histories of the mysteries of our Redemption" be instructive of "the articles of faith," and at the same time be inspiring "because the miracles which God has performed by means of the saints, and their salutary examples, are set before the eyes of the faithful; that so they may give God thanks for those things; may order their own lives and manners in imitation of the saints; and may be excited to adore and love God, and to cultivate piety."[18]

The purpose of hagiography, then, is to construct a narrative of a saint's life, including miracles, in such a way as to evoke a religiously transformative effect in the reader while maintaining historical credibility, usually by citing eyewitnesses or earlier accounts written by authorities in the tradition. As the historian Avaida Kleinberg argues, hagiography cannot be pure fiction or it would defeat its own purpose: "If the saint were to serve as evidence that perfection was humanly possible, he had to be more than a literary construct; he had to be real."[19] All the accounts of miracles performed by saints, during their lives or from their glorified positions in heaven, are accordingly instances of "writing faith" as textual signs of the saints' miraculous historical presence (in stories of visions) and power (in stories of healings and provision). While these popular accounts fail modern tests of historical confirmation, they fulfill the intention of miracle stories to the extent they evoke wonder and transformation in readers.

This purpose is evident in the story of the most dramatic of Francis's healings which occurred during his visit to a friary where the monks were providing what care they could for patients with many different diseases. One leper so resented his physical degeneration that he complained about lack of treatment, even cursing God and the Virgin Mary for the failure of the monks to attend to his needs. Francis knew "by divine revelation that this leper was possessed of the evil spirit," so he first prayed and then offered to wash the man's lesions. The account continues: "And by miracle divine, wherever St. Francis touched him with his holy hands the leprosy departed, and the flesh became perfectly whole."[20] More significantly, the man began to weep in penance as the healing proceeded; thus he was made whole in body and soul, as were those whom Christ healed. Divine compassion, extended through Francis to animals, here reached one who was pushed to the edge of human community and restored him.

As in other traditions, Christian miracle stories are sometimes employed for polemical purposes, even though it is hard to see how a saint's miraculous healings, as signs of divine compassion, could serve to establish theological standards. Nevertheless, tales of Francis's supernatural powers were cited not only as confirmation of his holy life but also as proof that the teaching of the Roman Catholic Church he upheld constituted normative Christian belief. Commenting on the enthusiastic welcome Francis received in every village he entered, Thomas noted, "Heretical depravity was confounded, the faith of the church was extolled, and while the faithful engaged in jubilation heretics went into hiding. For so many signs of sanctity appeared in him that no one dared to oppose his words."[21] The meaning of events of transcendent power, it seems, cannot be confined to the values and beliefs of the tradition in which they occur. Their significance is also relevant to defining the authority of that tradition over others. Francis's miracles established his holiness as consisting not only of spiritual virtue but also of political power: heretics were forced to withdraw from his presence and Catholics were inspired to greater devotion to their church.

After two decades of deprivations and ascetic rigor Francis began to suffer from frequent illnesses, but just as St. Paul's prayers for healing went unanswered, so Francis's unrelieved weakness was interpreted as a sign of his identity with Christ. That identity was dramatically confirmed in the miraculous appearance of wounds in his hands and feet and side, corresponding to those received by Jesus in his crucifixion. According to the account in *Little Flowers*, Francis spent one night in the woods in sorrowful prayer over the passion of Christ. His companions "saw him with his arms held in the form of a cross, and lifted up from the ground and suspended for a great space, and surrounded by a bright and shining cloud."[22] Miracles of levitation usually signify spiritual ecstasy in which the saint is "rapt" or "caught up," literally separated from the earth and concerns of this world. One monk, named Leo, witnessed Francis suspended in the air as far as the top of a beech tree "and surrounded by such dazzling splendor, that scarce could the eye behold him." As in the case of the Transfiguration of Christ on Mount Tabor, when he appeared to his disciples in clothes "dazzling white" and a "bright cloud" overshadowed them (Matthew 17:2, 5), Francis was enveloped in divine light. The next day a peasant provided the exhausted Francis with a donkey to ride, reminiscent of Jesus's entry into Jerusalem on an ass. These replications of biblical miracles prepared the way, in the narrative, for the climactic imitation of Christ.

Francis was praying in his solitary cell on the feast of the Most Holy Cross, asking to experience the agony of Christ as a way to feel the divine love for humanity, when he beheld a vision of a seraph (angel with six pairs of wings) nailed to a cross. As Francis stared in amazement at an immortal spirit suffering crucifixion, nails appeared, piercing his hands and feet, and a gaping wound opened in his right side so that his tunic was soon soaked with blood. As intense light illumined the countryside, Christ appeared to announce that he had given Francis "the stigmas that are the marks of my Passion, in order that thou be My standard-bearer." Christ then commissioned Francis to descend into purgatory once a year, on the day of his death, to lead the penitent of his order into paradise.[23] The narrator concluded that "this secret converse left in the heart of St. Francis a burning flame of divine love, exceeding great, and in his flesh, a marvelous image and imprint of the Passion of Christ." The meaning of the wounds was to signify the total consecration of Francis as a mediator of divine compassion. Just as his healings restored both body and soul, so his vision imprinted the divine presence in his spirit and on his body. Francis concealed the wounds from even his closest followers, regarding any display of the mysterious wounds as a temptation to take sinful pride in his own piety. This miracle was private, a gift of pain that Francis kept largely to himself. Perhaps he thought of his wounds as a corrective to the miraculous powers he had been given—like the apostle Paul, who also received "visions and revelations of the Lord," but then noted, "to keep me from being too elated, a thorn was given me in the flesh" (2 Corinthians 12:7).

Beginning with Francis, the Roman Catholic Church has regarded the spontaneous appearance of bleeding lacerations as signs of extreme devotion and special sensitivity to the suffering of Christ. This manifestation is called *stigmata* and has been experienced by many Roman Catholic saints.[24] The term is the same one Paul used to refer to his scars from persecution as "brands" that signified his belonging, as a slave, to Christ: "I carry the marks (*stigmata*) of Jesus branded on my body" (Galatians 6:17). The number of wounds, their locations, and the frequency with which they bleed vary from saint to saint. In addition to wounds in their hands, feet, and side, some manifested gashes on the head from Jesus's crown of thorns, some on the back where he was flogged by Roman soldiers, and bruises on the shoulder where the heavy cross left its impression. Francis was unusual in that jagged pieces of skin on the back of his hands and feet resembled nails and made walking painful.

As in the case of other saints, Francis appeared to his devotees after his death. According to one story, a friar desired to know what the angel told

Francis when he received the stigmata. After eight years of fervent prayer to the saint, the friar was called to show hospitality to two strangers, friars that appeared at the door, wet and covered with mud. While washing the feet of the older stranger, the friar uncovered wounds he recognized as stigmata. The stranger identified himself as "your father, Friar Francis," and proceeded to reveal that the angel had commissioned him each year to enter purgatory and lead to paradise any members of his order who were there. "This said, St. Francis and his companion vanished." Posthumous appearances of saints are often miracles granted to pious individuals, but in this case there were "eight friars that were present at the vision and heard the words of St. Francis."[25] The narrative form of this story follows biblical precedent where post-resurrection appearances of Jesus were also attested by multiple witnesses. What is remarkable is that Francis's elevation to heaven did not result in the healing of his wounds; he retained the marks of passion in his glorified body, just as the risen Christ did. The purpose of the indelible stigmata identified Francis as playing a continuing role in the salvation of the world, necessary as long as souls in purgatory are in need of deliverance. The meaning of this miracle is that divine mercy extends beyond death and that holiness and suffering are inseparable, as demonstrated in Catholic history of wounded saints.

The significance of the stigmata as the physical replication of Christ's crucifixion—the visible demonstration of his sacrifice which is invisible in the ritual of the Mass—led to an interpretation of saints' suffering as contributing to the salvation of others. Stigmata indicated that certain saints, even before they were elevated to heaven, exercised intercessory power. In this way stigmata take their place with other miracles as social acts and not only private tokens of devotion. The public significance of stigmata was clear in the case of Padre Pio (1887–1968), an Italian priest from the village of Pietrelcina. In 1918, he had a vision of a heavenly being that thrust a fiery sword into his body. He wrote to his spiritual director, "From that day on I have been mortally wounded. In the depths of my soul I feel a wound that is always open and that causes me to writhe continually." Soon after, he reported, "I am immersed in an ocean of fire. My wound, which was reopened, is bleeding, always bleeding. . . . O my God, why do I not die? . . . What am I saying?" [26]—the wounds of Christ and the emotional ambivalence they evoked would remain with Padre Pio for fifty years.

In the modern era Catholic authorities closely investigate claims of stigmata to determine whether they are genuine miracles or psychosomatic symptoms. Padre Pio's wounds were examined and photographed extensively, but no scientific explanation was confirmed for their recurrent bleeding (following the pattern of opening late on Thursday and closing on Saturday, corresponding to the time of Jesus's crucifixion). Padre Pio regarded the constant bleeding as an embarrassment and prayed that it would cease while the pain remained. "I . . . will not stop beseeching Him until, through His mercy, He withdraws from me not the torment, not the pain—because I think that is impossible and I want to intoxicate myself with pain—but these external marks that are the cause of indescribable and unbearable confusion and humiliation."[27] To understand this plea we turn to a request that Padre Pio made of his spiritual director early in his career as a priest: "to ask Our Lord to accept him as a victim soul to alleviate the sufferings of the souls in Purgatory and to win souls for Heaven."[28] There could hardly be a clearer statement of intention to participate in the redemptive suffering of Christ as the ultimate expression of compassion, specifically for those souls whose sins left them with painful penance to endure. By being wounded as Christ was, Padre Pio hoped to reduce their suffering and hasten their entrance into heaven. In Catholic interpretation his desire to be "intoxicated" with pain was not morbid or masochistic, but a holy wish to extend the benefit of Christ's sacrifice through his own body. In recognition of Padre Pio's posthumous miracles confirming his "heroic virtue" Pope John Paul II canonized him in 2002.[29]

In Christian tradition miracle stories promote the values of compassion and justice, particularly as shown in divine favor to the poor and deprived. Miracles of stigmata, while peculiar to Roman Catholic saints, are an extreme expression of compassion by which the saint continues the suffering of Christ for the world by taking on the physical marks of his crucifixion. If Jesus is the perfect embodiment of divine love, the saint is the next best thing: the human expression of God's suffering with, and for, the salvation of the world. In a paradox that St. Paul located at the center of Christian faith, the power of the saint lies in his or her weakness. That paradox is clearly demonstrated in the correlation of physical vulnerability and spiritual receptivity in the French peasant girl who became St. Bernadette.

Bernadette Soubirous (1844–1879) was the frail child of pious but impoverished parents, born in a remote village in southern France called Lourdes. It was a time of rising secular opposition to France's historic ties to Christianity and specifically to claims that the nation enjoyed the protection of the Virgin Mary. According to Bernadette's account, when she was fourteen, she set out to gather firewood with her sister and a friend. When they arrived at a convergence of two rivers, her companions waded across while Bernadette hesitated to enter the frigid water because of her asthma. When she looked across the stream she saw a grotto in a rocky cliff that local people believed to be enchanted. As she stared, the niche was suddenly illumined and a young woman appeared. "She wore a long white dress with a blue sash, a long white veil that concealed most of her hair, and a yellow rose on each bare foot. Hanging from her arm was a rosary with large white beads on a golden chain, finished by a large crucifix."[30] This image would serve as the likeness of Our Lady of Lourdes, but the apparition did not identify herself as the Virgin Mary and Bernadette referred to her merely as *Aqueró*, "that one." During the next fifteen days *Aqueró* appeared to Bernadette in the presence of a growing crowd of spectators, sometimes giving her messages to proclaim and, on one occasion, directing her to crawl on all fours and dig in the dank dirt of the cave until she discovered muddy water. When Bernadette drank the slurry, the townspeople thought she had gone mad. But soon the water began to run more clearly and one woman who plunged her paralyzed arm into the pool withdrew it fully functional again. The miracles of healing at Lourdes had begun.

Aqueró informed Bernadette of her wish to have a chapel built on the spot, but when Bernadette relayed the request to the parish priest he refused to believe that her visions were authentic. Still, people were flocking from all over France to the grotto. Popular enthusiasm for demonstrations of the presence of God, as usual, overwhelmed official opposition. Following a pattern we have seen elsewhere, church authorities then sought to regulate the miraculous phenomena. First the priest demanded to know the identity of the woman who requested the chapel be built. When Bernadette later asked the apparition her name, *Aqueró* answered, "I am the Immaculate Conception." When Bernadette, for whom the strange phrase held no meaning, repeated the words to the parish priest, he was stunned. While the Council of Trent had made the sinless perfection of the Virgin Mary an article of faith, Pope Pius IX had declared only four years earlier that she was conceived immaculately or without sin. The dogma (required belief of all Catholics) was a theological refinement far beyond the unaided mind of an illiterate peasant girl; her uttering this new title of the Virgin gave her testimony to visions new credibility.[31]

By 1862, even church authorities were convinced and issued this statement: "We hold that the Immaculate Mary, Mother of God, actually appeared to Bernadette Soubirous on the eleventh of February, 1858, and on the days following, to the number of eighteen times, in the grotto of Massabielle, near the town of Lourdes; that this apparition bears all the signs of authenticity and the faithful are free to consider it true."[32] What makes an apparition of

Mary credible is that the one who appears has some identifying mark of the "mother of God." In the case of Bernadette it was her new title bestowed by papal decree. But another distinguishing feature of visions of Mary is that they are given to the poor or children or women; Bernadette qualified on all three counts. It is entirely consistent with the story of Mary's own visions in the New Testament that she, the teen-aged wife of a carpenter living under foreign occupation, would have a special interest in those who suffer from poverty, injustice, and illness. Apparitions of the Virgin often come to those who have no other sources of saving power.

Initially, there was no direct connection between Bernadette's visions and the curative power of the water in the grotto. The apparition did not promise Bernadette that she would be healed, but the appearance of the Virgin Mary marked the grotto as sacred space. Further, those who entered the grotto and took its water into their bodies could hardly avoid thinking of the sacramental drinking of the wine of the Eucharist and so regarded the water at Lourdes as the divine remedy for mortal ailments. The connection was made explicit in the ritual parade of the consecrated elements introduced at Lourdes in 1888, called the Procession of the Blessed Sacrament. As priests carry the Host through the esplanade in front of the grotto, sick pilgrims cry out for healing and, after fervent responsive chanting of the litany, the presiding priest calls on those hoping for healing to rise from their wheelchairs and pallets and follow the sacrament.[33] While few are capable of doing so, the meaning of the ritual is to make explicit the parallel between the mystery of the divine presence in the sacrament and at Lourdes: as one awaits the final salvation promised in the Eucharist, so one endures with patience unrelieved suffering now. In both cases faith affirms the invisible grace at work, healing the spirit if not the body.

As construction began on a basilica above the grotto and ever-larger crowds thronged to bathe in its waters, Bernadette began to diminish even more in strength in a monastery three hundred miles away. Her monastic career was brief and much of it was spent in the infirmary as she suffered the ravages of asthma, cholera, and tuberculosis within the curtained bed she called her "white chapel."[34] Demonstrating the patient suffering that many regard as the decisive evidence of her sanctity, Bernadette refused her friends' offer to bring water from the grotto to ease her pain. Few miracles were attributed directly to Bernadette, but she provided a powerful example of serving God through compassion for others while enduring great and unrelieved affliction of her own. For her heroic virtue confirmed by posthumous miracles she was canonized in 1933 and her body, believed by the faithful to be incorrupt, lies in repose in the chapel at Nevers where she spent her last years. It is fitting that veneration of St. Bernadette typically involves prayers for the spiritual strength to endure illness and disability with grace rather than to escape them through miraculous deliverance.[35]

The area near Lourdes that surrounds the grotto where Bernadette received her visions is now an enormous complex, covering 120 acres.[36] Pilgrims come from across the world to seek the intercession of the Virgin Mary and St. Bernadette, many hoping for a miraculous cure of sickness or disability. Despite the high level of collective fervor at Lourdes, however, almost all pilgrims leave, as the Catholic writer Elizabeth Ficocelli notes, "much the way they entered, but with a new peaceful acceptance of their suffering."[37] She reports that "out of seven thousand cases of inexplicable cures on file with the Lourdes Medical Bureau today, the Church has only recognized sixty-seven of them as miraculous."[38] That statistic is remarkable when one recalls that six million pilgrims each year make their way to Lourdes, but the stringent medical criteria for miraculous cures require that the disease must be incurable and that patients must not have received prior medical treatment (conditions rarely met by people under modern medical care). Further, the standards do not allow for deliverance from depression or addiction to which many pilgrims bear witness in testimonies that include, like all miracle narratives, wonders of transformed character and disposition.

Our study of the lives of three Roman Catholic saints highlights the primary themes in Christian understanding of miracles as signs of divine presence, experienced as compassion shown toward the poor and powerless. Even when supernatural healings are withheld, Christians are assured by stories of miracles that God is still present in the world—whether in the sacred elements of the Eucharist, the healing waters of Lourdes, or the lives of the saints. For some Protestants, however, the power of divine healing is found elsewhere: in the ecstatic prayer of faith that invokes the Holy Spirit of God to restore the bodies of believers as well as their souls.

Healer: Protestant Charismatic Miracles

By the time of the Protestant Reformation the stories of miracles performed by Catholic saints were deeply embedded in the oral culture of Europe. Images of these holy ones filled churches, edifying narratives of their lives were composed and consumed with enthusiasm, and their earthly remains were parceled out among competing parishes in a lively process of acquisition and exchange. Relics were souvenirs of a saint's embodied holiness and they still carried the power of sanctity, the power to restore believers to spiritual wholeness and bodily health. Both in life and in death a saint's body—down to the bone—was a medium of transcendent power. Further, a saint's holiness was manifest in miracles worked from heaven in response to prayer. Popular devotion ascribed specific interests and competences to individual saints, identifying which saint was most likely to answer one's request or meet one's need. Saints constituted a growing host of heavenly mediators whose supererogatory merit provided a fund of grace from which penitent sinners could draw to satisfy divine justice and secure eternal life. Further, their focused attention on human needs extended beyond the spiritual to the physical and, on some occasions, resulted in miraculous healings.

Prayer for healing is a nearly universal practice in Christian tradition.[39] Nevertheless, Protestant reformers denied that whatever physical improvement ensued from prayer was a miracle wrought by saints; it was rather a "special providence" bestowed through the operation of natural forces under God's sovereign regulation. This distinction served the polemical end of denying that miracles confirmed Catholic teaching and practice. Protestants argued that the purpose of miracles was to establish the divine authority of the gospel as preached by Christ's apostles. When the last apostle died, the power of miracles was withdrawn and believers should not expect their recurrence. Writing about the Catholic practice of anointing with oil people who were near death, the Swiss reformer John Calvin (1509–1564) denounced the ritual as a "false sacrament," adding, "But that gift of healing, like the rest of the miracles, which the Lord willed to be brought forth for a time, has vanished away in order to make the new preaching of the gospel marvelous forever."[40] In Calvin's judgment it was proof of the deviation of Catholic tradition from the teaching of the Bible that its defenders think "they can confirm their faith by continual miracles!"[41] For Calvin, Catholic wonder workers were "magicians" whose alleged miracles were produced by the power of Satan. He even suggested that Catholic saints were demonic figures "disguised as angels of light."[42]

For three centuries the belief in a limited age of miracles allowed Protestants to reject Catholic claims of miracles as "superstition." As the historian Robert Mullin demonstrates, however, that argument could not be sustained in the mid-nineteenth century in the face of increasing interest among Christians in new forms of spiritual healing and the growing threat of materialist attacks on all religious faith. Protestant leaders found it necessary to begin defending contemporary miracles in alliance with Catholics to form a common apology for supernaturalism against modernists and materialists.[43] Further, the rise of the Pentecostal movement in the United States in the early twentieth century aroused a popular enthusiasm for miracles, particularly healing, that engaged a wide range of Americans, regardless of age, race, or class.

Their experience was modeled on the biblical account of the apostles in Jerusalem on the Jewish feast of Pentecost, when "suddenly from heaven there came a sound like the rush of a violent wind. . . . Divided tongues, as of fire, appeared among them, and a tongue rested on each of them. All of them were filled with the Holy Spirit and began to speak in other languages." As a result, each person in the audience "heard them speaking in the native language of each" (Acts 2:2–6). The apostles were miraculously endowed with the ability to speak foreign languages and those who heard them testified to their message: "we heard them speaking about God's deeds of power." Speaking in "other tongues" (also called *glossolalia*) confirmed the authority of the apostles to announce the coming of the "last days" before the return of Christ. While Pentecostal Christians do not interpret glossolalia as speaking in known languages, they do regard their ecstatic speech as miraculous, a sign that confirms the divine presence in history and identifies them as authentic witnesses to the divine message.

Speaking in tongues was included by St. Paul in his list of the "gifts of the Spirit" (*charismata*), but not as a mark of spiritual authority. On the contrary, he understood glossolalia as an expression of religious ecstasy; the individual participated directly in the divine Spirit through prayer that was as unintelligible to the one praying as to those who heard it. Because speaking in tongues is an individual experience not easily constrained by forms of communal worship, Paul insisted that public outbursts of the "tongues of angels" be accompanied by interpretation so that the entire "assembly" (*ecclesia*) could benefit. Paul referred to glossolalia as "ecstatic speech," and that is the understanding of tongues in Pentecostal churches today: inspired by the Holy Spirit, divinely caused, a miracle that often accompanies healings.

According to most historical accounts, the Pentecostal movement began with Charles F. Parham (1873–1929), a former Methodist preacher and itinerant healer, who founded the College of Bethel in Kansas. Under his teaching, students underwent the "baptism of the Holy Spirit," causing them to speak in tongues. Parham moved to Houston, and one of the students in his Bible school there was William Joseph Seymour (1870–1922), who later moved to Los Angeles and founded the Azusa Street Mission (incorporated as the Pacific Apostolic Faith Movement). He received the gift of tongues in 1906 and a revival began in his mission, the influence of which spread across the nation. Many made pilgrimages to Azusa Street to share in the miracle of restoring the supernatural power of the apostles to contemporary believers. Charles H. Mason (1866–1961) came from Tennessee and received the baptism of the Holy Spirit in 1907 under Seymour's preaching. Mason returned to Memphis and formed the Church of God in Christ, becoming its Chief Apostle, a title that affirmed connection with the authority of the early Church. This predominantly black Pentecostal denomination has a current membership of five million and holds beliefs in the final authority of the Bible, original sin, salvation as divine act, baptism of the Holy Ghost, and contemporary miracles, including tongues and healing.[44]

One young woman touched by the Azusa Street revival was Aimee Semple McPherson (1890–1944), who founded the denomination called Foursquare Gospel Church in Los Angeles in 1922. She derived the name from descriptions in the Bible of the temple in Jerusalem and the court of heaven as "foursquare." McPherson identified each square with an aspect of Jesus: as Savior, Baptizer with Holy Spirit, Healer, and Soon-Coming King.[45] Born on a farm in Canada, Sister McPherson (as she came to be called) went to China with her first husband, Robert Semple, as an evangelical missionary. After his death, she returned to answer what she believed was a divine call to ministry. McPherson built Angelus Temple in Los Angeles in 1923 with seating for 5,300 and filled it with audiences eager to hear her sermons and be transformed by their power. She was a dramatic and passionate preacher, who emphasized the power of the Holy Spirit to heal the body as well as save the soul. She preached a message of divine love, and tirelessly promoted social ministries and spoke at patriotic rallies. Ever alert to the possibilities of communication technology to spread the gospel, she purchased a radio station and soon her voice was heard throughout the nation. Perhaps her most successful appropriation of popular culture was her Sunday evening "illustrated sermons" that rivaled Hollywood productions in scale, costumes, and elaborate sets.[46] In these performances, McPherson played the starring role, enacting stories from her own life and from the Bible.[47] Many audience members, entering imaginatively into her narratives, felt themselves transformed in both spirit and body.

In a melodramatic autobiography published in 1927, McPherson described an outdoor healing meeting in San Diego with 30,000 people in attendance, including a vast throng of diseased and injured seeking healing. By noon, she wrote, there stretched before her "An ocean of humanity in intercession" and, at sunset, "Empty wheel-chairs—deserted stretchers—piled-up crutches."[48] Her description of the first healing of the day is worth considering in some detail. As the organ carried the hymn *Rock of Ages* across the scene, those seeking relief surged toward the stage, in McPherson's view, "carried beyond their pains and their aches, beyond their needy selves up, up to God . . . and felt themselves . . . filled with that transcending power." While the crowd was still in that ecstatic state, McPherson called a man healed in an earlier meeting to give his testimony. She recalled that "their ears strained for his every word. Mentally, they were all comparing their own ills with his, and lo! he stood before them, whole. They were all drinking it in. . . . The evidence was right before their eyes, they saw and they believed."[49] To be more precise, they *heard* and they believed. As with all compelling narrative, the man's personal story drew his listeners into the world of supernatural healing in which it transpired: a world in which Jesus the healer was still present. One of McPherson's favorite Bible verses was Hebrews 13:8: "Jesus Christ the same yesterday, today, and forever." She had the words emblazoned in gold letters behind the pulpit in Angelus Temple. On that biblical basis she insisted, "The age of miracles is still with us, since God, who performed those miracles, is with us still. The faith which of old could move mountains, can move mountains of affliction even yet."[50]

In that charged atmosphere the first person came to the stage: a middle-aged woman paralyzed from the waist down. "She was tense," McPherson wrote, "with the excitement of a wonderful expectation." Calling upon the divine will to heal her, the evangelist demanded whether the woman had any doubt that Christ could restore movement to her legs. When she responded, "I believe!" McPherson declared, in words cast in the diction of the King James Version of the Bible, "Then the Lord maketh thee whole. Arise and glorify His name!" The woman's legs began to stir and she haltingly rose; then, supported by attendants at each arm, she walked toward the stairs. For McPherson the healings that continued throughout the day were demonstrations of God's power and Christ's compassion, but they also served the function of attracting the attention of unbelievers and turning them to Christian faith. When curious scoffers repented and committed their lives to Christ, then was "wrought a double miracle": restoration of the body and conversion of the soul.[51] The healings revealed the love of God in Jesus, who is "willing and able to heal the body, as well as the soul and spirit in answer to faith."[52]

The style and success of McPherson's healing ministry raises the question: What role does impassioned and theatrical preaching play in setting the stage of miraculous healing? One answer may be that Pentecostal healers, like Puritan preachers in the Great Awakening, depend on what the historian Perry Miller called the "rhetoric of sensation," language that evokes within hearers the reality of what it describes. When the Puritan preacher and theologian, Jonathan Edwards (1703–1758), spoke of hell as a pit over which his listeners were walking on rotting planks which at any moment might splinter and send them plunging into the dark abyss, he evoked the primal fear of falling to provide the sensation by which the idea of hell became concretely intelligible and emotionally compelling.[53] For contemporary Pentecostal healing the anthropologist of religion Simon Coleman offers a related explanation: wondrous cures are examples of words at work in the "performative" mode of language. In listening to words from the Bible, "the Word can be made to 'live' as signs of language are externalized from the speaker and turned into physical signs of the presence of sacred power . . . words come to create the very reality which they purport to describe."[54] Thus, words about health become healing words.

While specific phrases and formulae, sometimes repeated continuously in healing sessions, may be effective in triggering physical changes, entire healing narratives—either in the form of biblical stories or personal testimonies—have an even greater effect. If our claims about the creative power of narrative are correct, then we would expect the response to miracle stories that construct a world in which divine healing is possible to evoke in hearers the externalization of the ideals of health portrayed in the stories.[55] In a similar way thousands experienced what they regarded as miraculous healings under the spell of Aimee Semple McPherson's "illustrated sermons" that engaged them in the narrative world of biblical miracles. The power of her language alone to shape the spirits and bodies of her listeners was evident in the success she had in evangelizing over the airwaves.[56] Telling stories is a form of sermon that appears in Christian tradition from Jesus's dramatic parables to testimonies of healing. Hearers are invited to identify with actors in the story and to imagine their lives transformed in the same way, restored to inner peace, physical health, and social relationships.

The theme of healing as a process of integrating all the aspects of one's life into a healthy and harmonious whole recurs throughout the history of charismatic Christianity. It is central to the career of the best-known healer of the twentieth century, Granville Oral Roberts (1918–2009). His name conjures the classic image of a Pentecostal preacher, shedding the tears and sweat of "Holy Ghost power," speaking in tongues and healing the sick. He testified to being healed from tuberculosis and stammering while in high school. The healings occurred at the same time during a tent revival meeting. After his sermon the evangelist walked over to the young Roberts and spoke directly and forcefully: "You foul disease, I command you, in the name of

Jesus Christ, to come out of this boy's lungs. Loose him and let him go!" The preacher conducted the healing as an exorcism, and Roberts later recalled that he felt strength flowing into his body and he began to breathe deeply and freely. When the young man began shouting that he was healed, the evangelist called upon him to testify. To his amazement, his stuttering was gone and he launched into the style of preaching that would mark his career as a revivalist: "I walked up and down the platform telling the people, over the microphone, exactly what Jesus of Nazareth had done for me." He claims his complete cure was later verified by medical tests at Oklahoma State Hospital.[57]

Ordained in the Pentecostal Holiness Church at age seventeen, Roberts was soon a successful pastor, but he left his church in 1947 to launch his own healing ministry. Moving to Tulsa, Oklahoma, Roberts launched publication of the magazine called *Healing Waters* and began weekly radio broadcasts during which he urged listeners to place their hands on their radios in order to receive the healing power he transmitted to them. According to seminary professor D. William Faupel, when Roberts held tent revivals across the nation, "Thousands attended every meeting with scores claiming healing in every crusade."[58] Early in his career Oral Roberts shifted into the Protestant mainstream by joining the Methodist Church, but he never abandoned his conviction in supernatural healing directed through his touch and words. As the founder of Oral Roberts University, including its extensive medical complex, Roberts recognized the value of medical science and wrote, "God heals in many ways. He heals through good doctors, through medicine, through nature and climate, through understanding and love." Yet when those means fail, "There is a healing power above the doctor's power, or nature or climate or any other form of healing. That healing power is by faith in God. 'The prayer of faith shall save [heal] the sick' (James 5:15)."[59]

Roberts' most startling claim of miraculous power was that he raised an infant from the dead. While he later admitted that there had not been a doctor present to declare the baby clinically dead, he and the mother were convinced that the child had died and that it was due to Roberts that he was restored to life.[60] The primary witness to this resuscitation was Richard Roberts, the evangelist's son, who continues to promote his father's teachings through Oral Roberts Ministries. On the Web site of the organization, disease is attributed to the devil and healing is promised to all who have faith. Although Christians filled with the Holy Spirit cannot be possessed by demonic forces, Roberts teaches, their bodies remain subject to the ravages of original sin and thus vulnerable to demonic "oppression" in the forms of disease and death.[61] The recommended means of escape from that oppression and of sustaining faith is to believe Jesus's words: "If you ask anything in My name, I will do it." The miracle of healing comes in response to faith in divine power to accomplish what appears to be impossible, whether instantaneous remission of terminal cancer, permanent reversal of debilitating depression, or raising the dead.

For Protestant charismatic healers, then, miraculous cures signify not only God's compassion toward the afflicted, but also God's power over the destructive oppression of Satan. According to the Epistle to the Hebrews, Jesus's victory over death destroyed "the one who has the power of death, that is, the devil, and freed those who all their lives were held in slavery by the fear of death" (2:14–15). Releasing the sick from physical diseases restores divine authority over the lives of believers and thus foreshadows the time when Christ will finally destroy the unjust powers of this world and establish divine rule in a paradise where "mourning and crying and pain will be no more" (Revelation 21:4). In Pentecostal tradition the ecstasy of tongues and the healing of the body combine as signs of the salvation that awaits believers in the age to come.[62] While not shared by all Christians, this interpretation of miracles provides another dimension of meaning: confirmation of the promise of redemption, the restoration of human life in the perfect unity of spirit, body, and community.

Even the most inspiring healers, however, cannot guarantee that their prayers will result in miraculous restoration. Aimee Semple McPherson candidly admitted, "Not all were healed, for either all have not yet the necessary faith or He in Whose hands are the issues of life and death and who numbers all our days, wills otherwise."[63] In Pentecostal theology healing is included in the salvation Christ secured in his atoning death, but the gift of entire restoration must be accepted by sincere and sustained faith. As Oral Roberts once warned, "What you did to get your healing, you must continue to do to keep your healing."[64] Roberts made repentance a necessary condition for healing in both body and soul, implying that the recipient of the miracle limits the possibility of its occurrence. For many—like those who left Angelus Temple or the Sanctuary at Lourdes or turned off their radios after listening to Oral Roberts unrelieved of their physical suffering—the luminous hope that God honored their faith and in his infinite wisdom ordained that they should bear their affliction a while longer was sufficient reward. For others, however, the silence of heaven seemed more like indifference than mystery. Why should my faith be insufficient to merit miraculous cure? What reason could God possibly have for allowing my child to die or continuing to burden me with paralysis or blindness or cancer? Robert Mullin expressed the problem bluntly: "Why did a loving God who promised healing not heal? . . . The question would stick to the Protestant healing movement like a tin can on a cat's tail."[65] As it turns out, that is only one of the reasons for dissent from belief in miracles in Christian tradition.

Dissent: From Gnostics to Moralists

Objection to belief in miracles arose early in Christian tradition and is a persistent feature of its history. St. Paul insisted that resurrection was a miracle of re-embodiment, but his interpretation was not accepted by all early Christians. One alternative view was promoted by a school of thought scholars locate under the general heading *Gnosticism*.[66] In brief, Gnostics held a version of Christian faith that denied religious significance to the suffering of Christ, regarded martyrdom as folly, affirmed the divinity of every believer, and found in revealed knowledge the basis of immortality. Gnostics taught that Jesus revealed heavenly wisdom (*gnosis*) that would enable the spirit, upon the death of the body, to ascend into the eternal realm of the unchanging divine One in which all distinctions would forever disappear. In their view resurrection is the return of the soul to God, making reanimation of the body unnecessary, even undesirable. "Now, since we are manifestly present in this world, the world is what we wear (like a garment). From the savior we radiate like rays; and being held fast by him until our sunset—that is, until our death in the present life—we are drawn upward by him as rays are drawn by the sun, restrained by nothing. This is resurrection of the spirit, which makes irrelevant . . . resurrection of the flesh."[67] As all-knowing Spirit, God does not sustain any relation to the material world; much less does God have an interest in intervening miraculously in its operation. Gnostic views of the body and the natural world as hindrances to spiritual advance undercut interest in miracles as a mark of attachment to the world and thus of spiritual immaturity.

Other Christian critics of belief in miracles take the opposite tack of arguing that great spiritual benefit can be gained from full participation in embodied existence. They maintain that those who pray for miraculous power to alter the forces of nature are missing the opportunity to develop virtue and wisdom that the trials of life are designed to cultivate within us. How better to grow in compassion, they reason, than to share in common human experiences of illness, failure, and suffering? How better to learn the central importance of justice in human affairs than to be afflicted by injustice? Further, to ask for divine deliverance from the conditions of human life is to deny the truth of the incarnation: that God became flesh in Jesus and bore the pain and anxiety of embodied existence. Grounded in central Christian beliefs, this objection weighs heavily against a desire for miracles.

But how do such critics deal with the fact that the Gospel accounts of Jesus's life include stories of his performing miracles? One answer is based on the principle that Jesus's spiritual insight transcended his historical embodiment and is detachable from his earthly career. This interpretation allows Christians to honor Jesus as a moral exemplar with a profound awareness of God, while also accepting the scientific view of the natural world as a closed system in which miracles are impossible. On this view, stories of miracles in the Bible are symbols of spiritual realities. The true miracle is the transformation of the spirit from self-interest to self-sacrifice, from indifference to compassion, and from ignorance to liberating knowledge in fulfillment of Jesus's promise: "You will know the truth, and the truth will make you free" (John 8:32). This approach of separating Jesus's teachings from his miracles was introduced by Enlightenment thinkers and readily adopted by modernist Christians in the twentieth century.

We have already considered David Hume's objections to miracle claims and Immanuel Kant's critique that reliance on miracles undercuts moral responsibility. We now turn to another Enlightenment critic, Gotthold Ephraim Lessing (1729–1781). Lessing intended to follow rational principles consistently and to establish religion on the basis of moral excellence. To that end he argued that stories of miracles are examples of truths revealed in imaginative accounts suited to untutored minds. Lessing thought of revelation as progressively replacing symbolic lessons with rational insights.[68] The truth of Christianity, then, is not dependent upon historical claims, but upon universal truths of reason and morality. Therefore, even if miracle stories in the Gospels were instructive fictions, Christianity remains true. The essence of Christianity is confirmed by inner moral power, not by the proof of miracles. The problem, Lessing wrote, is that by the eighteenth century that proof "has sunk to the level of human testimonies of spirit and power," but "reports of miracles are not miracles." At best, he argued, stories of miracles are "as reliable as historical truths ever can be," that is, less than absolutely certain and thus inadequate as the foundation of faith.[69] Lessing thus despaired of ever crossing "the ugly, broad ditch" of history which separated him from the founding miracles of Christianity.

In the next century Kierkegaard offered to point the way across the chasm by a leap of faith, but Lessing would have regarded Kierkegaard's passion as an irrational and dangerous impulse. For Lessing, what brings certainty and reality is what has power to promote virtue in an individual's life. Faith does not rest on metaphysics or on history—and certainly not on the suspension of reason and morality that Kierkegaard thought necessary for faith—but on its moral consequences, chiefly love.[70] The essence of Christianity, then, has nothing to do with miracles but rather consists of belief in one God and the intention to be regulated by the most worthy ideas of God in all one's thoughts and actions. Thus, morality is not only the test of religion; morality is the substance of religion.[71] Lessing's criticism of biblical texts consisted of separating their timeless moral teachings from the imaginative forms, such as miracle stories, in which they were cast. The forms were dispensable for Lessing as dated methods of presentation adapted to an elementary stage in the development of human understanding. It is a theme that would be sounded often in the subsequent application of historical and literary criticism to the Bible.

Beginning with D. F. Strauss (1808–1874), scholars began systematically to distinguish among literary forms used in the composition of the Bible, such as myth, poetry, legend, and history. In his revolutionary book, *The Life of Jesus, Critically Examined* (1835), Strauss interpreted Jesus with neither a rationalist dismissal of miracle stories as fiction nor a pietistic faith in supernatural intervention, but in light of messianic hopes expressed in the language of myth. He argued that the miracles of Jesus were cast in a narrative form because it conveyed a spiritual truth inexpressible in less imaginative discourse. While Strauss's work was attacked fiercely at the time, his method inspired a new approach to interpretation of the Bible. One of the most radical applications of this line of criticism to the New Testament was made by the biblical scholar Rudolf Bultmann (1884–1976). Bultmann argued not only that miracle narratives were cast in the "picture language" of mythology but also that each story was carefully crafted to serve the author's theological purpose in constructing his Gospel. The stories were not meant as literal accounts but as expressions of the author's faith.

Bultmann's exegetical work posed a serious challenge to traditional Christian belief in miracles—a challenge he made explicit in a brief work called *Jesus Christ and Mythology*. In this controversial book Bultmann proposed that, if the message of Jesus were to be understood in the modern world, it would have to be "demythologized" and translated into an idiom intelligible to twentieth-century readers. That new idiom, Bultmann believed, must express the one concern modern readers share with the authors of the New Testament: an interest in authentic existence. Influenced by the philosopher Martin Heidegger (1889–1976), Bultmann argued that to be human means to decide to take responsibility for one's existence without seeking guidance or assurance from others. The mythological worldview, however, encourages a false sense of security and dependence on supernatural powers. By contrast, "modern science does not believe that the course of nature can be interrupted or, so to speak, perforated, by supernatural powers."[72] What Christians call "acts of God," therefore, are not visible events "capable of objective, scientific proof," but internal transformations discernible only by faith.[73] "Statements which speak of God's actions as cosmic events are illegitimate," Bultmann wrote, because God's reality is no more demonstrable in natural events than is the human self as a center of freedom unconstrained by historical conditions.[74] (We hear an echo of Kant's noumenal self.)

Bultmann insisted that miracles can be experienced only as events of personal disclosure, not public demonstration: "the understanding of an event as a miracle is not a conclusion from what is perceived, but the perception itself apprehends the miracle. . . . Those into whose lives these events do not come with the faith-creating might of God's activity must obviously regard them not as miracle, but only as astonishing events."[75] For Bultmann only faith acknowledges the events through which God speaks as miracles, occasions of divine revelation to individuals calling them to encounter God through relationships with their neighbors. In this way Bultmann believed he retained the moral imperative of Jesus's radical call to love, without accepting the historicity of supernatural events.

Bultmann sought to exempt the religious truth of New Testament accounts of Jesus's miracles from historical criticism. In that enterprise he was joined by two other influential Christian theologians of the twentieth century.[76] Karl Barth (1886–1968) employed the method of distinguishing secular history (*Historie*), open to doubt and revision by empirical methods, from salvation history (*Heilsgeschichte*), the revelatory narrative of the Bible that becomes the Word of God to the one who reads it by faith. Paul Tillich (1886–1965) developed the view that all theological language was symbolic and always pointed beyond itself to the universal "ground of being" underlying historical reality. Bultmann, Barth, and Tillich were theological modernists, holding out for essentialist claims, the universal validity of reason, and the transparency of history. They worked with dualisms of fact and interpretation, history and myth, science and religion, reason and revelation. Each of these dialectical oppositions has been called into question by recognition that the first term in each set has no reality independent of the second term. For example, religion cannot be exempt from history because it emerges from history. Reason cannot transcend particular insights, whether from individual geniuses or communal experience (standard media of revelation), because it is composed of them. Therefore, neither religion nor reason is warranted in making universal claims. They cannot escape the matrix of historical conditions from which they were birthed, together, locked in sibling rivalry.

But while methods of de-mythologizing the Bible were not successful in exempting miracle stories from historical criticism, they did shift the interpretation of miracles from considerations of historical confirmation to questions of moral responsibility. We have noted ethical objections to reliance on miracles in other religious traditions: believers should not depend on transcendent power to grant them what they should earn through their own effort. As an example of its expression among Christians today we note the critique of Reverend Jose Cárdenas Pallares, a Mexican Roman Catholic priest and prison chaplain. Writing from the standpoint of liberation theology, which teaches that God is always aligned with the powerless in this world, promoting their struggles for peace and justice, he insists that interest in miracles is a distraction from the economic, social, and political problems of the poor. "The miracle fever the 'gringo' sects use," he writes, "to distract us from our vital problems—our living problems—have contributed to our loss of a true sense of miracle."[77] The "sects" he has in mind are new churches planted by Protestant evangelists, who convert Catholics to their form of Christianity with promises of physical healing and blessings of prosperity. As a minister whose parishioners face daunting economic and political challenges, Pallares distrusts appeals to heavenly power to solve earthly problems. He suggests that evangelicals represent another strategy of oppression by which North Americans dilute revolutionary consciousness among the poor by fantasies of divine deliverance. By contrast, he seeks to restore the "true sense of miracle" as a "sign of liberation" communicated through the material world: "The earmark of the Christian miracle is not that it is a prodigy but rather that it is an anticipation of the human being's deliverance from all harm. It is a challenge to conscience. It is an incitement to faith."[78]

As a Catholic priest, Pallares accepts Christ's miracles, but when he interprets the story of Jesus's healing a leper, he emphasizes the way Jesus's touch restores the man to community, not the wonder of transcendent power. Turning to the miracle of Jesus's feeding thousands from a few loaves of bread, Pallares calls for a revolutionary response to the story: action to create economic conditions where everyone is nourished freely. "Let us remember that the miracle of the Christ . . . is to reveal God's project to us, and to encourage and accompany us along the path of its accomplishment."[79] Pallares thus enlists the stories of Jesus's miracles in the service of recruiting active participants in the divine project of bringing the kingdom of God to earth—without expecting miraculous assistance in fulfilling that commission.

Summary

Miracles in Christian tradition are signs of divine presence in history enacting compassion and defending justice. For Christians, the primary manifestation of God is Jesus Christ, and his career as a wonder worker provided models for miracles associated with martyrs, saints, and healers. Jesus's miracles revealed and confirmed his divine nature and authority to those whose faith allowed them to perceive his wonders as signs and whose belief in him elicited his healing power on their behalf. The miracle of the resurrection of Jesus as the Christ provides the basis for Christians' hope of everlasting life. Saints demonstrate their identification with Christ by performing wonders. Their healings not only demonstrate divine compassion for the weak and powerless, but also serve the polemical role of affirming Catholic doctrine and practice. The careers of Protestant charismatic healers also reflect the themes of compassion and justice, articulated in biblical narratives and personal testimonies that evoke transformative responses in those who identify their own stories with those who are healed. The failure of even the most enthusiastic confidence to bring about cures in most cases, however, continues to be a source of dissent to belief in miracles among modern Christians who find the heart of their faith to be in following the moral teachings of Christ without reliance on supernatural aid.

Islam

Signs of Divine Authority

To write about miracles in Islamic tradition requires at the outset that we acknowledge that many Muslims insist the only miracle in their history was the revelation of the sacred text, the Qur'an ("recitation"), to the Prophet Muhammad in Arabia in the seventh century. Called the "standing miracle," it was an event of transcendent power that confirmed the authority of Muhammad to convey the words of God, and it evoked such wonder in those who heard the words recited that many reported being converted to the new faith by the power of the language alone. For Muslims, the inimitability of the Qur'an is proof of its divine origin.[1] The traditionalist scholar of Islam, Seyyed Hossein Nasr, represents most Muslims when he insists that Muhammad did not compose the sacred text from his own reflection or from other sources; rather, "his knowledge marks a direct intervention of the Divine in the human order, an intervention which is not, from the Islamic point of view, an incarnation but a theophany [divine appearance]."[2] The distinction suggests that the Qur'an is not the *presence* of God on earth (as Christ is for Christians) but a divine *manifestation* in the form of a revealed text (as Torah is for Jews). Islamic tradition regards the written Qur'an as the perfect expression in history of the eternal will of God inscribed in a book in heaven: "And, in truth, this Qur'an is an integral part of the Archetype of the Book (*umm al-kitāb* or "Mother of the Book"), which is there in Our Presence, Transcendent and all Wisdom" (43:4).[3] As the ninth-century scholar Abu Bakr al-Baqillani explained the divine nature of the Qur'an, the sacred text reveals "information about the invisible, since there is no way that human beings have the ability to acquire this level of knowledge."[4] The foundational miracle of Islamic tradition, then, is the revelation of divine truth to the uneducated Prophet Muhammad in the Arabic language. Because Muslims believe the eloquence of the revelation is incomparable they also maintain that the Qur'an cannot be translated; versions in other languages are called "paraphrases."

Most Muslims agree that the Qur'an is a miracle, and many accept the authenticity of miracle stories in the Qur'an,[5] but there is sharp controversy over contemporary miracle claims. The majority of Muslims are Sunnis, who follow traditions of faith and practice established by legal scholars called *ulama*. Sunnis largely deny miracles ascribed by Shiites, the minority group of Muslims loyal to successors of the family of the Prophet, to their charismatic teachers called *Imams*. Other Muslims, known as Sufis, belong to mystical orders under the guidance of masters called *shaykhs*, some of whom are regarded as *saints* or persons of extraordinary wisdom and virtue capable of miraculous works. All agree that miracles are signs of divine authority; they disagree on whether any leaders after Muhammad could perform miracles in support of their teachings. Despite the Sunni view that the Qur'an is the only miracle in the age inaugurated by Muhammad, miracle stories abound in Islamic tradition. Here is one story that demonstrates the authority of a Sufi shaykh to teach the basic truth of Islam.

> There once was a humble man who discovered the divine presence in his own heart. He applied to a religious order and those in charge gave him a small house in bad repair for himself and a single student. The inner radiance of this ordinary-looking teacher soon attracted a crowd of students and the authorities decided to test his understanding. Calling him before them, they demanded he explain the first truth of Islam: "There is no god, but God." The Sufi began with the first phrase, "There is no god," and disappeared from sight! Then the crowd heard him say, "but God," and he reappeared. He repeated this feat three times. On the fourth recitation of "There is no god," the entire assembly, including his examiners, disappeared, and when he said, "but God," they reappeared.[6]

The story of the overlooked master is an enacted commentary on the confession of faith: "There is no god, but God." The shaykh reveals the inability of his questioners to see the radical contingency of the world and the transitory nature of the human self: "Now you see me, now you don't. Now you appear, now you don't." For the Swiss Sufi master, Frithjof Schuon (1907–1998), the "quintessence" of Islam is disclosed only through "an indefinite play of veiling and unveiling."[7] The alternation of visibility and invisibility represents the state of the world, moment by moment brought into being anew by continuous divine creativity. Apart from God there is nothing, so the shaykh who is in total unity with God is literally "no thing" and thus not available as an object of sight. His ego is annihilated in the divine unity, and his realization of the Islamic claim "there is no god" is so powerful that his spectators also disappear. His performance is more than an object lesson; it is divine truth made actual in the world. Every created being is utterly dependent upon divine power for its perdurable reality; and the master grasped that fact, not as a matter of theoretical knowledge, but as experiential truth. The audience could recite the same confession as the master, but now they realized its meaning, both as individuals and as a community of common faith. The miracle was an exercise in spiritual pedagogy and social formation achieved through the divine authority of which it was the sign. Finally, the miracle marked the humble teacher as a genuine Sufi shaykh capable of discerning reality at its primal level. In the playful veiling and unveiling of the miracle, the shaykh disclosed what is otherwise hidden in the mind of God: he became, in that wondrous moment, a living revelation.

To interpret the event in that way, however, is to demonstrate what Sunni teachers find objectionable about attributing miracles to humans: such close identification of the shaykh with divine truth approaches the blasphemy of *shirk* or associating a creature with God. Al-Hallāj (d. 922) was one Sufi who made that claim by declaring, "I am *al-Haqq* (the Truth)!" By applying one of the names of God to himself, al-Hallāj announced the merging of his identity with Allah. But his bold assertion was thought by Sunni authorities to be self-idolatry and he was tortured and executed. Sunni ulama have similar trouble with the claims of some Shiites that their Imams are conduits of divine revelation. If the Qur'an is the definitive Word of God to humanity which corrects and clarifies all previous holy books, then subsequent claims to revelation are false. Further, if Muhammad is the final prophet sent to humanity, perfect in character and infallible in insight, as Sunni tradition understands his status, then subsequent claims to human mediation of divine truth are false. It follows that no miracle in support of such claims could be genuine. Thus, dispute over the story of the disappearing Sufi illustrates some of the divergence in Islamic tradition on the question of miracles. Before examining those differences, however, we will briefly consider beliefs and practices that Muslims hold in common as background for understanding the meaning of miracles in Islamic tradition as signs of divine authority.

Muhammad (570–630) was born in a time and place of widespread confusion. Arabia was in upheaval, and there was no central authority to adjudicate disputes or establish laws. Nomadic tribes raided each other's flocks, water-holes, and grazing lands; clans conducted feuds, following the age-old law of revenge. The religious situation was likewise fragmented: each tribe claimed its own spirit as its patron deity. What Muhammad brought into this "age of ignorance" was the message of perfect peace (*salaam*) known only to those who submit to the will of *al-ilah* (this Arabic term meaning "the God" is related to the Hebrew word for God, *El*). Muhammad was the messenger of God, who both taught and embodied the ideal way of life, and Muslims value his sayings and practice (*sunnah* or tradition) as a source of guidance second only to the Qur'an. As the exemplar of utter devotion to God he is honored as the "perfect man" whose life provides a model for Muslims worldwide.[8] In the Qur'an Muhammad was commanded: "Say: 'My prayers and my devotions, my life and my death, are all for God, Lord of the Universe: He has no peer. Thus am I commanded, being the first of the Muslims.'"[9] Because Muhammad's life was the paradigm of obedience to divine will, his companions collected stories about his words and deeds, called *hadīth*. The authenticity of a *hadīth* is determined by tracing its chain of transmission to its origin from the Prophet or one of his companions. Through this process Muslims can be assured that they have exact information about Muhammad's conduct to guide them (even though Sunnis and Shiites have somewhat different collections of *hadīth*). *Hadīth* are our primary source of stories about miracles ascribed to Muhammad and his companions.

The Qur'an and *hadīth*, along with consensus decisions made by authoritative leaders and new judgments based on analogies to cases in the Qur'an, constitute the four sources of guidance for most Muslims. Together, these sources produced the *Sharī'ah*, "the straight path" of Islamic law. The entire *Sharī'ah* covers most aspects of personal behavior and social conduct, but its principal requirements are contained in a popular summary called the *Five Pillars of Islam*:

1. Witness (*Shahāda*): "There is no god but God, and Muhammad is God's messenger."
2. Worship (*Salāt*): Prescribed prayers and recitation of the Qur'an five times daily.
3. Giving (*Zakāt*): Giving 2.5 percent of one's income to meet the needs of the poor.
4. Fasting (*Siyam*): During the month of Ramadan, from dawn to sunset.
5. Pilgrimage (*Hajj*): All Muslims, once in their lifetimes, are obligated to travel to Mecca and perform rituals during the designated month of the lunar calendar.

Muslims around the world regard these actions as marks of Islamic identity, even though there is considerable variation in the ways Muslims practice them.

Despite these broad areas of agreement, Muslims are divided on the question of miracles. While we found ambivalence toward miracles in Jewish tradition, in Islamic tradition fierce contestation developed between legal scholars who insisted on the divine authority of their jurisprudence and charismatic leaders who claimed miracles as divine credentials for their authority to issue pronouncements. As a means of regulating those claims, Sunni ulama instituted a system of professional training and accreditation for legal scholars and a process of formulating rulings that required strict adherence to established precedents. By the twelfth century, Sunni authorities succeeded in "closing the gates of *ijtihād* [legal reasoning]" by preventing those who were not certified from entering the realm of legitimate judicial deliberation. Shiites challenged this exclusion, declaring their Imams to be directed by divine illumination, apart from Sunni approval, to issue legal judgments that are infallible and irreversible—confirmed, as was the revelation that came through Muhammad, by miraculous signs.

The dispute reflects a fundamental division on the matter of authority within the early Islamic community immediately after the death of Muhammad. New religions often face a crisis of leadership after the death of the founder. Often, a community considers two alternatives: appoint a member of the founder's family on the principle of transmitted authority or select a leader from among the founder's disciples who seems best to understand and embody the original vision. Muslims split along this fault line: the Sunni majority elected to follow Muhammad's companion Abu Bakr, while the minority supported Muhammad's cousin and son-in-law, Ali, whom they believe the Prophet designated as his successor. They became known as the *Shī'at 'Alī* or "party of Ali."[10] It is important to note that the divisions within Islam are not based on disagreements about the authority of the divine words revealed to Muhammad, but—as was also the case within early Christianity—over who has the right to interpret the sacred text. Different forms of Islam identified different centers of authority: Sunnis relied on the consensual judgment of those trained in Islamic law and tradition; Shiites looked to Imams descended from the family of Ali; and Sufis followed masters of meditation and devotion, who also traced their spiritual lineage to Muhammad through Ali.[11] Miracles, as signs of divine authority, took on different meanings within these various communities of interpretation.

Early in Islamic history, Sunni ulama represented themselves as the normative interpreters of the Qur'an and the authentic preservers of tradition. The process by which a school of textual experts claimed to be the final authority in theological and legal questions for the entire Muslim community is parallel to that by which the rabbis assumed the role of custodians of normative Jewish belief and practice. As the rabbis surrounded the Torah with dense layers of commentary that they described as building a "hedge" around the sacred text, so the ulama constructed elaborate systems of legal decisions that only scholars trained in their schools could understand. It is not surprising that religions based on revelation in written form ascribe authority to a class of learned interpreters—and for most Muslims the ulama "help to create what the official meaning of Islam should be for members of any given society, and in that sense they establish the yardstick for locally defining what is Islam and what is not."[12]

But there is a danger in this strategy, as the anthropologist Michael Gilsenan points out. If the system of interpretation becomes so dense and rigid that ordinary people cannot understand or adapt it to their immediate needs, then they may create their own "men of authority" whose views may not conform to the orthodoxy of the scholars. In that context, "There could arise miracles and miracle workers, healers, mystical groups, new ritual forms, and a host of beliefs and symbols put together in a patch-work quilt to make sense of everyday life."[13] Out of that practical need people discovered or constructed their own leaders, some of whom were illiterate and instinctive rather than reflective. Sufi shaykhs and Hasidic *zaddikim*, regarded by their followers as the "center of the universe," often challenged established authorities (religious and political). For that reason Gilsenan underscores the fact that "the miracle is always potentially dangerous. Anything that opposes the given order of things, that disrupts causality, that confounds our ordinary expectations, and that, by definition, is not controlled but comes from an external, nonhuman, transcendent source is in essence subversive."[14] The renowned scholar of Sufism, Annemarie Schimmel, notes that in Arabic "the general term for anything extraordinary is *khāriq ul-ʿāda*, 'what tears the custom (of God).'"[15] Miracles rend the fabric of natural and social order, exposing both as frail artifices ultimately subject to transcendent power. In Islamic tradition miracles are signs of the only authority by which the customary operations of the created world could be interrupted and modified: the authority of the divine creator.

The story of the disappearing Sufi shows one way that the threat of miracles can be posed to social order: as a sign of divine authority in a figure lacking official credentials. The shaykh's lived demonstration of truth surpassed the formal learning and institutional control of his critics and so undermined their authority—and anyone retelling the story renews the challenge it issues. As we have seen in other contexts, a miracle story can serve the function of transforming those who enter into its narrative world by inspiring them to resist established orders of power. In the name of this unnamed Sufi, in the belief that his wondrous deed is a sign that divine authority resides even in the overlooked and impoverished, revolutionary consciousness may awaken.

Among the urban poor in Cairo a generation ago, Gilsenan experienced miracle stories functioning in that way. He reports that he frequently found himself, as a listener, responding to the stories with appropriate expressions of amazement and piety, participating in the recreation of the event: "because the miracle is performed each time it is retold . . . Miracles are made every day in cafés and conversations, and it is there that they are created, reproduced, and transformed."[16] Here is the same pattern we found in other traditions: miracles become real to those who enter the narrative world in which they transpire. Gilsenan highlights how that entrance opens invitingly to those who lack power in the social order and how those in control guard that entrance jealously. "We need not be surprised that the miracle is so often a weapon or refuge of the dominated, an essential part of the discourse, hopes, expectancies, and creations of the poor. It is no wonder that these miracles must be denied, stigmatized as superstition, and denied authenticity by the powerful."[17]

Because miracles provide visions of alternative possibilities for those whose lives are constricted by illness or oppression, they are either denied altogether or appropriated by religious and political leaders to sanction their own privilege and power. "Guardians of the holy law had to be quick to define the nature of the miraculous. They establish where it may be said to exist and hedge it around with a whole system of restrictions that as far as possible rule out its unauthorized and inconvenient presence."[18] But the presence of miracles, reenacted by retelling, has never been successfully banished from popular imagination by official suppression—and Islamic tradition is no exception to that general rule. Miracles are ascribed to the Prophet Muhammad, the Shiite Imams in succession from his family, and Sufi saints who are venerated as "friends of God." In each case, miracles function as signs of divine authority. For some Muslim thinkers, however, the seamless and immutable unity of God's creation is singular witness to divine authority and sufficient to inspire faith in all rational beings. For other Muslim critics, as for their counterparts in other traditions, hope for miracles cuts the nerve of the revolutionary impulse to enact the divine will in human society and, thus, betrays faith.

Prophet: Wonders of Muhammad

Muhammad is revered in Islamic tradition as the human instrument through whom God chose to reveal eternal and universal truth, specifically the divine will for personal conduct and social order. The choice of Muhammad rested entirely in the sovereign will of Allah, but Muslims believe that Muhammad's piety and character prepared him for his vocation as a prophet of the highest order. Seyyed Hossein Nasr observes that there are three levels of prophetic calling in Islam: *nabī*, one who speaks God's word at a particular time and place; *rasūl*, one who proclaims the message he received to a specific people; and *ūlu'l-'azm*, one called to found a new religion. Muhammad was a prophet in all three senses, and Nasr likens his status as bearer of divine law to the role of Christ as the Logos (John 1:1), the perfect expression of divine intellect that precedes his existence as a human being. To support this exalted view of Muhammad as "the norm of all perfection, the first of all beings" Nasr cites this *hadīth*: "He [Muhammad] was prophet when Adam was still between water and clay."[19] In Nasr's reading, shaped by his view of Islam as the expression of universal truth found in all spiritual traditions, Muhammad is the cosmic axis through whom divine reality intersects with human life in the form of a prophet. "The Prophet is outwardly the messenger of God to men; inwardly he is in permanent union with the Lord."[20] As such, Muhammad need not perform miracles; he *is* a miracle. Even if Nasr's view is somewhat overwrought, for many Muslims Muhammad's role as the instrument of God's final revelation makes him the point of miraculous intervention in human history—whether or not he possessed supernatural knowledge and power. They remember that in the Qur'an Muhammad is commanded: "Say: 'I do not tell you that I possess God's treasures or know what is hidden, nor do I claim to be an angel. I follow only that which is revealed to me'" (6.50).

Muhammad thus downplayed the significance of miracles, as Buddha and Jesus had done before him. Even though others interpreted his wondrous deeds as signs of authority, he regarded the transmission of the Qur'an as sufficient proof of his divine calling. In one *hadīth* he is reported to have said: "There was no prophet who was not granted the like of which would induce men to believe in him. What I have been granted is revelation which God imparted to me, and I trust I shall have the greatest congregation on the Last Day."[21] Moreover, witnessing a miracle is not a sufficient condition of faith.

According to the Qur'an, unbelievers may "solemnly swear by God that if a sign be given them they would believe in it. Say: 'Signs are only vouchsafed by God.' And how can you tell that if a sign be given them they will indeed believe in it?" (6:109). Thus, even if Muhammad worked miracles to signify his divine authority, others could not read the signs unless God enabled them to do so. On these grounds Sunni ulama reject miracles other than the revelation of the Qur'an.

As with founders of other traditions, however, wondrous events found their way into accounts of Muhammad's life, beginning with stories about his birth. In one account his mother heard a voice while still pregnant with him that announced her son was "the Lord of this people" and instructed her to name him Muhammad, meaning "laudable" or "praiseworthy."[22] Later in the pregnancy his mother saw a light emanating from her body so bright it illuminated the world.[23] In this narrative the unborn prophet radiated the "shining light" by which he would guide the world (Qur'an 33:46), referring both to the revelation that would come *through* him and the divine luminosity *within* him, praised by Muslim poets as the "light of Muhammad" (*nūr muhammadī*). Muslim theologians incorporated this image into the doctrine of Muhammad's pre-existence as God's primal creation in the form of a column of light, from which Adam was shaped. They also identified the luminous nature of Muhammad with the "lamp" in a niche created by the eternal light of God (Qur'an 24:35).[24]

The story of the "light of Muhammad" shining in his mother's womb provided a clue in the life of the Prophet for interpreting a puzzling metaphor in the Qur'an: why is God's light compared to the niche rather than to the lamp? The answer seems to be that divine light is the encompassing and sustaining power of being, always present even if not always seen, while Muhammad is the visible source of light in the form of the perfect man. The story may thus be read as a narrative representation of the Quranic teaching. In this way, the Canadian scholar Andrew Rippin argues, biographical accounts of Muhammad may have been composed in order to provide a "contextual framework for the revelation of the Qur'an."[25] Other miracle stories about Muhammad also seem to serve the purpose of clarifying elliptical references in the revelation by placing them in relation to an event in the life of the revelator. Miracle stories are thus not only interpreted events, but also serve as interpretive keys. Such keys are necessary because divine truth cannot be communicated directly; thus, as God explains in the Qur'an, "In such parables We speak to men, so that they may take thought" (59:21). Reflection, then, is required in order to read or hear the Qur'an with understanding—perhaps that was why

Muhammad counseled his followers to recite his revelations slowly. Little of value lies on the surface to be seen and grasped by the casual reader; only the one who makes the effort to break the reflecting surface of parables is able to reach the depth of meaning that revelation conceals from literal readers but opens to those who "take thought." As in other faiths, revelation in Islamic tradition is veiled in parables and stories that point—as signs (*ayat*)—to truth that lies beyond them. The language of revelation indicates the direction in which the seeker of truth should proceed; it is not the destination. Because every verse in the Qur'an is called a sign, the entire book requires interpretation in order for the reader to grasp anything of what is signified by it. In the interpretive process miracle stories prove to be significant "aids to reflection."

Two miracle stories about Muhammad are prominent in Islamic tradition. In one tale Muhammad was tending sheep with his foster brothers when two angels appeared. The angels laid him on the ground, split open his breast, removed a drop of black blood from his heart, and washed his internal organs with melted snow from a gold basin.[26] Annemarie Schimmel interpreted the story to mean that "God's special cleansing of Muhammad's breast endowed the Prophet with a unique degree of purity, so he could convey the divine message without defect."[27] This story provides narrative context for the opening line of Surah 94 of the Qur'an: "Did We not open [or expand] your breast?" This incident is another way of emphasizing that Muhammad was a transparent medium for divine revelation; there was nothing of his own desires or illusions to obscure God's message. The story is a symbolic counterpart to the traditional claim that Muhammad was illiterate—the "Unlettered Prophet" according to Qur'an 7:158—and, therefore, could not have composed the eloquent prose and poetry of the Qur'an. The story of initiatory cleansing serves as a dramatic illustration of the claim made in the Qur'an that Muhammad "does not speak out of his own fancy. This is an inspired revelation" (53:5).

In the other story the young Muhammad accompanied his uncle's caravan to Syria. On the way they passed the cave of a Christian hermit, named Bahīra, who was said to possess esoteric knowledge. Bahīra had always ignored passing travelers before; but on this occasion he watched the caravan approach and saw that a cloud overshadowed Muhammad, shading him from the sun. With an extravagant hospitality that astonished the travelers, he invited the entire party to a feast. The others gathered at the monk's invitation, leaving Muhammad behind to guard the baggage. Bahīra observed that none of his guests bore the identifying marks he expected from his study, so he inquired whether everyone in the caravan was present. When he was told that the youngest was left on guard duty, he insisted that he join in the meal. After the others left, Bahīra took Muhammad aside and questioned him to test whether his character and habits conformed to descriptions in his secret book. When Bahīra asked Muhammad to answer questions in the name of Arab gods, assuming he worshipped tribal deities, the boy replied that he would speak only in the name of the true God. The hermit then investigated Muhammad's back and "saw the seal of prophethood between his shoulders in the very place described in his book." Bahīra warned his uncle to guard the young man against the Jews, saying that "if they see him and know about him what I know, they will do him evil."[28] The story portrays the Christian hermit as detecting signs of Muhammad's future career as a great leader, confirming the Prophet's esoteric insight, proving his loyalty to one God, and forecasting opposition to his message that would require others to protect him. The story also fit the polemical context of the establishment of Muhammad's rule in Medina by representing a Christian holy man as accepting the authority of Muhammad while warning that Jewish tribes would oppose him.

The Prophet's authority was also confirmed by his performing miracles as previous prophets had done. Islamic tradition distinguishes those miracles that confirm a prophetic message (mu'jizāt) from acts of grace (karamāt). Schimmel translates mu'jizāt as "deeds that render [others] unable to match them."[29] Gilsenan adds that mu'jizā indicates a "sign that makes it impossible to contest someone's prophetic or saintly claims . . . . The notion of challenge and contest is very strong."[30] The intention to confirm Muhammad's authority in the face of resistance is evident in many miracle stories set in the context of battles waged in the dual cause of defending Medina and subduing Mecca to Islamic rule. As military and spiritual leader, Muhammad performed several miracles in order to supply his troops under conditions of crisis that no human power could resolve. On one occasion he produced water for his soldiers to drink and to use for ablution before praying by taking a small dish with the little water that was left and placing his palm on it. As water gushed out between his fingers, seventy men performed their ritual washing.[31] Another time his thirsty force came upon a dry well. A witness reported, "The Prophet sat on the edge of the well, prayed and rinsed out his mouth, then spat into the well. We were able to draw water until each had his fill and we watered all the mounts. We were about 1,400 men."[32]

During a time of drought, a nomad interrupted Muhammad's Friday sermon to demand that he pray for rain. The prophet stretched out his hand and a torrential rain began that lasted for a week. The next Friday a man rose to plead that Muhammad pray for the rain to stop. "Smiling, the Prophet said, 'Around us, but not on top of us.' Suddenly the clouds parted, forming a circlet around Medina."[33] All of these astonishing deeds were done in public, as signs of divine interest in the success of Muhammad's military expeditions and in the protection of the city Muhammad governed. That is, the miracles invested divine authority in the Islamic society Muhammad established in Medina and in his own person. Thus, the three primary factors in the historical founding of Islam—Book, Prophet, and City—were confirmed by miraculous events.

For early Muslims battles waged in defense of Medina were fraught with symbolic meaning because they believed history was the arena in which God's will was revealed, often on the field of combat in strenuous defense of Islam against its enemies. One of the early conflicts held special significance for Muslims as a sign of the divine authority of their Prophet and their enterprise: the battle of Badr in 624. What began as a fairly routine raid on a caravan headed for Mecca turned into the most decisive turn of events in the formation of the Muslim community. Outnumbered three to one, Muhammad's forces fought with discipline and courage, eventually routing the disorganized tribal warriors of Mecca. From that moment on Badr became a confirmation of divine approval of the Islamic cause; some fighters later remembered seeing angels coming to their aid. The victory was interpreted as a miracle, the sign that God will support the righteous few, even against overwhelming odds. Badr lives on as a symbol of the divine authority of *jihad* (even in the names of some contemporary Islamist movements). Karen Armstrong observes that in Judaism, Christianity, and Islam, "current events became theophanies and God was believed to reveal Himself in battles, political reverses and achievements."[34] In the case of Badr the battle was the occasion for revelation coming to Muhammad in the form of Surah 8 of the Qur'an, including the divine promise, "I am sending to your aid a thousand angels in their ranks."

In this surah Muhammad was also instructed to recite, "It was not you, but God, who slew them" (8:17). According to tradition, the turning point of the battle came when Muhammad threw a handful of dust at the Meccan forces, and this revelation made clear that the efficacy of the gesture depended on divine action. As Schimmel commented, "This [verse] points to the divine activity that needs no secondary causes: it was God who moved the Prophet's hand."[35] God's intervention in the battle was not by remote control, but by joining the Muslims in combat, imparting to their bows and swords deadly efficiency. While a theology of divine participation in history can sanction ruthless warfare, it can also inspire initiatives of peace, as when Muhammad concluded the treaty of Hudaybiyyah with the Meccans while he was on pilgrimage. Unfortunately, they violated the pact and in retaliation Muhammad marched on Mecca and took control of the city without resistance. Even that surrender had religious value in that the Prophet destroyed the idols in the Ka'bah (the square stone building located in the center of Mecca) and dedicated it as the site of Islamic pilgrimage. In each case, historical events were interpreted as signs of divine authority and in that process took on transcendent meaning as revelatory media. When battle narratives are retold as acts of God, the line between history and miracle is erased.

One report that continues to generate debate among Muslims over its historicity is the best known of the wonders associated with Muhammad: his Night Journey (isrā') and Ascent (mi'rāj or ladder).[36] In the traditional story Muhammad was transported on the back of a supernatural steed through the night sky from Mecca to Jerusalem, referred to in the Qur'an as the "Farthest Mosque."[37] Stepping from a rock which Muslims believe still bears his footprint (today covered by the Dome of the Rock on the Temple Mount), Muhammad ascended through seven heavens, accompanied by Gabriel. When they approached the throne of God, Gabriel withdrew for fear his wings would burn, indicating that the purity of soul required to commune with God face-to-face surpassed the spiritual attainment of the archangel. Sufis regard the story as a metaphor for the ascent of the soul to God through graduated stages of discipline and meditation by, in the words of Seyyed Hossein Nasr, "ascending the ladder of the universal hierarchy of being to the Divine Presence." Nasr continues, "the Prophet accomplished this journey not only 'mentally' or 'spiritually' but also 'physically.' This implies that the journey symbolizes the integration of his whole being including the body just as resurrection is also bodily and, in another context, the Qur'an was received in the body of the Prophet."[38] What for Muhammad was a literal assumption into heaven, however, is for Sufis a spiritual experience only—although climbing the ladder of spiritual growth may require commitment and discipline fully as difficult as defying gravity. In Sufi interpretation the unique purity of Muhammad's body allowed him to enter the Divine Presence, whereas other humans can only aspire to a similar purity of spirit.

For most Muslims, however, the story was less about strenuous mystical exercises and more a sign that Muhammad was uniquely authorized by God to direct the practice of the Muslim community and to proclaim the divine will for the present age. The story of the mi'rāj is the narrative illustration and confirmation of the doctrine that Muhammad is the "seal of the prophets" (Qur'an 33:40). During his Night Journey Muhammad met earlier prophets, including Enoch, Moses, and Jesus, indicating that he travelled the same path they did but he reached its highest end, surpassing them in knowledge of God. In one *hadīth* concerning his audience with Allah, Muhammad declared, "I have a time with God to which even Gabriel, who is pure spirit, is not admitted." Schimmel comments, "This remark is interpreted as pertaining to the mystery of the heavenly journey, in which the Prophet was taken out of serial, created time and touched the Eternal Now of God."[39] To reach the divine throne Muhammad stepped off the top rung of the ladder, so to speak, leaving behind linear progression and knowledge accumulated by retracing prophetic history. At that point Muhammad was miraculously removed from history and drawn into the timeless moment of divine reality.[40]

In that meeting, beyond earth and heaven, he realized his true nature as "light of the world," filled with knowledge of God unmediated by language and undivided by thought. In that moment Muhammad experienced what Sufis call *fanā'* or annihilation of self; it was awareness that cannot be attained within the divisions and distractions of time and space and so exceeded what any prophet had achieved before him. As the scholar of esoteric Islam, Frederick Denny, remarks, "It was of course one thing, and marvelous, to have had revelation *descend* from God to Muhammad; it was quite another, and more wonderful and auspicious, for God to have caused Muhammad to *ascend* to his presence."[41] The difference was that Muhammad did not receive additional items of revealed truth as he did in his role as prophet; rather, he entered directly the mind of God where universal and eternal knowledge is not learned in successive fragments but known as a single whole. In this reading the story of the *mi'rāj* provides narrative interpretation of the Islamic doctrine of *tawhīd* (divine unity) that can be entered only through spiritual insight not by bodily intrusion. Thus, on the question of the historicity of the event, it is perhaps best to give the last word to Muhammad's wife, Ā'isha: "The apostle's body remained where it was but God removed his spirit by night."[42]

As is true of all miracle stories in Islamic tradition, the Night Journey also has both exoteric and esoteric levels of significance. Its outer meaning (*zāhir*) is that God ordered Muhammad to change the direction in which Muslims prayed from Jerusalem to Mecca and to fix the number of prayers at five a day. In addition to confirming Muhammad's general authority as a prophet, this reading of the story invests distinctive Islamic ritual practices with divine sanction. The inner meaning (*bātin*) of the miracle is, in the words of Nasr, as "the prototype of all spiritual wayfaring and realization."[43] The story of the *mi'rāj* invites the reader to embark on a pilgrimage inward and upward, through stages of ever-widening awareness, toward the transcendent wisdom that religious traditions warn cannot be attained by human understanding but awaits anyone willing to abandon self-interest for the consuming love of God. As the Persian Sufi poet Jalal al-Dīn Rūmī (1207–1273) interpreted the goal of Muhammad's journey, "the Far Mosque, is not built of earth and water and stone, but of intention and wisdom and mystical conversation and compassionate action."[44] Muhammad may have reached what was left of Herod's Temple in Jerusalem by miraculous translocation, but for Sufis that is the exoteric meaning of the journey, designed for mass consumption and public validation. The esoteric meaning can be grasped only by the individual, in a moment of such concentrated "mystical conversation" with God that all temporal concerns disappear and the self with them.

At that time beyond historical duration, Muhammad stood alone before the throne of God. The story of his ascent thus provides a narrative representation of the incomparable status of the Prophet of God. At least that is one meaning of the story which the majority of Muslims accept. In some Shiite traditions, however, Muhammad was accompanied into the divine presence by Ali ibn Abu Talib, the first Shiite Imam.[45] Shiites regard Ali as so closely identified with the Prophet that he shared this moment of highest insight, knowledge, and authority—a spiritual legacy, they believe, Ali bequeathed to his successors.

Shiite Imam: Miracles of Knowledge

In Islamic tradition, as we have seen, miracles are signs of divine authority; as such, they are particularly important to minority groups within the Muslim community. Miracles provide sanction for their departures from the beliefs and practices of the majority. In Shiite tradition the power of Imams to work miracles is relative to their level of esoteric knowledge. The scholar of Islamic theology, John Renard, summarizes the relationship this way: Imams "enjoy preferential awareness of both seen and unseen worlds as well as of hidden meanings of divine revelation in all its manifestations. . . . They can restore life to the dead, heal all ailments, and be transported great distances instantly." Shiite tradition refers to these wondrous feats as "amazing things" (*a'ājīb*) and "power" (*qudra*).[46] Miracle stories are especially associated with the twelve Imams in succession from Ali. Along with Muhammad and his daughter Fatima, these figures are known as the Fourteen Infallible

Ones, preserved from cognitive error and moral failure, and their authority to intercede with God on behalf of sinful humanity is signified by their miracles.[47]

For example, the eleventh Imam, al-Hasan al-Askarī (d. 873), is said to have provided gold to needy petitioners by drawing figures on the ground, healed a blind boy, restored the dead to life, transported himself instantaneously to any place he desired ("earth shrank its distance under his feet"), replied to an unwritten letter by reading the writer's mind, tamed wild animals sent to tear him to pieces ("tiger, lion, fox, and bear . . . bowed their heads on Imam's feet"), and caused chains to dissolve and prison doors to open so that he could miraculously meet with Shiites in various locations. All of these powers over forces of nature, animal instincts, and human injustice were produced, Shiites believe, from the Imam's inner illumination. As one contemporary Shiite poet expressed the conviction: "Even though he was sleeping / His miracle was manifesting / His handsome face was very bright / Shining from him was divine light."[48]

In general Muslim usage, *imam* refers to a leader of prayers; but, as Nasr explains, Shiites use the term "in the special sense of someone who bears the Muhammadan Light (*al-nūr al-muhammadī*) and the power of initiation within himself and who is master of both the exoteric and esoteric sciences."[49] As the living representative of the Prophet, the Imam is "the sustainer and interpreter *par excellence* of the revelation."[50] For various branches of Shiite Muslims the legitimacy of their leaders or Imams is grounded in their possession of the esoteric wisdom Ali received from Muhammad and passed on to his descendants. While Shiites ascribe mastery over nature and time to some Imams, the primary miracle of an Imam is his divine investiture with insight into truth hidden from ordinary believers. That insight is beyond human capability and, as the illumination of the mind by divine light, is a transcendent event. Thus, in terms of this study, the secret and infallible knowledge given to Shiite Imams is a miracle, the undeniable sign of their divine authority to both teach and embody eternal truth.

The first Imam was Ali, the Prophet's cousin and husband of his daughter, Fatima. Ali was the first, following Muhammad's wife Khadijah, to accept the message revealed to Muhammad; and Shiites believe the Prophet selected Ali to be his successor. They claim that the authority of Ali and his lineage to govern the Islamic community is grounded in the Qur'an. The Lebanese academic Fuad Khuri notes that this "textual Imamate" is traced to the command in 26:214: "Admonish your nearest kinsfolk." Shiites "insist that upon this revelation, the Prophet gathered his folk in his house, and after they had eaten, he said to them while pointing to Ali, 'This is my guardian and successor, listen to him and obey his order.'"[51] Further, near the end of his life, one *hadīth* records Muhammad's declaration: "Whoever takes me as lord, Ali is his."[52] In a Shiite *hadīth* the Prophet is reported as saying, "Ali is with the Truth (*haqq*) and the Qur'an, and the Truth and the Qur'an are also with Ali, and they will be inseparable until they come upon me at Kawthar [in Paradise]."[53] The formative miracle of Islamic tradition is the revelation of eternal truth in the language of the Qur'an, and for Shiites, Ali was the living edition of the text, a flesh and blood miracle.

According to another tradition, when the Prophet was returning to Medina from pilgrimage to Mecca he stopped at a pool of water called Ghadīr Khumm and declared, "I am the city of knowledge and 'Alī is its gate. Therefore, whosoever seeks knowledge should enter through its door."[54] The Iranian Shiite teacher, Muhammad Husayn Tabātabā'ī, notes that the authority of Ali and Imams descended from him rests not on political power but on insight into "religious science."[55] Further, since Imams are chosen to guard and transmit the truth disclosed to the Prophet, they must also be inerrant, their judgment guaranteed by God to be flawless with regard to the exoteric content of the Qur'an and its esoteric meaning. Such transcendent wisdom makes the Imam transparent to the divine reality that sustains his being and inspires his spiritual perfection. Tabātabā'ī continues, "Through Divine guidance he becomes adorned with moral and spiritual virtue and pure actions which are the same as Islam itself, the submission to God, the religion that is in the primordial nature of things." In this way, "the knowledge of God and of the Imam are inseparable in the same way that the knowledge of God is inextricably connected to the knowledge of oneself. For he who knows his own symbolic existence has already come to know the true existence which belongs solely to God."[56] The French interpreter of Islamic mysticism, Henry Corbin (1903–1987), argued that the Imam is the appearance in human form of not only the knowledge, but more importantly the love, that constitutes "the inner, esoteric meaning of the Qur'anic Revelation." It is through the Imam, as the "Face of God," that humans can know what it is possible to know about the hidden deity, what Corbin called "the secret of the Treasure that is hidden but aspires to be known." "The Imam is this Treasure becoming knowable and the object of love."[57]

But what does it mean to say the Imam knows the divine being which is utterly hidden from human sight? What is the content of this miraculous knowledge? From the Shiite perspective such a question may seem naïve at best and presumptuous at worst because the Imam's knowledge is, by definition, hidden from those not initiated into its secrets. But we can gain some fragmentary understanding by examining briefly one Shiite sect, called the *Isma'ilis*. This group traces its spiritual lineage to Ismā'īl al-Mubārak, a son of the sixth Imam who was rejected by other Shiites as the legitimate heir of Ali because he died before his father and could not, they insisted, serve as his successor. Isma'ilis, nevertheless, acknowledge Ismā'īl as the seventh Imam (thus they are also called "Seveners"), but believe that he went into "occultation" (or hiding) and will reappear at the end of history as the savior (*mahdi*) who will restore justice and peace to the world. Until then, they maintain, the Hidden Imam, while sustaining the being of the universe, also inspires their leaders, called Aga Khans, with esoteric knowledge.[58]

Like other Shiites, Isma'ilis believe that Imams possess souls that were created before all other beings, from pure light. According to the fifth Imam, Ali explained the supernatural origin of Imams this way: "[God] uttered a word which became a light. From that light He created Muhammad and created me and my progeny. Then God uttered another word which became a spirit, which He made to dwell in that light and the light He made to dwell in our bodies. Thus we [the imams] are the spirit of God and His words."[59] On the basis of this tradition, Isma'ilis hold that the esoteric knowledge of Imams, to the limited extent it can be expressed in human language, is insight into the creative mind of God. It is important to note that the light from which all being emerged was also created by divine speech. The elaborate symbolism of Isma'ili cosmology thus points to the primacy of knowledge in salvation, not exoteric understanding of the world *as it is*, but esoteric insight into the origin of the world and the ideal of unity with God from which humanity has fallen. As Nasr explains, the seventh Imam "is the Mahdi or 'Imam of Resurrection.'" When he reappears, then "comes the 'Great Resurrection' upon which man and his celestial prototype are re-instated in their original condition."[60] While Nasr emphasizes the cyclic nature of cosmic and personal renewal, the Western scholar of Islam, Marshall Hodgson, argues that, for Isma'ilis, individual resurrection was "an essentially spiritual matter based on transformation of the personality through the truth, while the great historical resurrection was to include the political establishment of truth and justice in the world."[61] The two approaches may be synthesized by viewing the Isma'ili hope as confidence that the power of the "inner meaning" of the history of prophetic revelations will overcome all resistance, whether intellectual skepticism or moral rebellion. The emergence of the Imam from centuries of occultation will be an event of transcendent power, evoking wonder in all who witness his appearance, and providing the ultimate sign of his divine authority.

In the meanwhile, Isma'ilis believe, God inspires spiritual leaders, called *pīrs*, to guide the community in devotion and obedience. One such leader in the twelfth century, Hadrat Pīr Shams al-Dīn Sabzawārī, composed eloquent hymns of praise filled with the imagery of light. In one cycle of poetic verses, recited in the midst of a Hindu audience who were moved to abandon their worship of "idols" to become Muslim, the Pīr sang of his faith in language employing key terms from both Hindu and Islamic traditions: "Serve the Light (*nūr*) of Satgur [from Hindi for "True Guru"]! The Guru who is the master of Divine Light. . . . Believe in the manifestation (*avatār*) of 'Ali! Then you will reap fruit." In another hymn, he proclaimed, "The name of the final Prophet was Muhammad—[bearer of] Divine Light (*nūr*). . . . The Imams are from Light; they are ever-present (*qā'im*) in the world. Listen to this true wisdom (*jñāna*) and serve [them]. Then you will reach the other shore and attain Heaven (*svarga*)."[62] The authority of the Pīr to represent the Light of Muhammad that brings salvation was confirmed by miracles. In one story, when he led prayer, the minarets of the mosque bowed in reverence. In astonishment, the people fled from what they feared was the imminent collapse of the building. When he emerged from the place of prayer, the Pīr explained, "My mind is the prayer mat and the judge; and my body is the mosque." The master's devotion compelled even the physical building to conform to his intention.[63] On other occasions, he raised the dead son of a king to life by his command, peeled off his own skin and continued on his way, and brought the sun close enough to earth to cook his meal. When the people complained of the intolerable heat, Pīr Shams ordered the sun to return to its place in the sky. This hagiographical account of the Pīr's life ends with the note: "In India, wherever he went to give wisdom, he composed *gināns* [hymns] and *garbīs* [songs of praise] in beautiful language to disclose the true religion, thus winning many followers." Thus, both outer miracles of controlling natural forces and inner miracles of transforming loyalties served as signs of the authority of Pīr Shams, proving him to be the embodiment of supernatural knowledge and power.

What makes the esoteric knowledge of which Isma'ilis regard themselves as custodians miraculous or supernatural is that it discloses the origin and the end of creation, including the fate of human beings. According to one tradition, the Prophet inquired about the welfare of a visitor named Hārithah, who answered, "I live as a true believer." When Muhammad pressed him to explain, Hārithah answered that he had turned from the world. "It seems as if I am gazing at the Throne of my Lord and the account has been settled, and as if I am gazing at the people of paradise who are visiting each other in heaven, and as if I hear the cry of the people of hell in the fire." This *hadīth* continues, "Then the Prophet of God said, 'This is a servant whose heart God has illuminated.'"[64] This vision of life after death is one example of Shiite teaching that "religion contains truths and verities above the common comprehension of man."[65] In religious traditions the beginning and end of the world are subjects of divine revelation since neither can be deduced from any known state of the world. As in heavenly visions in Jewish and Christian apocalypses, the human mind must be informed of primordial conditions either preceding or following the order of nature by which all our human experience and knowledge is shaped. Seeking knowledge of the beginning of the world is futile as long as we are limited by the established laws of the world, and the same is true of inquiring about the state of things after the universe ceases to exist. About such matters, we have literally no way of knowing; the question takes us beyond all reference points. Therefore, only revelation, illumining the human mind from a source beyond the limits of the physical universe, could provide information about the beginning and end of the world. Shiites claim that Imams have been so illumined— for Isma'ilis they are indwelt by divine light—and thus their knowledge is a miracle.

In our final example, we consider Twelver Shiites, the majority Muslims in the Islamic Republic of Iran today. They recognize as the Hidden Imam the twelfth in the line of Ali, Muhammad ibn al-Hasan al-'Askari, who disappeared at the age of five in the year 874. Twelvers believe that he went into occultation and selects representatives to guide believers until his reappearance as Mahdi on the Day of Judgment. The miracle of the Hidden Imam inspires Shiites living as a persecuted minority in most Muslim societies as a symbol of enduring divine protection. As Shiites interpret the history of the descendants of Muhammad, Sunni authorities sought to eradicate the line of Ali, beginning with his eldest son, Hasan, who had retired to Medina. While Sunnis insist that Hasan died in his sleep, all agree that Ali's youngest son, Husayn, was killed by Umayyad troops at Karbala in Iraq in 680. The anniversary of Husayn's death is a major Shiite religious holiday, called *Ashura*, during which Husayn's martyrdom is reenacted in a passion play. *Ashura* is observed on the tenth of Muharram (the first month in the Islamic calendar) with public memorial services. In some locales, the ritual includes self-laceration to identify with the suffering of Husayn.

The tenth of Muharram is also the date on which Twelvers believe the Hidden Imam will miraculously return to restore ideal Islamic society. Awaiting that transcendent event, Twelver Shiites believe that their leaders represent the Hidden Imam; the most honored among them are called "signs of God" (*ayatollahs*). We see again the parallel between living manifestations of divine truth and the sacred text of the Qur'an, every verse of which is also called a "sign." As descendants of Ali, Imams possess esoteric insight into the inner meaning of the Qur'an that Shiites believe no Sunni teacher could ever grasp. Thus for Shiites the designation of Imams cannot be left to human judgment because it is a gift of supernatural knowledge bestowed by God. Yet, as in other religious traditions, miracles are social acts and require witnesses to attest to their authenticity. While the miracle of the Imam's transformed consciousness is invisible, its effects appear to believers in the public forms of discipline and virtue. Their acknowledgment of the Imam's total conformity to divine will constitutes an essential element in their recognition of him as a "sign of God." That is, to call the Imam's knowledge a "miracle" involves social confirmation of his illumination as a transcendent event. He cannot declare himself to be a bearer of the "light of Muhammad"; that status must be ascribed to him by others who perceive his supernatural insight reflected in wisdom, compassion, and justice.

In Shiite tradition, knowledge of God is proved by submission to divine guidance and miracles are a sign of the Imam's authority to proclaim that guidance unerringly. In the tradition of Sufi saints, to which we now turn, mystical insight also produces miracles as signs of the authority available to all believers willing to develop their own intimate friendship with God.

Sufi Saint: Miracles by "Friends of God"

In Islam any believer can in principle become a saint, a holy man or woman through whom God's blessings (*barakat*) may flow to others in the form of miraculous healing or knowledge. Yet God chooses the instruments of *baraka* by his sovereign and mysterious wisdom, so no one should presume to claim that status and power for oneself. Such extraordinary persons are called "friends of God" (*awliyā'*; singular *walī*). Prophets and Imams also perform miracles as signs of their divine authority, and so are recognized as *awliyā'*, but this section focuses on the meaning assigned to the wonders of Sufi saints. Their name comes from the Arabic word for wool and refers to the coarse garments worn by the early Sufis, perhaps in imitation of Christian hermits in Syria. The Sufi movement began as a protest against Islamic rulers whom Sufis saw as more interested in gaining and keeping political power in this world than in seeking a closer union with God. So while they are often referred to as Muslim mystics, Sufis are not other-worldly. They have been very engaged in the affairs of this world and, as our opening story in this chapter demonstrates, the miraculous powers of their shaykhs often challenged established authorities.

As we have seen, Roman Catholic tradition developed strict procedures for identifying saints, but in Muslim communities there is no centralized regulation of the process of declaring someone a saint. That recognition is often the result of local veneration, inspired by the saints' miracles or benefits received by those who pray at their tombs. As in other traditions, Islamic sainthood is socially constructed. In his study of Sufis in modern Pakistan, the scholar of religion, Robert Rozehnal, describes the process this way: "sainthood is an ascribed status. It is negotiated in public discourse *before* it is inscribed in sacred biographies, assimilated within institutional structures, and narrated in story-telling networks. To a large extent, a spiritual leader's reputation depends on the response of her/his followers."[66] Without followers who are transformed by the leader's wisdom or power, there is no community of interpretation in which the saint's divine authority is acknowledged, remembered, and transmitted. Miracle stories are a central element in that process. As Renard notes, "Because Friends stand between humankind and God they often function as mediators or intercessors. Wielding the gift of marvels, Friends perform countless deeds that benefit and astonish their constituencies, including healing and managing otherwise untamed elements of nature."[67] As in Christian tradition, ascription of miracles to Islamic saints was the result of perceptions of the divine powers of *awliyā'* in which local enthusiasm for holy men and women often overruled official regulation of miracle claims.

A story from the life of al-Hallāj illustrates the saint's relationship with his followers in which he met their needs by miraculous provision.

> On a desert sojourn, Hallāj and four hundred companions had nothing to eat. The crowd asked the shaykh for a lamb's head, whereupon he produced a roast head for each, along with two loaves of bread. When the people asked for ripe dates, Hallāj instructed them to throw him heavenward, and a shower of dates came down. Thereafter, every thorn bush Hallāj leaned upon produced ripe dates.[68]

In a familiar pattern of later miracles replicating earlier ones in a tradition, Hallāj provided food for his companions as Muhammad supplied his troops with water. Stories of producing or multiplying supplies of food are common in many religious traditions and constitute signs of the miracle worker's drawing upon divine creative power. What is important in this story is that the miracle benefitted witnesses whose response of wonder and gratitude (assumed but unrecorded) constituted the social ground for acknowledging Hallāj as a saint. That response, in turn, was strengthened by their prior conviction of his selfless devotion to the divine will.

The theologian ʿAlī ibn ʿUthmān Hujwīrī (d. 1072) introduced his analysis of miracles of Sufi saints by insisting that "only individuals whose lives are consonant with Revealed Law are capable of performing 'supernatural' acts and that such deeds testify to the individual's authenticity."[69] That is, miracles function as signs of divine authority only when linked to a saint's moral perfection, as already established in the judgment of the witnesses. The social confirmation of any miracle, then, is the result of a specific history between a saint and his or her companions. While saints were made through local negotiations, it was common for those processes to involve exhibitions of moral virtue by saints. From that nearly universal connection believers draw confidence in the saint's power and benevolence—what Rozehnal calls "the dual nature of sainthood. The Friend of God combines piety and sanctity with power and authority. Though he lives, works, and worships in the world, the Sufi saint is unbound from the laws of nature by virtue of his intimacy with God."[70]

That intimacy empowers the saint to exercise divine authority over human and natural forces. While there are accounts of saints performing preternatural acts, such as walking on water,[71] flying through air, and instantaneously translocating across great distances, it is common for saints themselves to emphasize the more important struggle, what Muhammad called the "greater jihad," to overcome pride and submit without qualification to God's will. A miracle story from the life of the saint Rābiʿa al-ʿAdawīya (d. 801) of the Iraqi port of Basra makes the point. One day, when she and another renowned mystic, Hasan, were walking by a river, he cast his prayer mat on the water and called upon Rābiʿa to pray with him mid-stream. Instead, Rābiʿa flung her mat into the air and sprang onto it—a feat impossible for the crestfallen Hasan, who had not yet attained the necessary degree of spiritual advancement. "Hasan," said Rābiʿa, "that which you did, a fish can do . . . and that which I did, a fly can do. The real work (for the saints of God) lies beyond both of these and it is necessary to occupy ourselves with the real work."[72] That "real work" was, in Rābiʿa's mind, the effort to know God directly and exclusively, with no other motive than pure love.

One test of Rābiʿa's unconditional reliance on God came during a trip to Mecca when her donkey suddenly died. Waving aside her companions' offer to carry her few belongings for her, the saint waited in the desert in utter dependence on God. Then, in Renard's retelling, "She asks God why he, a king, is so harsh to a woman with so few resources. After all, God called her on this pilgrimage. The donkey immediately rises, and she continues the journey."[73] Her biographer, Farīd ad-Dīn ʿAttār (d. 1220), then added that someone reported seeing the donkey for sale in the market, adding the element of social confirmation necessary in miracle stories. The story added to the impression of Rābiʿa's profound piety, even as it served as a narrative commentary on the exhortation of the Qur'an to trust in God alone.

In another story Hasan and friends visited Rābiʿa at a time when she had no lamp. "Rābiʿa blew upon the tips of her fingers, and throughout that night, until daylight came, her fingers gave forth light like a lamp, and they sat until morning in the illumination."[74] Rābiʿa's glowing fingers were a sign of her authority to reflect the primal light of divine knowledge and to be herself a source of enlightenment by interpreting the hidden meaning of the Qur'an otherwise veiled from human understanding.

On occasion transcendent insight into the true nature of reality empowers the saint to perform outer miracles as well, following the Sufi maxim, "Whosoever obeys God completely, everything created is bound to obey him."[75] The Sufi master Jalal al-Dīn Rūmī demonstrated that power in responding to the question whether human beings are integrated as organisms by the blood in their veins or by the mercy of God alone. Physicians of the time maintained that blood was the vital element since, if it were drained, the body would die. In defense of the belief that God alone sustains life, Rūmī ordered a blood-letter to draw his blood until it ran yellow, nearly depleted, far past the point where humans would normally die. The physicians were forced to acknowledge God's grace was the sole condition of human existence. Rūmī, the story concludes, "went to his bath; and was afterward joined in the chanting and singing of mystical verses, as if nothing unusual had occurred."[76] In this act of utter confidence Rūmī risked his life in order to demonstrate the truth of prophetic revelation and, thereby, to confirm his authority to declare that all existence depends upon divine power.

Rūmī also demonstrated that truth by using miraculous power to collapse space and time in an event traditional sources call "folding the earth."[77] In the story Rūmī, also known by the honorific *Maulana* ("our Master"), asked a merchant on his way to Istanbul to convey greetings to a Christian monk there. On arrival the merchant located the monk "in profound contemplation with a halo of righteousness around him." Looking about the cloister, the merchant was astonished to see Rūmī, wearing the same clothes and bearing the same expression he had when the merchant left him. The merchant fell unconscious with astonishment. When he awoke the monk told him that if he could "become aware of the mysteries of the 'free' he would become higher in spiritual level." The monk then asked him to send greetings to Rūmī. Returning home, as he approached the master, Rūmī said, "Look, and you will see wonder!" The merchant glanced at a corner of the room and there sat the monk from Istanbul. The story concludes: "The merchant tore his clothes in the ecstasy of the whole scene for the thing had passed all human comprehension."[78]

This glimpse into the relativity of time and space was a fragmentary grasp of the hidden meaning of reality veiled by the seeming inflexibility of natural laws. Behind the façade of immutable order, the material world is subject to the power of spirit, supremely exercised by God but also available to saints. This miracle of translocation was a transcendent event, evoking stupor in the witness, and signifying the divine authority of the one who performed it. The meaning of the miracle is that those who dissolve their egos in contemplation of divine unity, whether Muslim or Christian, are indistinguishable on the plane of ordinary perception.

As in other traditions, however, miracles also serve a polemical role of confirming the truth of Islam over other religious viewpoints. Schimmel recounts the story of Abu'l-Adyan in the tenth century, who argued with a Zoroastrian priest that fire had no inherent, much less sacred, reality because it burned only by divine permission. The Sufi master then passed through a blazing pyre unhurt to establish the point that "there is no real causality, but that God gives or withholds the capacities of the elements to which mankind is accustomed: He creates these qualities and capacities anew every moment."[79] The Zoroastrian was persuaded that Abu'l-Adyan's version of Islamic metaphysics was correct. At the same time, the miracle confirmed the Sufi's authority as *walī Allāh*, friend of God, who enjoyed special protection from danger. What the British historian, Josef Meri, said of saints in medieval Syria is true of "friends of God" in many other settings: "They were God's agents on earth."[80]

Nevertheless, Muslim wonder workers, following the example of Muhammad, often regard miracles as obstacles to spiritual progress. Rābi'a, for example, explained her reluctance to receive visitors as fear that people would later concoct stories of miraculous events associated with her. The Sufi master Bāyazīd al-Bistāmī (d. 875), when asked by an old woman to help her carry a bag of flour, summoned a lion to bear the burden because he was too weak to do so. But when he asked the woman what she would tell her friends about the incident, she replied that she would report meeting a "nasty show-off." As Renard retells the story:

> Taken aback, Bāyazīd admits that his treatment of the lion was unkind and that his desire to have people think that the lion followed his commands was indeed arrogant. From that day on, Bāyazīd asks God to offer a special sign to show his presence in every marvel. Thereafter, God sends down a light inscribed with the names of five witnessing prophets (Muhammad, Noah, Abraham, Moses, and Jesus) each time Bāyazīd performs a marvel, until at length the Friend no longer needs confirmation.[81]

In another cautionary tale, a variation on similar stories in other traditions, Bāyazīd approached the Tigris River and its waters parted for him. He preferred, however, to pay a ferryman to take him across, implying that he was unwilling to squander miraculous power for such a trivial purpose. In both incidents the saint is keenly aware of the temptation miraculous powers pose to one who seeks freedom from worldly concerns. Schimmel remarks that this view is "typical of the sober, high-ranking mystics throughout history; they regard interest in miracles as one of the three 'veils' that can cover the hearts of the elect (the two others being too much attention to works of obedience and hope for heavenly reward)."[82] Renard notes that saints often caution their disciples not to be impressed by miraculous powers, remembering that Satan can fly through the air as well. "The dawning of faith in the heart is a far more important marvel."[83]

Despite that elevated sentiment, ordinary Muslims, like believers in other traditions, pray for miracles to meet primary human needs for food, protection, justice, and compassion. When natural resources are scarce and appeals to wealthy neighbors are futile, when one's beliefs are shaped by profound confidence in one God who brings all things out of nothing and disposes the fate of every being, and when one acknowledges divine gifts in the "friends of God," both living and dead, then no degree of official disapproval or spiritual snobbery can prevent believers from crying to heaven for supernatural relief. At such times, one may take comfort in the *hadīth* that attributes to Muhammad these words: "He who does not ask Allah (for favors) Allah is annoyed with him."[84] If God is gracious and merciful, then surely human need is an opportunity for him to demonstrate those virtues in events of transcendent power. But it is precisely that form of religious reasoning that has been criticized and chastened by voices of faithful dissent to belief in miracles from nearly the beginning of Islamic tradition.

Dissent: Rationalist and Revolutionary Critics

In Islamic tradition, as in other traditions we have considered, belief in miracles has been criticized on both rational and ethical grounds. Muslims committed to the strongest version of *tawhīd* (unity) of God maintain that the order of creation is sustained by the immutable divine will; therefore, natural laws are invulnerable to suspension or modification by human insight or virtue. Only God could produce a miracle, and for the majority school of Muslims, the Sunnis, such an extraordinary event happened only once: in the revelation of the Qur'an to Muhammad. In that final disclosure of divine will for personal and social life, they argue, humanity has all the direction and motivation needed to establish peace and justice in the earth, the restoration of universal *salaam* that God intends us to achieve through our own reason, moral determination, and compassion—without reliance on supernatural assistance. Further, where there is resistance to the divine will, it may be necessary for the faithful to engage in militant action against enemies of the faith, in what the Prophet called the "lesser *jihad*" of armed defense of Islam. We will consider briefly both rationalist and revolutionary objections to belief in miracles as the intervention of transcendent power into the order of nature and the drama of history.

A recurrent theme of this book is that the use of reason to reflect critically on religious belief is not exclusively a modern concern. In particular, we have found ancient voices of dissent to belief in miracles in other traditions, and we hear them in the early traditions of Islam. One group of faithful dissenters were the *Mu'tazilites*, who flourished in the ninth century in Iraq. Their name means "those who stand aloof" because they refused to take sides in the question of whether a "grave sinner" should be expelled from the Muslim community; but they called themselves "the people of (divine) justice and unity," indicating their conviction that God's revealed will supported human freedom and was coherent with human reason. "They rejected the image of an all-powerful divinity who arbitrarily and unpredictably determined good and evil, and instead declared that a just God could command only that which is just and good."[85] Further, God could reveal only what was consistent with reason; thus it would be irrational, they argued, to suppose that the eternal God would act in time. They rejected miracle stories, understood as historical effects of divine agency, as anthropomorphic representations of God and, as such, idolatrous. To enforce their viewpoint as normative, the Mu'tazilites initiated a political movement, requiring an oath of loyalty to their imperial patron, Caliph al-Ma'mun (813–833). Finally, in Denny's words, "its abuses were so great and its ideas so unacceptable to grass-roots Muslim religious consciousness that it was finally toppled and driven into hiding as a continuing but minority school of thought with a wide variety of styles and emphases."[86]

Among those enduring emphases is the insistence that reason and revelation are complementary, a principle of religious understanding they shared with Jewish and Christian thinkers who were likewise influenced by the ideal of systematic and comprehensive thought pursued by Greek philosophers. The Mu'tazilites' quest for a coherent understanding of nature and history was based on their primary conviction that the eternal unity of God was maintained in every aspect of creation; therefore, no event could constitute what the Sufis called *khāriq ul-'āda*, "what tears the custom (of God)." Specifically, that means no human in a body of flesh and blood could traverse great distances instantaneously or rise into the heavens. Thus, Mu'tazilites interpreted the Night Journey and Ascent of Muhammad as "a vision and admitted only of the possibility of a spiritual journey,"[87] whereas most other Muslims interpreted the events as undertaken by the Prophet in his perfected body. For Mu'tazilites the admission of miracles was tantamount to the denial of divine unity by breaking the order of nature and the harmony of reason and revelation.

The most controversial Mu'tazilite application of rationalist method in theology was their argument that "the Qur'an was created since, if it were eternal, it would exist with God as though it were another eternal thing, and this would constitute a second God, and this multiplication of eternal things runs the risk of ending in polytheism."[88] The Mu'tazilites were opposed by a rival school of thinkers called Ash'arites, who maintained that the Qur'an was uncreated and, therefore, its revealing to Muhammad was a transcendent event: a miracle that could not be grasped by human reason. Ash'arites cited passages in the Qur'an (13.39 and 85.22) that mention an eternal archetype of the revealed Qur'an in heaven.[89] The Ash'arite view won the day among ordinary believers, who were concerned that the Mu'tazilite position compromised the divine nature of the Qur'an. As we shall see, the same concerns surface today about Islamic rationalists who seek to interpret the Qur'an as a discursive production, relative to its historical context and shorn of miracles.

Support for the Mu'tazilite movement was grounded in a strong Sunni disposition to insist, in the words of the historian Massimo Campanini, that "Islam is in fact a religion without mystery, especially as regards God." While that claim may seem odd at first glance, it is a way of asserting that God has made clear, in the order of creation, the text of the Qur'an, and the person of the Prophet his moral will for humanity. Apart from that guidance, humans do not need to know anything else about God. Campanini contrasts the Sunni position with the Christian claim to more extensive understanding of the divine nature: "There is nothing to be revealed about God, no incarnation, no Trinity, no sacrament. The openness of God is guaranteed by the fact that the human mind is able to apply itself to science and nature. Hasan Hanafi (b. 1935) said that it is useless to speculate on the essence of God; the important thing is to struggle for the progress and liberation of humanity. So there is no room for the miracle that surprises and stupefies the naive, and conditions and distorts faith."[90] The rejection of miracles from this viewpoint is a necessary condition for the development of mature faith.

Islamic thinkers of the late nineteenth and early twentieth centuries continued the rationalist critique of belief in miracles, emphasizing the consonance of reason and nature. The modernist reformer in India, Sayyid Ahmad Khan (1817–1898), argued that Islam was entirely compatible with modern science and that stories of miracles in the Qur'an and *hadīth* should be interpreted metaphorically or allegorically. "I do not deny the possibility of miracles because they are against reason," he wrote, "but because the Qur'an does not support the happening of events or occurrences that are against the laws of nature or violate the usual course of things."[91] Rashīd Ridā (d. 1935), a leading figure in the *Salafiyya* ("pious ancestors") movement of reform that called for applying Islamic principles to the totality of life, rejected any *hadīth* that recorded miracles associated with the Prophet because those stories "violate a key element of *salafi* dogma—that Muhammad's only miracle was the Qur'an." Other reformers, less willing to attack directly such popular beliefs, argued that "the time of miracles (*mu'jizā*) is finite. Muhammad brought in the epoch of reason. Miracles were necessary at the time of the infancy of humanity."[92] This view recalls the Protestant notion of a limited age of miracles and reflects an evolutionary view of history reminiscent of Lessing's "education of the human race." Consequently, these Islamic reformers condemned "all superstitions such as . . . the cult of saints, as aspects of popular religiosity."[93]

The rejection of miracles as the fantasies of the masses went along with a generally more disciplined form of Islamic thought and practice in the rigorously conservative movement led by Muhammad Ibn 'Abd al-Wahhāb (1703–1792). The Wahhābīs recognized the legal decisions made in the first three centuries of Islamic tradition as normative and rejected all ideas and practices that deviated from them as heresy. As they read the tradition, veneration of Sufi saints or Shiite claims of divine revelation were particularly offensive and they set themselves fiercely against both. As Denny notes, "the early Wahhābīs did succeed in razing any mosques, shrines, and tombs that were in any way dedicated to the memory or centered in the ongoing cult of [friends of God]."[94] Inasmuch as the disclosing of the Qur'an to Muhammad is the unique transcendent event that provides the final knowledge of God, for Wahhābīs all subsequent reflection on the divine will must conform to it, as interpreted in the early tradition. Thus, no contemporary miracle could authorize the slightest deviation from that interpretation. On the basis of such thinking, the Wahhābīs resist innovation, including claims of miracles, in order to preserve tradition in the form of a fixed interpretation of the Qur'an.

While modern liberal Islamic thinkers agree with conservatives in rejecting miracles, their basis for doing so is entirely different. They argue that the Qur'an must always be re-interpreted in light of the discoveries of reason and the conditions of history. Thus, no interpretation could capture divine truth in its immutable entirety, and no particular regime of meaning could be universal or final. An example of such a thinker is Mohammed Arkoun, emeritus professor of the Sorbonne, born in Algeria, who defends a dynamic view of revelation that requires new interpretations as historical conditions change. What Arkoun calls the "liberating vista of revelation" opens a horizon on which new understandings of divine presence and action appear.[95] By contrast, closed canons of sacred texts and putatively infallible interpretations of divine truth narrow religious vision and inevitably require the imposition of power to retain their place of privilege (a need that even rationalists like the Muʿtazilites felt compelled to satisfy).

Arkoun sees such a process at work in Islamic history when the third caliph ʿUthman selected the authoritative text of the Qur'an and then destroyed all other compilations of the Prophet's recitations. The establishment of the fixed text, in Arkoun's judgment, resulted in the persistent Muslim resistance to applying historical critical methods to the Qur'an. He attributes that resistance to the political interest in appealing to the Qur'an as absolute authority in the legitimation of new states and to the psychological appeal of identifying the written Qur'an with the infallible Word of God. "The written Qur'an thus has become identified with the Qur'anic discourse or the Qur'an as it was recited, which is itself the direct emanation of the Archetype of the Book."[96] As a modern thinker, committed to the historical origin and cultural shaping of all forms of discourse, Arkoun rejects this absolutist view of the Qur'an. The distinction between eternal divine knowledge, ultimately unknown to humans, and contingent historical speech, intelligible only as interpreted, is crucial to Arkoun's analysis. The Qur'an as recitation in Arabic during the seventh century in the politically charged settings of Mecca and Medina was not the direct disclosure of immutable truth, but the revelation of divine guidance mediated by the Prophet and transmitted in the Book. That is, the ineffable Word of God, symbolized as "Mother of the Book," comes to the reader through the triple mediation of the person of Muhammad, the Arabic language, and the official compilation of Qur'anic verses by 'Uthman.

Arkoun believes it would be irresponsible for a modern thinker not to acknowledge that historical process and subject its various elements to critical analysis. What he assumes, like his counterparts in Western biblical criticism, is that the religious value of the text becomes clearer as it is freed from fixed and outmoded meanings and allowed to produce "the psychological operations that the Qur'an locates in the heart," what we have called the transformative response of readers who enter imaginatively into the narrative world of the text. As Rippin observes, Arkoun is "asking questions not of 'what really happened' (in the formulation of the discipline of history) but of how it is that certain ideas came to be a part of the social imagination and of the role that ideas play in the construction of reality for society."[97] For Arkoun the question whether any miracle, including the revelation of the Qur'an, was a transcendent event—an intrusion of divine agency into natural order—is not the right question to ask. As historical beings we can only inquire into how the idea of miracle shaped and reflected the social world in which it functioned as part of daily discourse. The result of that inquiry increases our understanding of the historical conditions in which Islam arose and, simultaneously, frees contemporary Muslims to formulate the "meaning" of the Qur'an, including its miracle stories, for themselves.

While Arkoun acknowledges that "ancient testimony contains aspirations toward the transcendence of social and cultural context," he thinks secular conditions of modern life have rendered such aspirations impotent or ludicrous. "The experience of the divine," he writes, "can no longer seek support in symbolic capital, a sense of miracle, a mythical universe, and a capacity for bewitchment. All such assets have been neatly destroyed not only by our surroundings of concrete, factories, and public housing but by a replacement myth of secular and republican origin characteristic of our current societies."[98] For Arkoun the loss of "a sense of miracle" is one result of the general collapse of confidence in the unchanging meaning of Qur'anic discourse. Modern Muslims no longer inhabit a narrative world in which God is present, revealing divine knowledge, extending healing power, or turning the course of battle. The fact that even the language of revelation is heard within the flux of history requires readers to accept responsibility for discerning (or creating) its meaning for their individual lives. The implication of Arkoun's analysis is that the Word of God *in itself* may be immutable, but *as revealed* it must be interpreted in a process as individuated as each believer's private relationship to God and as malleable as shifting historical circumstances. The former world of sacred narrative, in which miracles provided assurance of the authority of Imams and saints to provide unerring guidance, has passed away. We must accept that inevitable conclusion of reason and be prepared for the profound responsibility that is now ours.

One Islamic revolutionary thinker willing to accept that responsibility was Sayyid Qutb (1906–1966), an Egyptian radical whose challenges to the piety and morality of ruling authorities led to his execution. Influenced by the Pakistani reformer, Sayyid Abul A'la Maududi (1903–1979), Qutb interpreted the Qur'an as practical, not theoretical: "The doctrine is essentially praxis, practical action in order to further the realization of a new moral, social and political order."[99] He emphasized the revolutionary power of the revelation as the divine blueprint for ideal human society. The utopian vision of the Qur'an should, in this interpretation, mobilize Muslims to enact the divine plan. Conceiving of Islam as a movement toward the unrealized goal, rather than as a static legal and social order, these radical thinkers emphasize human responsibility. They argue that God revealed his will and sustains dedicated effort (*jihad*) to realize it; further divine assistance should not be desired or expected.

Qutb deduced from the foundational belief in the unity of God that natural, personal, and social orders are governed by divine will. For him that doctrine requires humans to accept their place within nature and not seek power to transcend it: "the task of living beings is not to contend with Nature, for they have grown up in her bosom, and she and they together form a part of the single universe which proceeds from the single will."[100] Within the system of creation, humans alone are invested with the power of self-determination: "[God] chose that his divinely ordained path for human life should be realized through human exertions, within the limits of human capacities."[101] Only by taking full responsibility for enacting the divine will within political and social order can a Muslim attain personal authenticity. Where existing governments prevent humans from choosing whether or not to obey the commands of the Qur'an, they must be cleared away, by violence if necessary. In that *jihad*, radical reformers may rely on divine support, as Muhammad and his companions did in the establishment of the first Islamic city; but they should not count on miraculous intervention. Even the first generation of Muslims "had no expectations during the course of this life, because they knew the decision between the Truth and falsehood would be made in the Hereafter."[102] For Qutb, the test of authentic faith is whether one's success is achieved within the limits of human capacities, while respecting divine sovereignty that determines the outcome of all efforts to realize the divine will on earth.

Summary

Miracles in Islamic tradition serve as signs of divine authority, interpreted as such by the community of believers who ascribe events of transcendent power to prophets, Imams, and saints. For many Muslims the only miracle in the present age was the revelation of the inimitable Qur'an to the illiterate Prophet Muhammad. As the final revelation of divine guidance to humanity, Sunnis believe that the Qur'an is the decisive intervention of God in history. Miracles associated with the life of Muhammad are signs of his divine authority and of his perfection in both body and spirit. For Sunnis, however, the significance of those signs is confined to the founding events of the Muslim community. For Shiites, miracles continue to have meaning as signs of authority invested in their Imams as guardians of the esoteric meaning of the Qur'an entrusted to Ali and transmitted through the spiritual lineage of his family. The power of that knowledge enabled Shiite leaders to perform miracles, including healing, resuscitation, translocation, and telepathic insight. In the mystic tradition of Sufism, miracles are ascribed to saints, whose authority is signified by their transcendent powers, such as levitation, healing, and translocation. Among Shiite and Sufi miracle workers, however, there is a common concern that popular enthusiasm for wonders poses an obstacle to spiritual development. Finally, despite the persistence of miracle stories in all branches of Islamic tradition, rationalists object to belief in miracles on the ground that natural order reflects the immutable will of God and revolutionaries criticize hope for miracles as an illusory interruption of the earnest and self-sacrificing effort required to defeat oppressive governments and restore human autonomy under perfect obedience to the will of God. In their view, focused effort on earth must not be distracted by desperate glances toward heaven.

Afterword

The meanings of miracles in the five religious traditions we have considered are derived from their role as signs of transcendent reality. The narratives that recount these miraculous events represent worlds in which human life is transformed by power and wisdom from "elsewhere" than the world shaped by conventional perception and expectation. Miracle stories give dramatic form to what believers could expect to happen if their belief in the transcendent were true. In the final analysis, then, does religious faith require belief in miracles as a condition of its credibility?

In light of the internal dissent to miracles each tradition generates, it might seem the answer is *no*. Revisionary critics offer alternative interpretations of miracle stories from those recorded in founding scriptures to those told about founders and leaders, interpretations that affirm the primary values of each tradition while denying the historical veracity of miracles. Consider these examples: Hindu commitment to the fundamental fairness of the universe, articulated in the doctrine of karma, holds firm even if no yogi ever exercised paranormal powers. Jewish faith in the justice of God and the integrity of his covenant continues despite the absence of miraculous deliverance from Nazi genocide. Buddhist belief in the ultimate emptiness of things as the refuge from fear and suffering persists even when hope in the wondrous acts of Bodhisattvas fades. Christian commitment to follow Jesus's example of compassionate sacrifice does not waver even when the resurrection of Christ is understood as a symbol of the enduring power of love rather than a literal re-embodiment. Islam remains firmly based on the moral guidance of the Qur'an as the way to salvation in the Day of Judgment even when the Night Journey of Muhammad is interpreted as an allegory of mystic ascent to unity with God. But note that, in each tradition, religious critics replace miracles with other signifiers of transcendence, such as metaphysical insight or moral wisdom.

The focus of this book has been on those who believe that miracles *really* happen. We have seen that such events must be interpreted within broader systems of meaning in order to confirm belief in transcendent reality. Many affirm belief in miracles in the face of sneering dismissals by secular intellectuals, domesticated revisions by idealistic moralists, accusative exhortations by impatient reformers and revolutionaries, scoldings about childish fantasies by psychological analysts, and even this well-intentioned re-reading of traditional stories as "transformative narratives" (that gently sets aside the question of historicity). Nevertheless, believers persist in retelling the old stories—and in adding new ones, since gurus, rebbes, bodhisattvas, saints, and Imams have not disappeared from the scene. Religious communities continue to ascribe wondrous power, transcendent wisdom, and divine virtue to men and women. These are miracle workers in our midst, subjects of new stories based on old patterns: narratives of healing, raising the dead, mastery over natural forces, and communicating with animals.

The popular enthusiasm for miracles in every tradition we have considered is so potent a personal and social force that established authorities devote much energy and ingenuity to constraining it where possible and co-opting it where necessary. The degree of effort put forth to control and regulate miracle claims is one indication of the force of the *idea* of transcendent power, let alone its exercise, to disrupt existing arrangements of social order. That effect is, of course, precisely why so many people tell and retell miracle stories. They are signs that nothing on earth must remain exactly as it is; everything can be different, renewed, restored, made right—if not in this life, then in another domain of reality now visible only to the eye of faith.

For those able and willing to inhabit the worlds their narratives construct, miracle stories confirm that faith by demonstrating its hope is not an illusion. Once the settled order of things is broken, either disrupted from beyond the reach of its systematizing power or imploded from within by the force of liberated mind, the illusion of its permanence and immutability is shattered. Miracle stories sustain the hope that every routine can be disrupted and radically new possibilities can be realized. The system that imprisons and constricts human life may be undeniable addiction, crippling disease, paralyzing depression, social persecution, or political tyranny. For religious believers, stories of the defeat of such evils by miracle workers wielding transcendent power keep hope alive under soul-sapping oppression.

Another value of miracle stories is that they evoke what Descartes called the "primitive passion" of wonder: a wide-eyed attention to everything that presents itself for consideration, a receptive hospitality to the new, the different, the other—"a sudden surprise of the soul." Wonder is the disposition every miracle story seeks to evoke in its implied reader or listener. A miracle story invites us to enter a world in which transcendent power illumines, liberates, saves, and heals—and to consider, in a state of wonder, that such events are not impossible in our world. At the very least, miracle stories nurture in their audiences openness to being astounded, willingness to entertain novelty, and freedom from the prescriptive view of reality composed by their own experience, habits, and cultural consensus. Miracle stories challenge established views of what is possible and impossible, and in so doing shatter the modern illusion that scientific constructions of reality are absolute.

We come back to the question: does religious faith require belief in miracles? While I am sympathetic to some of the faithful dissenters on this question, I am inclined to answer *yes*. Since practically every page of this book runs the risk of over-simplification, let me not shrink from it here. If religion is distinguished from other cultural activities, the mark of distinction is belief in what we have been calling *transcendence*. This final reflection seems perhaps unsophisticated, but I find it irresistible: if religion offers human beings anything other than what is already achieved in politics, art, literature, ethics, psychology, and social order, then that added value must somehow derive from the transcendent. Even if all that religion contributes is an interpretive overlay that enables believers to critique other cultural activities, that standard requires a point of view from "elsewhere" to distinguish it from that of astute and morally sensitive humanists.

The naturalist critic of religion, Russell McCutcheon, takes as a "useful research assumption" that "some human behaviors can be described as being religious insomuch as people ascribe motivations or goals to their actions and beliefs that take into account, for instance, nonempirical beings or states of existence."[1] Because McCutcheon rejects claims that cannot be tested by empirical means, he denies that religion has any distinctive content. The alternative seems fairly stark: *either* there is transcendent reality and miracles (or other events) are signs of its presence *or* transcendence is an empty category and religious claims are fraudulent. Yes, some believers regard themselves as "spiritual" because they feel moved by awe or inspired to virtue or filled with confidence by a power beyond their own. Yet, as modern thinkers, they insist that miracles are impossible because scientific accounts of reality leave no room for the transcendent. As I have tried to show, however, transferring the site of radical transformation from public events to private dispositions does not escape the question of the transcendent. Buddha's insight and Jesus's healings alike require transcendent sources because they both disrupt the order and transgress the limits of customary reality.

Religious faith that does not affirm access to power and wisdom from "elsewhere" than human creativity or the system of nature seems hardly worth the exclusive devotion, rigorous discipline, and self-denying sacrifice most religious traditions require. It is not surprising that those who enthusiastically embrace religion today are largely those for whom miracles signify possibilities that exceed the limits of natural resources, including human ingenuity and good will. That is the primary meaning of miracles in world religions: as signs of transcendence.

Whether or not one perceives this world as intersected by miraculous power is not finally a difference that can be resolved by reasonable debate—for each side represents a foundational commitment to what is, and what is not, possible for human beings. As the Polish philosopher Leszek Kołakowski wrote in another context, "This is not a confrontation of metaphysical doctrines of which the rightness or wrongness could be ascertained by logically sound arguments, but rather the expression of two opposite kinds of experience, both of which may be called mystical insofar as the ultimate truth about the world is touched (and not just asserted) in them."[2] How you assess the meanings of miracles set out in this book, then, may depend on what kind of mystic you are.

Notes

PREFACE

1. For one example, see William E. Paden, *Religious Worlds: The Comparative Study of Religion* (Boston: Beacon Press, 1994).

2. Leszek Kołakowski finds this idea central to religion: "The crucial insight we find in religious experience, repeatedly recurring in various sacred books, may be summed up in one single word: alibi—elsewhere" [*Metaphysical Horror* (Oxford: Basil Blackwell, 1988), 28].

3. *Transcendence* is a contested category in religious thought, and I am using it here to indicate "what lies beyond," however that is construed in the religious traditions we are considering. For current discussion of the term, see the essays in *Transcendence and Beyond: A Postmodern Inquiry*, edited by John D. Caputo and Michael J. Scanlon (Bloomington: Indiana University Press, 2007).

4. Alfred North Whitehead, *Process and Reality: An Essay in Cosmology* (1929), edited by David Ray Griffin and Donald W. Sherburne (New York: Free Press, 1978), 244.

5. Lenworth M. Jacobs, Karyl Burns, Barbara Bennet Jacobs, "Views of the Public and Trauma Professionals on Death and Dying from Injuries," *Archives of Surgery* 143:8 (August 2008), 730–735.

6. Charlotte J. Martin argues this point eloquently in *Dynamics of Hope: Eternal Life and Daily Christian Living* (Collegeville. MN: Liturgical Press, 2002).

CHAPTER 1

1. William James, *The Varieties of Religious Experience: A Study in Human Nature* (New York: Longmans, Green, 1902, 1928), 518–519.

2. The inclusion of faithful dissent is one difference between this book and the fine survey by Kenneth L. Woodward, *The Book of Miracles: The Meaning of the Miracle Stories in Christianity, Judaism, Buddhism, Hinduism, and Islam* (New York: Simon & Schuster, 2000).

3. John Ciardi, *How Does a Poem Mean?* (Boston: Houghton Mifflin, 1959).

4. Wolfgang Iser, *The Implied Reader: Patterns of Communication in Prose Fiction from Bunyan to Beckett* (Baltimore: Johns Hopkins University Press, 1974), 282.

5. *The Implied Reader*, 284.

6. Richard H. Davis, ed., *Images, Miracles, and Authority in Asian Religious Traditions* (Boulder, CO: Westview Press, 1998), 5.

7. George Butte, an original narrative theorist, thoughtfully explores the reflexive state of modern consciousness in *I Know That You Know That I Know: Narrating Subjects from Moll Flanders to Marnie* (Columbus: Ohio State University Press, 2004).

8. "Miracles," *The Brill Dictionary of Religion*, edited by Kocku von Stuckrad (Leiden: Brill Publications, 2007), volume 3, 1233.

9. This sentence from Sam Harris is typical: "Religious faith represents so uncompromising a misuse of the power of our minds that it forms a kind of perverse, cultural singularity—a vanishing point beyond which rational discourse proves impossible" [*The End of Faith: Religion, Terror, and the Future of Reason* (New York: W. W. Norton, 2004), 25].

10. *End of Faith*, 110.

11. "Modern Power and the Reconfiguration of Religious Traditions," *Stanford Electronic Humanities Review* 5, 1 (1996). Posted online at http://www.stanford.edu/group/SHR/5-1/text/asad.html. Accessed 14 November 2007.

12. Talal Asad, *Genealogies of Religion: Discipline and Reasons of Power in Christianity and Islam* (Baltimore: Johns Hopkins University Press, 1993), 236.

13. Martin Marty and Scott Appleby, *The Power and the Glory: Fundamentalisms Project* (Chicago: University of Chicago Press, 1998), 34–35.

14. Corrine G. Dempsey, "Lessons in Miracles from Kerala, South India: Stories of Three 'Christian' Saints," *History of Religions* 39:2 (November 1999), 150–176.

15. Nicole Winfield, Associated Press, in *Chicago Sun Times* (14 March 2006).

16. Text is from *Present Procedure in Causes of Beatification and Canonization*, section 18, posted online at: http://www.vicariatusurbis.org/Beatificazione/Causaen.asp.

17. "Any solemn celebrations or panegyric speeches about Servants of God whose sanctity of life is still being legitimately examined are prohibited in Churches" (*Norms to be Observed in Inquiries by Bishops in the Causes of Saints*, 7 February 1983, section 36).

18. *Divinus Perfectionus Magister*, section 15.

19. *Divinus Perfectionus Magister*, section 12.

20. *Norms to be Observed in Inquiries by Bishops in the Causes of Saints*, section 21. a): "The Bishop or his delegate is to call some witnesses ex officio, who can contribute to completing the inquiry, if it be the case, *particularly if they are opposed to the cause*" (emphasis added).

21. Peter Brown, *The Cult of Saints: Its Rise and Function in Latin Christianity* (Chicago: University of Chicago Press, 1982), 9.

22. Michael Walzer, *Interpretation and Social Criticism* (Cambridge, MA: Harvard University Press, 1987), 39.

23. Thich Nhat Hanh, *The Heart of the Buddha's Teaching* (New York: Broadway Books, 1998), 162.

24. David Hume, "Of Miracles," *An Enquiry Concerning Human Understanding* (1748), section 10, part I.12, n. 23, in Tom L. Beauchamp, *An Enquiry Concerning Human Understanding: A Critical Edition* (New York: Oxford University Press, 2000), 87.

25. Robert J. Fogelin develops a forceful argument against the common reading of Hume's criticism of miracles as circular by pointing out that Hume allows for the possibility of testimony to a miracle claim establishing its veracity. What Hume asserts is that the testimony for any religious miracle has, as a matter of historical fact, never been strong enough to outweigh confidence in the uniform operation of natural laws. That assertion,

Fogelin insists, is empirical, not a priori [*A Defense of Hume on Miracles* (Princeton, NJ: Princeton University Press, 2003), 29].

26. "Of Miracles," part II.27. Flat statements like this give one pause in fully endorsing Fogelin's analysis. Hume recognized that, as an empiricist, he could not insist on the impossibility of miracles in general; but his antipathy toward religious enthusiasm was so profound that he simply assumed testimony to religious miracles will always be promoted by "the help of vanity and a heated imagination," and thus unreliable ("Of Miracles," part II.29).

27. "Of Miracles," part II.35.

28. "Of Miracles," part II.38. J. L. Mackie (1917–1981) sought to improve Hume's theory of testimony by arguing that multiple independent witnesses to a miracle constitute evidence more valid than Hume allowed although still, in Mackie's judgment, inadequate to override the probability that the alleged miracle had an unknown natural cause [*The Miracle of Theism* (New York: Oxford University Press, 1982)].

29. C. S. Lewis, *Miracles: A Preliminary Study* (New York: Macmillan, 1947), 19.

30. Richard Swinburne, *Miracles* (New York: Macmillan, 1989), 9.

31. Immanuel Kant, *Critique of Practical Reason* (1788), tr. L. W. Beck (Indianapolis: Bobbs-Merrill, 1956), 126–136.

32. The quotation is from Kant's *Lectures on Ethics*, 110. Most of the commentary in this section is based on Immanuel Kant, *Religion Within the Limits of Reason Alone* (1793), tr. T. M. Greene and H. M. Hudson (New York: Harper Torchbooks, 1960).

33. In *Training in Christianity* (1850), Kierkegaard invites readers to imagine themselves as "contemporary" with Christ, without the benefit of 1,800 years of accumulated evidence and tradition, and then face the decision whether to believe Christ is the "God-Man" or take offense at his claim. "The miracle can prove nothing; for if you do not believe that he is what he says he is, you deny the miracle. A miracle can make one attentive—now thou art in a state of tension, and all depends upon what thou dost choose, offence or faith. It is thy heart that must be revealed" [tr. Walter Lowrie (Princeton, NJ: Princeton University Press, 1967), 99].

34. Davis, *Images, Miracles, and Authority*, 4.

35. Davis, *Images, Miracles, and Authority*, 8.

36. Descartes, "Passions of the Soul," II.70, in *The Philosophical Writings of Descartes*, tr. J. Cottingham (Cambridge: Cambridge University Press, 1985), vol. 1, 353. Subsequent references will be enclosed in parentheses.

37. Mary-Jane Rubenstein observes that Martin Heidegger located the "beginning of thought" in wonder as a primal awareness of being itself, in contrast to calculative explanation of individual beings [*Strange Wonder: The Closure of Metaphysics and the Opening of Awe* (New York: Columbia University Press, 2008), 31].

38. Wendy Doniger, ed., *Merriam-Webster's Encyclopedia of World Religions* (1999), s.v.

39. Davis, *Images, Miracles, and Authority*, 9.

40. Jonathan Z. Smith, *Relating Religion: Essays in the Study of Religion* (Chicago: University of Chicago Press, 2004), 9, 64.

41. *Relating Religion*, 246.

42. Here I am following the lead set by Wendy Doniger in her argument that behind the visible web of contextual meanings of myths there is an "implied spider" at work, spinning stories from common human experience [*The Implied Spider: Politics and Theology in Myth* (New York: Columbia University Press, 1998), 60–64].

43. "Permanent Significance of Miracle," *Harvard Theological Review* 8, no. 3 (July 1915), 298–322.

44. Benedicta Ward, writing of Christian tradition, distinguishes between a miracle "as a wonder to be marveled at" and "as a sign to be explored and understood"—but acknowledges that these two views are "intertwined in all Christian consideration of the miraculous" ["Monks and Miracles" in John C. Cavadini, ed., *Miracles in Jewish and Christian Antiquity: Imagining Truth* (Notre Dame, IN: University of Notre Dame Press, 1999), 128, 135]. We shall see in this study that the movement from wonder to interpretation is typical of response to miracles in all traditions.

45. Michael D. Bailey, *Magic and Superstition in Europe: A Concise History from Antiquity to the Present* (New York: Rowman & Littlefield, 2007), 44.

46. "Islamic folklore has associated the jinn with fabled performances of magic" [Richard C. Martin, *Islamic Studies: A History of Religions Approach* (Upper Saddle River, NJ: Prentice-Hall, 1996), 101].

47. Barbara Stoler Miller, tr., *The Bhagavad-Gita: Krishna's Counsel in Time of War* (New York: Bantam Books, 1986), 7:14–15 [73].

48. "Permanent Significance of Miracle," 312.

49. Kenneth Woodward reports a tendency among contemporary religious people to understand miracles as "private rather than public events" and so cast their stories in the form of testimonials. As a result, "most modern miracle stories lack the cultural resonance, style, and structure of the classic stories" (*The Book of Miracles*, 365).

50. Shah Abdul Latif of Bhit, cited in Annemarie Schimmel, *Mystical Dimensions of Islam* (Chapel Hill: University of North Carolina Press, 1975), 213.

51. Linda Trinkaus Zagzebski points out that the probability value of a miracle claim "crucially depends upon background data," including prior belief "in a supernatural realm" or in a benevolent God that increases the likelihood of miracles [*Philosophy of Religion: An Historical Introduction* (Malden, MA: Blackwell, 2007), 221]. But many believers' experience provides background evidence that counts against miracles occurring and thus changes the calculus of probability that they will benefit from one directly. What is remarkable is that such low probability does not significantly discourage belief in miracles.

CHAPTER 2

1. *The Bhagavad-Gita: Krishna's Counsel in Time of War*, 10.41, tr. Barbara Stoler Miller (New York: Bantam Books, 1986), 95. Subsequent references to this translation will be placed in parentheses.

2. *Krishna: The Beautiful Legend of God, Śrīmad Bhāgavata Purāna, Book X*, tr. Edwin F. Bryant (London: Penguin Books, 2003), ix. Subsequent references will be placed in parentheses in the text.

3. *The Rig Veda: An Anthology*, tr. Wendy Doniger O'Flaherty (New York: Penguin Books, 1981), 137. Subsequent references will be placed in parentheses in the text.

4. *Rig Veda*, 132.

5. Christopher Chapple and Yogi Anand Viraj, *The Yoga Sutras of Patanjali* (Delhi: Indian Books Centre, 1990), III:3, 81. Compare the translation by Rama Prasada: "[Meditation] when shining with the light of the object alone, and devoid, as-it-were, of itself, is trance

(or contemplation)" [*Patanjali's Yoga Sutras with the Commentary of Vyasa and the Gloss of Vachaspati Misra. The Sacred Books of the Hindus*, 4 (Allahabad: Indian Press, 1912), 181].

6. Sondra Hausner reports little tolerance among lay Hindus in South Asia for hypocritical yogis in her ethnography, *Wandering with Sadhus: Ascetics in the Hindu Himalayas* (Bloomington: Indiana University Press, 2007).

7. Ravīndra-svarūpa dās (William H. Deadwyler), "The Scholarly Tradition in Caitanyite Vaisnavism: India and America," *ISKCON Review* 1:1 (Spring 1985), 16.

8. Śri Caitanya-caritamrta, *Ādi-līlā*, chapter 7, 60–61, tr. A. C. Bhaktivedanta Swami Prabhupada, vol. 2 (New York: Bhaktivedanta Book Trust, 1973).

9. Max F. Müller, *Ramakrishna: His Life and Sayings* (New York: Scribner, 1899), 134.

10. This account is posted online at: http://caitanya.krishna.org/Articles/2001/08/013.html. Accessed 30 July 2008.

11. This account is posted online at: http://caitanya.krsihna.org/Articles/2001/05/00304.html. Accessed 30 July 2008.

12. http://caitanya.krishna.org/Articles/2000/06/00016.html. Accessed 30 July 2008.

13. Kirin Narayan, *Storytellers, Saints, and Scoundrels: Folk Narrative in Hindu Religious Teaching* (Philadelphia: University of Pennsylvania Press, 1989), 82.

14. *Storytellers*, 84.

15. Karen Pechilis, ed., *The Graceful Guru: Hindu Female Gurus in India and the United States* (New York: Oxford University Press, 2004).

16. *Graceful Guru*, 10.

17. http://www.amritapuri.org/health/index.php. Accessed 13 July 2008.

18. Swami Amritaswarupananda, *Mata Amritanandamayi: A Biography* (Kerala, India: MAM Trust, 1996). Less detailed information is available on Web sites: www.ammachi.org and www.amritapuri.org.

19. Maya Warrier notes, "Her claims to spiritual knowledge and enlightenment are based on systematic striving within any of the established devotionalist and/or renunciatory orders in Hindu religious traditions, but on the strength of her spontaneous ecstatic visions and mystical states" [*Hindu Selves in a Modern World: Guru Faith in the Mata Amritanandamayi Mission* (New York: RoutledgeCurzon, 2005), 3].

20. *Hindu Selves*, 3.

21. *Hindu Selves*, 3.

22. http://www.amritapuri.org/amma/whois.php. Accessed 11 July 2008.

23. *Hindu Selves*, 3.

24. http://www.amritapuri.org/cultural/guru/message.php. Accessed 11 July 2008.

25. http://www.amritapuri.org/cultural/guru/presence.php. Accessed 11 July 2008.

26. http://miraclesacrchives.amritapuri.org/amma/2001/rct010608.php. Accessed 13 July 2008.

27. *Hindu Selves*, 114.

28. "In the Hindu context, at least, the lack of any overarching institutional framework for monitoring ascetic behavior would seem to make stories about charlatan *sādhus* [wandering ascetics] an important means of setting limits on the extent to which *sādhus* could dupe trusting disciples" (*Storytellers*, 246–247).

29. I. C. Sharma, *Ethical Philosophies of India* (Lincoln, NE: Johnsen Publishing, 1965), 105.

30. *Ethical Philosophies of India*, 109.

31. Lawrence McCrea argues that the Mīmāṃsā critique of paranormal yogic powers was in part based on the argument that yogis are constituted with the same perceptual abilities as other humans; therefore, "it is sheer fantasy to imagine that there are or ever were people capable of perceiving things radically beyond the perceptual capacities of 'persons like ourselves'" ["Just Like Us, Just Like Now": The Tactical Implications of the Mīmāṃsā Rejection of Yogic Perception" in *Yogic Perception, Meditation, and Altered States of Consciousness*, ed. Eli Franco (Vienna, Austria: Austrian Academy of Sciences, 2009). I am indebted to Michael Mallen for this reference.

32. Swami Vivekananda, *The Complete Works of Swami Vivekananda* (Calcutta: Advaita Ashrama, 1964–68), vol. 1, 528.

33. *Works of Vivekananda*, vol. 1, 334f.

34. *Works of Vivekananda*, vol. 3, 495f.

35. *Works of Vivekananda*, vol. 4, 32f.

36. *Works of Vivekananda*, vol. 4, 32.

37. *Works of Vivekananda*, vol. 3, 495f.

38. Swami Vivekananda, *Rāja-Yoga* (New York: Ramakrishna-Vivekananda Center, 1982), 99.

39. *Rāja-Yoga*, 100.

40. *Rāja-Yoga*, 175.

41. *Rāja-Yoga*, 191.

42. *Rāja-Yoga*, 198f.

43. *Rāja-Yoga*, 195f.

44. S. Radhakrishnan, *The Hindu View of Life* (New York: Macmillan, 1973), 37.

45. *Hindu View of Life*, 25.

46. *Hindu View of Life*, 41.

47. *Hindu View of Life*, 54f.

48. *Hindu View of Life*, 52.

CHAPTER 3

1. Cited by Alexander Guttmann, "The Significance of Miracles for Talmudic Judaism," *Hebrew Union College Annual* 20 (1947), 376.

2. Adapted from Gershom Scholem, *The Messianic Idea in Judaism* (New York: Schocken Books, 1971), 291–292. Source is *Bavli Tractate Baba Mesia*, 1.15–16, in Jacob Neusner, *Talmud of Babylonia: An Academic Commentary*, vol. 21:A, University of South Florida Academic Commentary Series (Atlanta: Scholars Press, 1996), 286–287.

3. Louis Jacobs, *A Concise Companion to the Jewish Religion* (Oxford: Oxford University Press, 1999), 156.

4. *Messianic Idea*, 291.

5. *Bavli Tractate Baba Mesia*, l.16, *Talmud of Babylonia*, 287.

6. At least, that became the dominant view represented by Joshua ben Hananiah in our story. Jacob Neusner relates Eliezer's position to the larger question of how to understand divine involvement in human affairs: "You cannot close off the possibility of divine participation in the arguments of men, of rabbis. If you do, you say God is no longer interested . . . It is not easy to resolve this question, for within it are fundamental issues

facing religious people" [Neusner, *Invitation to the Talmud* (New York: HarperCollins, 1973), 187].

7. *Messianic Idea*, 295.

8. Michael Walzer, *Interpretation and Social Criticism*, 32.

9. Susan A. Handelman, *The Slayers of Moses: The Emergence of Rabbinic Interpretation in Modern Literary Theory* (Albany: State University of New York Press, 1982), 204.

10. *Bavli Tractate Baba Mesia*, l.16, *Talmud of Babylonia*, 287.

11. Jack Miles demonstrates that Yahweh, considered as an actor in a play, does a slow fade in the narrative world of the Hebrew Bible in *God: A Biography* (New York: Vintage Books, 1996).

12. Michael A. Signer, "Musings on Miracles in Rabbinic Judaism," in John C. Cavadini, ed., *Miracles in Jewish and Christian Antiquity: Imagining Truth*, 121.

13. In Jewish tradition the name is sacred. Orthodox Jews do not pronounce the name and many Jews refer to the deity in English as "G-d." In place of YHWH Jewish ritual language substitutes the generic Hebrew term for deity, *Elohim*, or the term *Adonai* meaning "my Lord." In the New Revised Standard Version of the Bible the sacred name is printed in small capitals as LORD. Richard Kearney helpfully distinguishes the ontological reading of God's self-declaration ("I am what I am"), favored by Christian theologians like Thomas Aquinas, from the eschatological version ("I will be what I will be") offered by Jewish thinkers like Maimonides [*The God Who May Be: A Hermeneutics of Religion* (Bloomington: Indiana University Press, 2001), 20–31].

14. A New Testament writer followed the Dead Sea Scrolls in naming the magicians Jannes and Jambres and identifying them as prototypes of evil men in the last days (2 Timothy 3:8).

15. Philo, *Moses*, I.156, tr. F. H. Colson (Cambridge, MA: Harvard University Press, 1935), 357.

16. Cited in Martin Buber, *Tales of the Hasidim: The Later Masters* (New York: Schocken Books, 1948), 316.

17. Cited in Martin Buber, *Tales of the Hasidim: The Early Masters* (New York: Schocken Books, 1947), 71.

18. Avivah Gottlieb Zornberg, *The Particulars of Rapture: Reflections on Exodus* (New York: Doubleday, 2001), 135.

19. *Particulars of Rapture*, 203.

20. Emil L. Fackenheim, *God's Presence in History: Jewish Affirmations and Philosophical Reflections* (New York: Harper Torchbooks, 1972), 25.

21. Jonathan Sacks, *To Heal a Fractured World: The Ethics of Responsibility* (New York: Schocken Books, 2005), 149.

22. *To Heal a Fractured World*, 150.

23. Theodore Weinberger makes a similar point by noting that in the *Siddur* (Jewish prayer book) one prayer of thanksgiving refers to miracles "bestowed" daily. Because the Hebrew root of the verb also means "to wean," he finds a parallel between God and a mother who denies her child breast milk for more mature nourishment. "God has weaned the Jewish people away from miracles that require a clear rupture of the natural order of the world . . . A Jew who today seeks supernatural miracles is told in the *Siddur* to grow up. God no longer nourishes the Jews with those kinds of miracles" [Dan Cohn-Sherbok,

ed., *Divine Intervention and Miracles in Jewish Theology* (Lewiston, ME: Edwin Mellen Press, 1996), 67–68].

24. *Particulars of Rapture*, 266, 269.

25. Once, when Aaron and Miriam challenged Moses, God rebuked them with these words: "When there are prophets among you, I the Lord make myself known to them in visions: I speak to them in dreams. Not so with my servant Moses; he is entrusted with all my house. With him I speak face to face—clearly, not in riddles; and he beholds the form of the LORD" (Numbers 12:6–8).

26. Moses ben Maimon (Maimonides), *Guide of the Perplexed*, tr. M. Friedlander (New York: Hebrew Publishing, 1946), III: 51.

27. Karen Armstrong, *A History of God: The 4,000 Year Quest of Judaism, Christianity, and Islam* (New York: Ballantine Books, 1993), 17.

28. *Tales of the Hasidim: Later Masters*, 229.

29. Enoch's disclosures supplement biblical revelation with information about the role of end-time actors, like the "watcher angels" who corrupted the earth at the time of Noah (Genesis 6:1–4) and exhortations about how to live in moral and ritual purity. See D. S. Russell, *Divine Disclosure: An Introduction to Jewish Apocalyptic* (Minneapolis: Fortress Press, 1992), 37–42, 53–54.

30. For detailed study of the Qumran community and its apocalyptic teaching, see John J. Collins, *The Scepter and the Star: The Messiahs of the Dead Sea Scrolls and Other Ancient Literature* (New York: Doubleday, 1995).

31. *Avot de Rabbi Natan*, chapter 6. Quoted in Jacob Neusner, *Between Time and Eternity: The Essentials of Judaism* (Belmont, CA: Wadsworth Publishing, 1975), 33.

32. Josef Meri notes that divine powers ascribed to *zaddikim* were exercised primarily "on behalf of Israel" [*The Cult of Saints among Muslim and Jews in Medieval Syria* (New York: Oxford University Press, 2002), 74].

33. Joseph Dan argues that the status of miracle-workers as hereditary leaders of Jewish communities was an innovation of twentieth-century Hasidism ("The Contemporary Hasidic Zaddik: Charisma, Heredity, Magic and Miracle," *Divine Intervention and Miracles in Jewish Theology*, 197).

34. A. I. Baumgarten, "Miracles and Halakah in Rabbinic Judaism," *Jewish Quarterly Review*, 73:3 (January 1983), 241.

35. Cited by Ruth Birnbaum, "The Polemic on Miracles," *Judaism* 33, 4 (Fall 1984): 440.

36. Baruch M. Bokser, "Wonder-working and the Rabbinic Tradition: The Case of Hanina ben Dosa," *Journal for the Study of Judaism in the Persian, Hellenistic and Roman Period* 16 (1985), 42. Subsequent references to the traditions regarding Hanina are drawn from this source.

37. "Miracles: Elisha and Hanina ben Dosa," *Miracles in Jewish and Christian Antiquity*, 70.

38. Even the popular accounts of making rain by one Honi, who drew circles around himself and presumptuously refused to leave until God caused rain to fall, were eventually recast to present Honi as a rabbi whose wondrous powers were the result of his Torah study (Bokser, "Wonder-working and the Rabbinic Tradition," 81).

39. Elie Wiesel, *Four Hasidic Masters and Their Struggle with Melancholy* (Notre Dame, IN: University of Notre Dame Press, 1978), 84.

40. Yaffa Eliach, *Hasidic Tales of the Holocaust* (New York: Vintage Books, 1982), 193.

41. *Hasidic Tales of the Holocaust*, 4.

42. *Hasidic Tales of the Holocaust*, 184.

43. Stories in this section are adapted from the collection edited and retold by Meyer Levin, *Classic Hasidic Tales* (New York: Penguin Books: 1932, 1975).

44. *Classic Hasidic Tales*, 186.

45. Some Hasidic teachers explained the power of miracle stories, especially those in the Bible, as derived from the creative vitality in the foundation of the written text, the Hebrew letters. One rabbi claimed that "the telling of a story about miracles influences the 'root of the miracles' and causes the repetition of the miracle mentioned in the biblical story" by re-presenting the primordial event in the present [Moshe Idel, *Hasidism: Between Ecstasy and Magic* (Albany: State University of New York Press, 1995), 186]. Mircea Eliade argued for a similar relation between retelling a myth of healing and effecting a miraculous cure in *The Sacred and the Profane: The Nature of Religion* (New York: Harcourt, 1957), 80–85.

46. *Tales of the Hasidim: Later Masters*, 27.

47. *Tales of the Hasidim: Later Masters*, 28.

48. Theodore Weinberger, "'And for Your Miracles That Are With Us Every Day': On Miracles and the *Siddur*" in *Divine Intervention and Miracles in Jewish Theology*, 59f.

49. Matthew Stewart notes that Spinoza's excommunication at age twenty-four was "among the harshest ever issued by his community" [*The Courtier and the Heretic: Leibniz, Spinoza, and the Fate of God in the Modern World* (New York: W. W. Norton, 2006), 33–34].

50. Benedict de Spinoza, *Theological-Political Treatise* (1670), ed. Jonathan Israel (New York: Cambridge University Press, 2007), 10.

51. *Theological-Political Treatise*, 82.

52. *Theological-Political Treatise*, 96.

53. Mordecai M. Kaplan, *Judaism as a Civilization: Toward a Reconstruction of American-Jewish Life* (1934) (New York: Schocken Books, 1967), 39.

54. *Judaism as a Civilization*, 42, 43.

55. *Judaism as a Civilization*, 316.

56. Richard Rubenstein, *After Auschwitz: Radical Theology and Contemporary Judaism* (Indianapolis: Bobbs-Merrill, 1966), 82.

57. Elie Wiesel, *Night* (1960), tr. Stella Rodway (New York: Bantam Books, 1982), 32.

58. Michael Walzer, *Interpretation and Social Criticism*, 39.

59. Richard Rubenstein, *After Auschwitz*, 181.

60. *After Auschwitz*, 245.

CHAPTER 4

1. The only reference to the "Twin Miracle" in the Pali canon of Buddhist scriptures is in *Patisambhidā-magga*, I, 53. The event is briefly described by the fifth-century commentator, Buddhaghosa [*Visuddhimagga*, XII.84, in *The Path of Purification*, volume 1, tr. Bhikkhu Ñyāynamoli (Berkeley: Shambala Publications, 1976), 431]. Other references to the miracle in Buddhist literature demonstrate its wide appeal and distribution in the tradition. See list at http://www.palikanon.com/english/pali_names/y/yamaka_paatihaariya.htm. Accessed 25 November 2008.

2. The version given here is from Robert Allen Mitchell, *The Buddha: His Life Retold* (New York: Paragon House, 1989), 75. Mitchell (1917–1964) was an independent scholar and recluse who devoted much of his brief life to the study of the career of the Buddha, seeking to present as comprehensive an account as possible. To that end he included stories of wondrous events that are dismissed in academic biographies as legend or myth. The Zen master Philip Kapleau, however, commended Mitchell for presenting elements of the Buddha's story rich in symbolic significance: "a story that conceals truths so majestic, so profound that they cannot be encompassed within mere fact" (x). Kapleau expressed the Buddhist conviction that "mere facts" are not bearers of ultimate truth. Since the wisdom that liberates from suffering is *transcendent*, it cannot be expressed in direct or univocal terms, but only in indirect forms of communication, such as parable and story. Accepting the principle that eternal and universal wisdom lies beyond transitory appearances clears the way to receive the vision of what is enduring. Because Mitchell followed this principle, there is much in his biography relevant to our search for the *meaning* of miracles in Buddhist tradition (although I have sought to verify that his "retellings" are grounded in primary sources).

3. This account is found in *The Mahāvastu*, volume 3, tr. J. J. Jones (London: Luzac & Company, 1956), 109–116. This text dates from the second century B.C.E. and reflects the views of the Transcendentalist school that held Buddha entered the world as a preternatural, fully perfected being.

4. Barbara Stoler Miller, *Yoga: Discipline of Freedom* (New York: Bantam Books, 1998), 97.

5. Peter Harvey, *An Introduction to Buddhism: Teachings, History and Practices* (New York: Cambridge University Press, 1990), 194.

6. Robert Brown, "Expected Miracles: The Unsurprisingly Miraculous Nature of Buddhist Images and Relics," in *Images, Miracles, and Authority in Asian Religious Traditions*, 23–35.

7. *Buddha* is a title meaning "Enlightened One." Buddhism teaches that there are many who hold that title, past and future. Siddhartha Gautama earned the title in the present age and is qualified to be the teacher of wisdom for the entire world.

8. "Falling from the host of beings in Tushita heaven, and illumining the three worlds, the most excellent of Bodhisattvas suddenly entered at a thought into her womb . . .to destroy the evils of the world" [*The Buddha-Karita of Aśvaghosha* (*Acts of Buddha*), I.19–20, tr. E. B. Cowell (1894), *The Sacred Books of the East*, vol. 49, reprinted in *Buddhist Mahayana Texts* (New York: Dover Publications, 1969), 4].

9. In the Nan Tien Temple in Australia, the ritual takes on the spiritual purpose of clearing the mind of impurity in order to "cleanse and beautify our society and country, transform this land of suffering into one of bliss, and guide the stray and evil minds onto the path of virtue. This is the true meaning of 'Bathing the Buddha'" [http://www.nantien.org.au/en/activities/buddhas_birthday.asp. Accessed 30 October 2008]. This interpretation transforms the miracle of fragrant rain into the wonder of personal dedication to Buddha's ideals.

10. *Buddha-Karita*, 2.29.

11. *Buddha-Karita*, 5.20.

12. *Buddha-Karita*, 12.101.

13. Douglas A. Fox, *The Heart of Buddhist Wisdom: A Translation of the Heart Sutra with Historical Introduction and Commentary* (Lewiston, NY: Edwin Mellen Press, 1985), 81.

14. *Buddha-Karita*, 14.65.

15. *Buddha-Karita*, 14.66–68.

16. *Heart of Buddhist Wisdom*, 79.

17. *Mahāparinibbāna Sutta* (*The Great Passing*), 2.26, 6.1, 6.7 in *The Long Discourses of the Buddha: A Translation of the Dīgha Nikāya*, tr. Maurice Walshe (Boston: Wisdom Publications, 1995), 245, 270.

18. *The Lotus Sutra*, tr. Kubo Tsugunari and Yuyana Akira (Berkeley: Numata Center for Buddhist Translation and Research, 1993), chapter 1 (24): "And that night the Buddha entered nirvana, like a fire that goes out when the wood is exhausted." A similar metaphor is used for others who attain enlightenment: "Later they will enter nirvana just as smoke dies away when the flame of a candle is extinguished" (chapter 14, 219).

19. *Lotus Sutra*, chapter 5 (112).

20. *Diamond Sutra*, 3, tr. Edward Conze in *Buddhist Wisdom Books* (London: George Allen & Unwin, 1958), 25.

21. *Buddha-Karita*, 14.72.

22. *Dhammapada Stories*, 15.197–199, tr. Daw Mya Tin, Burma Pitaka Association (1986), posted online at: http://zencomp.com/greatwisdom/ebud/dhp/i.htm. Accessed 30 October 2008.

23. H. Saddhatissa, *The Life of the Buddha* (New York: Harper & Row, 1976), 80.

24. *Buddha-Karita*, 17.21–23.

25. *Introduction to Buddhism*, 26.

26. *The Long Discourses of the Buddha*, 105. The passage occurs in *Sāmaññaphala Sutta* (*The Fruits of the Homeless Life*), 87. For the techniques required to achieve each of these miraculous powers, see the commentary by Buddhaghosa, *Path of Purification*, chapter 12.

27. Buddhaghosa recounts stories of several of Buddha's disciples exercising supernormal powers, duplicating his own (*Path of Purification*, chapter 12), confirming Woodward's observation that often a miracle "in some way repeats or echoes previous miracles within the same tradition" (*Book of Miracles*, 23).

28. *Therīgāthā*, 10.1, tr. Andrew Olendzki, posted online at: http://www.accesstoinsight. org/noncanon/comy/thiga-10-01-a00.html. Accessed 10 December 2006.

29. *Dhammapada* (*Path of Teaching*), a collection of sayings attributed to Buddha, established as authentic in 240 B.C.E. by the emperor Aśoka, translated by Irving Babbitt in 1936 (New York: New Directions, 1965), 12.

30. Posted online at: http://www.accesstoinsight.org/tipitaka/kn/thig/thig.10.01.than. html. Accessed 16 June 2009.

31. Charles S. Prebish, *Buddhist Monastic Discipline* (University Park: Pennsylvania State University Press, 1975), 11.

32. *Suttanibhanga*, *The Book of Discipline*, volume 1, tr. I. B. Horner (London: Luzac & Company, 1970), 113, 189.

33. *Buddhist Monastic Discipline*, 52, n. 27.

34. *Cullavagga*, *The Book of Discipline*, volume 5, tr. I. B. Horner (London: Luzac & Company, 1963), 149–152. For Buddha's words I have used Mitchell's more accessible translation in *Life Retold*, 124.

35. *Kevatta Sutta* in *Digha-nikaya* (*Collection of Long Discourses*), 2. This text is posted online at: http://www.buddhismtoday.com/english/texts/digha/dn11.html. Accessed 20 October 2008. Subsequent references are to this version. The text is also available in *The Long Discourses of Buddha*.

36. *Lotus Sutra*, chapter 2 (38).

37. *Lotus Sutra*, chapter 21 (285).

38. Harvey, *Introduction to Buddhism*, 122–124.

39. The *Kāśyapa Chapter* of *Mahāaratnakūta* (*Great Pile of Jewels*) in Donald S. Lopez, Jr., ed., *Buddhist Scriptures* (New York: Penguin Books, 2004), 352.

40. Karen M. Andrews, "Avalokiteśvara and the Tibetan Contemplation of Compassion" (1993), posted online at http://www.dharmaweb.org/index.php/Avalokitesvara_and_the_Tibetan_Contemplation_of_Compassion. Accessed 17 November 2008.

41. *Lotus Sutra*, chapter 25 (316–318).

42. My comments summarize the detailed introduction to a sample of these miracle tales collected and posted online by Robert Ford Campany, Professor of Religion and East Asian Languages and Culture at the University of Southern California at http://cla.calpoly.edu/~bmori/syll/Hum310china/Guanyin.html.

43. Tan Peng Yau, "Guan Shi Yin Bodhisattva and Buddhism," posted online at http://www.siddham.cn/yuan_english/sharing/sharing020101.html.

44. Nyogen Senzaki, *The Iron Flute: 100 Zen Koans* (Boston: Tuttle Publishing, 2000), 69–70.

45. Adapted from Bokar Rinpoche, *Chenrezig, Lord of Love: Principles and Methods of Deity Meditation* (San Francisco: ClearPoint Press, 1991), 28–32, posted online at http://www.khandro.net/deity_Chenrezig.htm. Accessed 5 November 2008.

46. Venerable Shangpa Rinpoche, "Arya Avalokiteśvara and the Six Syllable Mantra #3," posted online at http://www.dhagpo-kagyu.org/anglais/science-esprit/chemin/medit/methodes/avalokitesvara_shangpa3.htm. Accessed 12 November 2008.

47. Venerable Shangpa Rinpoche, "Arya Avalokiteśvara and the Six Syllable Mantra #5," posted online at http://www.dhagpo-kagyu.org/anglais/science-esprit/chemin/medit/methodes/avalokitesvara_shangpa5.htm. Accessed 5 November 2008.

48. Statement of His Holiness the Dalai Lama on the Forty-ninth Anniversary of the Tibetan National Uprising Day, March 10, 2008, posted online at http://www.tibet.net/en/index.php?id=d_tnud&rmenuid=1. Accessed 18 November 2008.

49. Interview published in *Indian Express* (July 6, 1999), posted online at http://www.tibet.com/DL/next-reincarnation.html.

50. *Cakkavatti-Sīhanāda Sutta* (*The Lion's Roar on the Turning of the Wheel*) in *Long Discourses of the Buddha*, 404.

51. Donald S. Lopez, Jr., introduction to "Maitreya Describes the Future," *Buddhist Scriptures*, 90–98.

52. Heinz Bechert and Richard Gombrich, eds., *The World of Buddhism* (London: Thames and Hudson, 1984), 87.

53. *The World of Buddhism*, 256–257.

54. Lama Anagarika Govinda, *Foundations of Tibetan Mysticism* (San Francisco: Weiser Books, 1969), 53.

55. Kānha, *Dohākosa* (*Treasury of Songs*), translated by Donald S. Lopez, Jr., *Buddhist Scriptures*, 485.

56. *The World of Buddhism*, 260. For a symbolic interpretation of this yoga as creating the flame of transcendent consciousness that pervades the body and mind of the meditator, see *Foundations of Tibetan Mysticism*, 166–178.

57. *Foundations of Tibetan Mysticism*, 163f.

58. Adapted from Tulke Thondup, *Masters of Meditation and Miracles: Lives of the Great Buddhist Masters of India and Tibet* (Boston: Shambhala, 1999), 66.

59. Harvey explains this enlightened perception: "As an analogy, the *Dharma*-body can be seen as a dazzling flash of light. Only a Buddha can see this in an unobstructed fashion. The obstructions remaining in the minds of Holy *Bodhisattvas* mean that the light is filtered and they see it as Enjoyment-body Buddhas. In ordinary beings, the light is even more filtered, so that they can only see it in the form of Transformation-bodies" (*Introduction*, 128).

60. *Transforming One's Body into the Realm of Enlightenment* in *Buddhist Scriptures*, 502f.

61. A.G.S. Kariyawasam, "The Bodhisattva Concept," Bodhi Leaves Publication No. 157 (Sri Lanka: Buddhist Publication Society, 2002), posted online at http://www.buddhanet.net/budsas/ebud/ebdha238.htm. Accessed 5 November 2008.

62. Paul Reps, ed., *Zen Flesh, Zen Bones: A Collection of Zen and Pre-Zen Writings* (Garden City, NY: Anchor Book, n.d.), 68.

63. *Zen Flesh, Zen Bones*, 81.

64. Malcolm David Eckel, "Contested Identities: The Study of Buddhism in the Postmodern World" in Kimberly Patton and Benjamin Ray, eds., *A Magic Still Dwells: Comparative Religion in the Postmodern Age* (Berkeley: University of California Press, 2000), 55–62. See also Brown, *Images, Miracles, and Authority*, 38. The irony of Blavatsky's role in promoting "modernist Buddhism" is that she claimed to exercise paranormal powers, including divine inspiration.

65. Walpola Rahula, *What the Buddha Taught* (New York: Grove Press, 1959, 1974), 87.

66. Stanley Tambiah, cited by Eckel, "Contested Identities," 60. Harvey notes that one promoter of modernist Buddhism, Don David Hewavitarne (1864–1933), linked the resurgence of Buddhism to Sinhalese nationalism (*Introduction to Buddhism*, 291).

67. Thomas A. Tweed and Stephen Prothero, eds., *Asian Religions in America: A Documentary History* (New York: Oxford University Press, 1999), 161.

68. D. T. Suzuki, *Essays in Zen Buddhism* (New York: Grove Press, 1961), 57f.

69. *Zen Buddhism*, 47.

70. *Zen Buddhism*, 84. Italics added.

71. *Zen Buddhism*, 41.

72. Thich Nhat Hanh, *The Miracle of Mindfulness: An Introduction to the Practice of Meditation*, tr. Mobi Ho (Boston: Beacon Press, 1975, 1987), 17.

73. *Miracle of Mindfulness*, 58.

74. *Fourteen Precepts of Engaged Buddhism*, from *Interbeing* (Berkeley: Parallax Press, 1993), posted online at http://buddhism.kalachakranet.org/resources/14_precepts.html. Accessed 9 December 2008.

75. Thich Nhat Hanh, *The Heart of the Buddha's Teaching* (New York: Broadway Books, 1998), 160.

76. *Dhammapada*, tr. Irving Babbitt, 60.

CHAPTER 5

1. Adapted from Gospel of Mark 6:46–51 in the New Revised Standard Version (1989).

2. Simon Samuel, *A Postcolonial Reading of Mark's Story of Jesus* (London: T & T Clark, 2007), 127.

3. Most scholars concur that Mark was written after the destruction of the temple in Jerusalem in 70 C.E., so the hope Mark's readers held for victory over the Romans might well have been apocalyptic, grounded in Jesus's teaching about the coming to earth of the messianic Son of Man "in clouds with great power and glory" (Mark 13:26).

4. Howard Clark Kee, *Jesus in History: An Approach to the Study of the Gospels* (New York: Harcourt Brace Jovanovich, 1977), 140.

5. Matthew quoted from the Greek translation of the Hebrew Bible (called the Septuagint) where the Hebrew for "young woman" (*'almah*) is rendered by the Greek word for "virgin" (*parthenos*). Matthew took advantage of the shift in meaning to introduce the miraculous element into what was originally a prediction of an ordinary birth.

6. Saint Athanasius, *On the Incarnation*, translated by a Religious of C.S.M.V. [Sr. Penelope Lawson] (London: A. R. Mowbray, 1953), 34.

7. Marcus Borg, the popular Christian author and scholar, insists that Jesus's miracles are "part of the *history of Jesus*, and not simply part of the church's *story about Jesus*." Borg believes it is "firmly attested" that Jesus was a successful healer and exorcist [*Jesus A New Vision: Spirit, Culture, and the Life of Discipleship* (San Francisco: Harper & Collins, 1987), 60, 67].

8. For a modern scholarly argument that Jesus attracted attention because of magical practices, see Morton Smith, *Jesus the Magician* (New York: HarperCollins, 1978).

9. Harvey Cox, *When Jesus Came to Harvard: Making Moral Choices Today* (Boston: Houghton Mifflin, 2004), 180.

10. "Gender and Power in the Gospel of Mark: The Daughter of Jairus and the Woman with the Flow of Blood," *Miracles in Jewish and Christian Antiquity*, 100–101. This essay sets the two healings in the context of Jewish and Roman views of the power and danger of menstrual blood.

11. "Gender and Power in the Gospel of Mark," 98.

12. Krister Stendahl, *Paul Among Jews and Gentiles* (Philadelphia: Fortress Press, 1976), 40–52.

13. We have not had space to consider the role of saints in Orthodox churches, but in general there is less official regulation of their status and more acceptance of local veneration. See the explanation of canonization at the Web site of the Orthodox Church of America posted online at: http://www.oca.org.

14. Papal declaration posted online at: http://www.franciscan-archive.org/bullarium/g9mira.html. Accessed 10 April 2009.

15. *First and Second Lives of St. Francis*, tr. David Burr. Copyright (C) 1996, David Burr. Posted by On-line Reference Book for Medieval Studies: http://www.the-orb.net/encyclop/religion/monastic/francis/francis.html. Accessed 10 April 2009. The next two stories are taken from this source as well.

16. Kathleen Ashley and Pamela Sheingorn, *Writing Faith: Text, Sign, and History in the Miracles of Sainte Foy* (Chicago: University of Chicago Press, 1999), 1.

17. *Writing Faith*, 10.

18. *The Canons and Decrees of the Sacred and Oecumenical Council of Trent*, Session 25, (December, 1563), tr. J. Waterworth (London: Dolman, 1848), 75–91. Posted online at: http://history.hanover.edu/texts/trent/ct25.html. Accessed 25 April 2009.

19. Avaida Kleinberg, *Prophets in Their Own Country: Living Saints and the Making of Sainthood in the Later Middle Ages* (Chicago: University of Chicago Press, 1992), 53.

20. *The Little Flowers of St. Francis of Assisi* (London: J. M. Dent, 1973), 44–46.

21. *First and Second Lives of St. Francis.* Copyright (C) 1996, David Burr.

22. *Little Flowers,* 102.

23. *Little Flowers,* 115.

24. As the first to receive the stigmata, Francis was transformed "from an imitator to a model of imitation" [Avaida Kleinberg, *Flesh Made Word: Saints' Stories and the Western Imagination,* tr. Jane Marie Todd (Cambridge, MA: The Belknap Press, 2008), 216].

25. *Little Flowers,* 128–130.

26. *Secrets of a Soul: Padre Pio's Letters to His Spiritual Directors,* tr. Elvira G. DiFabio (Boston: Pauline Books, 2003), 165, 168. Photographs of the stigmata are posted on the Web page of the Padre Pio Foundation of America at: http://www.padrepio.com.

27. *Secrets of a Soul,* 14.

28. Joan Carroll Cruz, *Mysteries, Marvels, Miracles in the Lives of the Saints* (Rockford, IL: Tan Books and Publishers, 1997), 229.

29. Padre Pio was a controversial candidate for sainthood. At one point the Vatican denied him permission to perform Mass during an investigation of charges against his character, including the allegation that he used acid to inflict wounds upon himself and applied cologne to produce the "odor of sanctity" that many saints are said to exude. Nevertheless, Pope John Paul II elevated him to sainthood after a comparatively brief period of inquiry into his qualifications. (The process is described online at: http://www.ewtn.com/padrepio/saint/saint.htm.) In 2004, John Paul II dedicated the Padre Pio Pilgrimage Church in San Giovanni Rotondo, and in 2008, Pio's body was exhumed and now lies in a crystal sepulcher for public viewing. In the case of this saint popular enthusiasm for miracles continues to sustain intense devotion to him, even in death, as a visible sign of divine presence.

30. Elizabeth Ficocelli, *Lourdes: Font of Faith, Hope, and Charity* (New York: Paulist Press, 2007), 22. Ficocelli is a Catholic writer whose account of Bernadette's life is a modern hagiography, but she is constrained by interests in historical veracity and reports the initial opposition by Catholic authorities to Bernadette's claims of visions.

31. Ficocelli concludes that by giving Bernadette that name, "the Lady in the grotto accomplished three things: She affirmed the new dogma, she acknowledged her heavenly identity, and she legitimated Bernadette's visions" (*Lourdes,* 35).

32. *Lourdes,* 45–46.

33. Suzanne K. Kaufman, *Consuming Visions: Mass Culture and the Lourdes Shrine* (Ithaca, NY: Cornell University Press, 2005), 106.

34. *Lourdes,* 55.

35. Pope Benedict XVI, on the 150th anniversary of Bernadette's visions, urged pilgrims to Lourdes to keep their hope not only in conditions of illness but also under injustice and torture (Associated Press, 15 September 2008).

36. *Lourdes,* 144.

37. *Lourdes,* 68.

38. *Lourdes,* 92.

39. Amanda Porterfield demonstrates that, despite the vast array of theologies and rituals in Christian communities, healing is a unifying theme: "a driving force in the construction of Christianity as an ongoing historical tradition" [*Healing in the History of Christianity* (New York: Oxford University Press, 2005), 4].

40. John Calvin, *Institutes of the Christian Religion*, Book IV, chapter 29, section 18, tr. Ford Lewis Battles (Philadelphia: Westminster Press, 1960), vol. 2, 1467.

41. Prefatory Address to King Francis I of France, section 3 (*Institutes*, vol. 1, 16–17).

42. Calvin alluded to 2 Corinthians 11:13–15. Helen L. Parish surveys the way Protestants recast Catholic saints and their miraculous powers as "symbols of the magic that was inherent in the faith and traditions of medieval Catholicism" in *Monks, Miracles and Magic: Reformation Representations of the Medieval Church* (New York: Routledge, 2005).

43. Robert Bruce Mullin, *Miracles and the Modern Religious Imagination* (New Haven, CT: Yale University Press, 1996).

44. See the Web site of the Church of God in Christ at: http://www.cogic.org.

45. See the Web site of the Foursquare Gospel Church at http://www.foursquare.org.

46. R. Laurence Moore comments that "her Church of the Foursquare Gospel set a standard for media savvyness that only a very few later religious entrepreneurs surpassed" [*Touchdown Jesus: The Mixing of Sacred and Secular in American History* (Louisville, KY: Westminster John Knox Press, 2003), 87].

47. Matthew Avery Sutton, *Aimee Semple McPherson and the Resurrection of Christian America* (Cambridge, MA: Harvard University Press, 2007), 66–89.

48. Aimee Semple McPherson, *In the Service of the King: The Story of My Life* (New York: Boni and Liveright, 1927), 221.

49. *In the Service of the King*, 224–225.

50. *In the Service of the King*, 243.

51. *In the Service of the King*, 226–230.

52. Statement of doctrine posted online at: http://www.foursquare.org/landing_pages/4,3.html. Accessed 8 May 2009.

53. Perry Miller, *Errand into the Wilderness* (New York: Harper & Row, 1956), 167–183. The sermon in which Edwards develops the image of hell is "Sinners in the Hands of an Angry God" (1741).

54. Simon Coleman, *Globalisation of Charismatic Christianity: Spreading the Gospel of Prosperity* (Cambridge: Cambridge University Press, 2000), 131.

55. In the medieval world the British monk and historian, the Venerable Bede (c. 673–735), claimed that he was healed while chanting the stories of miracles performed by St. Cuthbert [Deirdre Jackson, *Marvellous to Behold: Miracles in Medieval Manuscripts* (London: British Library, 2007), 76].

56. *Aimee Semple McPherson and the Resurrection of Christian America*, 78–82.

57. The entire autobiographical account can be found in Oral Roberts, *Don't Give Up! Jesus Will Give You that Miracle You Need!* (Tulsa: Oral Roberts Evangelistic Association, 1980), 41–65.

58. "Roberts, Granville Oral" in *The Encyclopedia of Protestantism*, ed. Hans Hillebrand (New York: Routledge, 2004), vol. 3, 1613–1614.

59. Oral Roberts, *Deliverance from Fear & Sickness: The Master Key to Your Healing* (Irving, TX: Benny Hinn Ministries, 1954, 2007), 39–40.

60. Richard Ostling, Barbara Dolan, and Michael P. Harris, "Raising Eyebrows and the Dead," *Time* (July 13, 1987), posted online at: http://www.time.com/time/magazine/article/0,9171,964970-1,00.html. Accessed 9 May 2009.

61. Richard Roberts, "Healing," posted online at: http://www.orm.cc/?p=603. Accessed 9 May 2009. Other references in this paragraph come from the same source.

62. Grant Wacker shows that early Pentecostals regarded "supernatural signs and wonders," including tongues and healing, as evidence that the return of Christ was imminent [*Heaven Below: Early Pentecostals and American Culture* (Cambridge, MA: Harvard University Press, 2001), 252–256].

63. *In the Service of the King*, 228.

64. *Deliverance from Fear & Sickness*, 73.

65. *Miracles and the Modern Religious Imagination*, 96–97.

66. A vast body of scholarly literature now exists on Gnosticism. The texts discovered in 1945 were translated and published as *The Nag Hammadi Library in English*, ed. James M. Robinson (San Francisco: Harper & Row, 1988). Elaine Pagels discusses the Gnostic understanding of Christ in her early work, *The Gnostic Gospels* (1979), as well as in her recent book, *Beyond Belief: The Secret Gospel of Thomas* (New York: Random House, 2005).

67. "Treatise on Resurrection," *The Gnostic Scriptures: Ancient Wisdom for the New Age*, tr. Bentley Layton (New York: Doubleday, 1987), 321. A modern version of this view can be found in the *Manual for Teachers* in *A Course in Miracles* in which resurrection is explained as the final unity of the human spirit with the divine (Mill Valley, CA: Foundation for Inner Peace, 1992), 68–69.

68. See the essays "On the Proof of the Spirit and of Power" and "The Education of the Human Race" in *Lessing's Theological Writings*, tr. Henry Chadwick (Stanford. CA: Stanford University Press, 1957), 82–98.

69. *Lessing's Theological Writings*, 52.

70. This theme is set out eloquently in his essays, *The Testament of John* and *The Religion of Christ*.

71. Accordingly, Lessing speculated about a "Nazarene Gospel" in which Christ is presented as a teacher of moral law, much as the ancient sect of the Ebionites taught. See his essay *New Hypothesis Concerning the Evangelists*.

72. Rudolf Bultmann, *Jesus Christ and Mythology* (New York: Charles Scribner's Sons, 1958), 15.

73. *Jesus Christ and Mythology*, 63.

74. *Jesus Christ and Mythology*, 69.

75. Rudolf Bultmann, *Jesus and the Word* (New York: Charles Scribner's Sons, 1934), 177.

76. Roger Trigg, *Rationality and Religion: Does Faith Need Reason?* (Oxford: Blackwell, 1998), 91–99.

77. Jose Cárdenas Pallares, *A Poor Man Called Jesus: Reflections of the Gospel of Mark*, tr. Robert R. Barr (Maryknoll: Orbis Books, 1986), 28.

78. *A Poor Man Called Jesus*, 30.

79. *A Poor Man Called Jesus*, 38.

CHAPTER 6

1. "Since the Quran is God's book, the text of the Quran, like its author, is regarded as perfect, eternal, and unchangeable. This is the basis for the doctrine of the miracle of inimitability of the Quran, which asserts that the ideas, language, and style of the Quran cannot be reproduced. The Quran proclaims that even the combined efforts of human

beings and jinns [spirits] could not produce a comparable text (17:88). The Quran is regarded as the only miracle brought by the Prophet. Muslim tradition is replete with stories of those who converted to Islam on hearing its inimitable message and of those pagan poets who failed the Quranic challenge (10:37–38) to create verses comparable with those contained in the Quran" [John Esposito, *Islam: The Straight Path* (New York: Oxford University Press, 1998), 19].

2. Seyyed Hossein Nasr, *Ideals and Realities of Islam* (San Francisco: Aquarian, 1966, 1994), 84.

3. Translation by Mohammed Arkoun in *Rethinking Islam: Common Questions, Uncommon Answers*, tr. Robert D. Lee (Boulder, CO: Westview Press, 1994), 31.

4. Cited in Massimo Campanini, *The Basics: The Qur'an*, tr. Oliver Leaman (New York: Routledge, 2007), 31–32.

5. Surah (chapter) 18, "The Cave," contains several miracle stories. The Qur'an also refers to the virginal conception of Jesus and his ability to defend his mother's purity and declare his destiny as a prophet while an infant (19:16–34), his healing of blindness and leprosy and his raising the dead to life, as well as the apocryphal story of his creating live birds from clay (3:45–51, 5:110). While the Qur'an denies that Jesus was crucified, it does record his ascension into heaven (4:157–158).

6. Adapted from Shems Friedlander, *Ninety-Nine Names of Allah* (San Francisco: HarperCollins, 1993), 16–18.

7. Frithjof Schuon, *Sufism: Veil and Quintessence* (Bloomington, IN: World Wisdom Books, 1981), 12.

8. *Ideals and Realities of Islam*, 82–83.

9. Qur'an 6.163 in *The Koran*, translated with notes by N. J. Dawood (New York: Penguin Books, 1997). Subsequent references to this version will be enclosed in parentheses in the text.

10. Frederick M. Denny, *An Introduction to Islam* (New York: Macmillan, 1985, 1994), 83.

11. Carl Ernst, *The Shambhala Guide to Sufism* (Boston: Shambhala Publications, 1997), 138.

12. Michael Gilsenan, *Recognizing Islam: Religion and Society in the Modern Middle East* (London: I. B. Tauris, 1982), 32.

13. *Recognizing Islam*, 33.

14. *Recognizing Islam*, 75.

15. *Mystical Dimensions of Islam*, 206.

16. *Recognizing Islam*, 75.

17. *Recognizing Islam*, 77.

18. *Recognizing Islam*, 77.

19. *Ideals and Realities of Islam*, 88.

20. *Ideals and Realities of Islam*, 89.

21. Cited in John Burton, *Introduction to the Hadith* (Edinburgh: Edinburgh University Press, 1994), 100.

22. In Islamic tradition Muhammad is closely associated with God as worthy of praise. For a detailed analysis of the names of the Prophet, see Annemarie Schimmel, *And Muhammad Is His Messenger: The Veneration of the Prophet in Islamic Piety* (Chapel Hill: University of North Carolina Press, 1985), 105–122.

23. The stories in this section are taken from the earliest extant biography of Muhammad by Ibn Ishaq (d. 767) as edited by Ibn Hishām (d. 833). The work is available in English under the title, *The Life of Muhammad: A Translation of Ishāq's Sīrat Rasūl Allāh* (London: Oxford University Press, 1955) by Alfred Guillaume. Ishaq's account is supported by carefully selected traditional sources, but it is a hagiography. E. F. Peters argues that the opening line—"This is the biography of the Apostle of God"—is modeled on the beginning of the Gospel of Mark and that the attempt "to demonstrate the authenticity of the Prophet's calling by the introduction of miracles" was "a motif that was almost certainly a by-product" of Ishaq's contact with Jews and Christians [*Muhammad and the Origins of Islam* (Albany: State University of New York Press, 1994), 263].

24. For a survey of devotional and theological interpretations of the "Light of Muhammad," see *And Muhammad Is His Messenger*, 123–143.

25. Andrew Rippin, *Muslims: Their Religious Beliefs and Practices. Volume 1: The Formative Years* (New York: Routledge, 1990), 31.

26. *The Life of Muhammad*, 72.

27. *And Muhammad Is His Messenger*, 68.

28. *The Life of Muhammad*, 79–81.

29. *And Muhammad Is His Messenger*, 67.

30. *Recognizing Islam*, 79. While the distinction is carefully maintained in the tradition, John Renard insists that there is also "continuity between prophetic miracles and saintly marvels," the latter understood as in succession to the former [*Friends of God: Islamic Images of Piety, Commitment, and Servanthood* (Berkeley: University of California Press, 2008), 95].

31. Several *hadīth* attest to this miracle being performed in various settings. See *Sahih Bukhari*, Volume 4, Book 56, Numbers 772–779, tr. M. Muhsin Khan. Posted online at: http://www.muslimaccess.com/sunnah/bukhari/Sahih-al-Bukhari.html. Accessed 26 May 2009.

32. This story and the following two are from traditional sources cited in *Introduction to the Hadith*, 97–99.

33. It should be noted that in another *hadīth*, Muhammad stated that he, like other humans, did not possess prescient knowledge: "Allah's Apostle (p.b.u.h.) said, 'Keys of the unseen knowledge are five which nobody knows but Allah . . .nobody knows what will happen tomorrow; nobody knows what is in the womb; nobody knows what he will gain tomorrow; nobody knows at what place he will die; and nobody knows when it will rain'" (*Sahih Bukhari*, volume 2, book 17, number 149, tr. M. Muhsin Khan).

34. Karen Armstrong, *Muhammad: A Biography of the Prophet* (New York: HarperSanFrancisco, 1992), 177.

35. Annemarie Schimmel, *Rumi's World: The Life and Work of the Great Sufi Poet* (Boston: Shambhala Publications, 2001), 117.

36. Schimmel summarizes the competing views on whether the journey was physical or spiritual in *And Muhammad Is His Messenger*, 161–167.

37. Qur'an 17:1 in *The Meaning of the Glorious Qur'an*, tr. Abdullah Yusuf Ali (Cairo: Dar Al-Kitab Al-Masri, 1934), volume 1, 693. The story is pieced together by Ibn Ishaq from traditional sources in *Life of Muhammad*, 181–187.

38. *Ideals and Realities of Islam*, 133.

39. *And Muhammad Is His Messenger*, 169.

40. In one seventeenth-century Sufi text a mystic ascends through nine planetary spheres, in imitation of Muhammad's *mi'rāj*, only to be told that "the hidden world where God resides" is "no-place" [Carl W. Ernst, tr., *Teachings of Sufism* (Boston: Shambhala Publications, 1999), 71–76].

41. *An Introduction to Islam*, 69.

42. Cited in *Life of Muhammad*, 183.

43. Seyyed Hossein Nasr, *The Heart of Islam: Enduring Values for Humanity* (New York: HarperSanFrancisco, 2002), 31.

44. Jalal al-Dīn Rūmī, *The Essential Rumi*, tr. Coleman Barks (New York: HarperSanFrancisco, 1995), 191.

45. *And Muhammad Is His Messenger*, 170.

46. *Friends of God*, 274.

47. Heinz Halm, *Shi'a Islam: From Religion to Revolution* (Princeton, NJ: Markus Wiener Publishers, 1997), 31.

48. Posted online by *Jafariya News*, self-described as "Largest Shia News Website" at: http://www.jafariyanews.com/articles/2k9/4march_miracles_Imam_askari.htm. Accessed 12 June 2009.

49. *The Heart of Islam*, 66.

50. *Ideals and Realities of Islam*, 162.

51. Faudi I. Khuri, *Imams and Emirs: State, Religion, and Sects in Islam* (London: Saqi Books, 1990), 108.

52. Cited in *Imams and Emirs*, 109.

53. Cited in Muhammad Husayn Tabātabā'ī, *Shī'ah*, tr. S. H. Nasr (Qum, Iran: Ansariyan Publications, 2006), 201.

54. From *al-Bidāyah wa'l-Nihāyah*, 7:359, cited in *Shī'ah*, 55, f.n. 2.

55. *Shi'ah*, 201.

56. *Shi'ah*, 248.

57. Seyyed Hossein Nasr, Hamid Dabashi, and Seyyed Vali Reza Nasr, eds., *Shi'ism: Doctrines, Thought, and Spirituality* (Albany: State University of New York, 1988), 169–177.

58. "If there were no imam, according to Shi'i belief, the cosmos would immediately cease to exist. This idea is . . .often used as evidence of the existence of the Hidden Imam. The fact that world continues to exist is considered proof that must be a Hidden Imam" (*Shi'a Islam*, 33).

59. From a collection of sayings gathered by the Iranian scholar al-Majlisī, cited in *Shi'a Islam*, 32.

60. *Ideals and Realities of Islam*, 171.

61. *Shi'ism: Doctrines, Thought, and Spirituality*, 92.

62. Tazim R. Kassam provides a translation of these hymns, long hidden from public view, in *Songs of Wisdom and Circles of Dance; Hymns of the Satpanth Ismā'ilī Muslim Saint, Pīr Shams* (Albany: State University of New York, 1995). The quotations are taken from Hymns 80–82.

63. Kassam translates the account of Pīr Shams's miracles in *Songs of Wisdom*, 375–380.

64. Cited in *Shi'ah*, 211.

65. *Shi'ah*, 209.

66. Robert Rozehnal, *Islamic Sufism Unbound: Politics and Piety in Twenty-First Century Pakistan* (New York: Palgrave Macmillan, 2007), 41.

67. *Friends of God*, 9.

68. *Friends of God*, 102.

69. *Friends of God*, 271.

70. *Islamic Sufism Unbound*, 43.

71. It was reported of the Iraqi ascetic saint, Abū Idrīs al-Khawlānī, "Among his miracles was that he used to walk on the Tigris with people watching him and his feet would not get wet" [Joseph Meri, *The Cult of Saints among Muslims and Jews in Medieval Syria* (New York: Oxford University Press, 2002), 77].

72. From Farid al-Din 'Attar (d. 1221), *The Memoirs of the Saints*, cited by Margaret Smith, *Rabi'a: The Life and Work of Rabi'a and Other Women Mystics in Islam* (Oxford: Oneworld Publications, 1994), 56–57.

73. *Friends of God*, 112.

74. *Rabi'a*, 57.

75. *Mystical Dimensions of Islam*, 207.

76. From traditional sources translated by Indries Shah in *The Hundred Tales of Wisdom* (London: Octagon Press, 1978), 56.

77. *Friends of God*, 115.

78. This story is taken from *The Hundred Tales of Wisdom*, 70–73.

79. *Mystical Dimensions of Islam*, 209.

80. *The Cult of Saints among Muslims and Jews in Medieval Syria*, 39.

81. *Friends of God*, 97. The following story is from the same source.

82. *Mystical Dimensions of Islam*, 211.

83. *Friends of God*, 116.

84. From the collection by Jami' Tirmizi translated by Abdul Hamid Siddique, *Selection from Hadith* (Safat, Kuwait: Islamic Book Publishers, 1983), 63.

85. *Islam: The Straight Path*, 72.

86. *An Introduction to Islam*, 180.

87. *And Muhammad Is His Messenger*, 162.

88. Campanini, *The Qur'an*, 13–14.

89. There may be parallels to the reference in Proverbs 8 to Wisdom who was with God from before the creation of the world as the architect of natural and moral order and thus the eternal source of Torah, as well as to Christian belief in the pre-existence of Jesus as the eternal Word of God in John 1.

90. Campanini, *The Qur'an*, 105.

91. From his commentary on the Qur'an, cited in Esposito, *Islam: The Straight Path*, 136.

92. Daniel Brown, *Rethinking Tradition in Modern Islamic Thought* (Cambridge: Cambridge University Press, 1996), 131.

93. Campanini, *The Qur'an*, 105.

94. *An Introduction to Islam*, 325.

95. Mohammed Arkoun, *Rethinking Islam*, 34.

96. *Rethinking Islam*, 36.

97. Andrew Rippin, *Muslims: Their Religious Beliefs and Practices. Volume 2: The Contemporary Period* (New York: Routledge, 1993), 23.

98. *Rethinking Islam*, 83–84.

99. Campanini, *The Qur'an*, 121.

100. Sayyid Qutb, *Social Justice in Islam* (1949), tr. John B. Hardie (New York: Octagon Books, 1970), 19. Also posted online at: http://onlineislamicstore.com/syedqutb.html. Accessed 15 June 2009.

101. From *This Religion of Islam*, 3–4, cited in Robert D. Lee, *Overcoming Tradition and Modernity: The Search for Islamic Authenticity* (Boulder, CO: Westview Press, 1997), 91.

102. Sayyid Qutb, *Milestones* (1964), tr. Ahmad Zaki Hammad (Indianapolis: American Trust Publications, 1990), 137.

AFTERWORD

1. Russell T. McCutcheon, *Manufacturing Religion: The Discourse on Sui Generis Religion and the Politics of Nostalgia* (New York: Oxford University Press, 1997), 63.

2. Leszek Kołakowski, *God Owes Us Nothing: A Brief Remark on Pascal's Religion and the Spirit of Jansenism* (Chicago: University of Chicago Press, 1995), 193.

Bibliography

Arkoun, Mohammed. *Rethinking Islam: Common Questions, Uncommon Answers.* Translated by Robert D. Lee. Boulder, CO: Westview Press, 1994.

Armstrong, Karen. *Muhammad: A Biography of the Prophet.* New York: HarperSanFrancisco, 1992.

———. *A History of God: The 4,000 Year Quest of Judaism, Christianity, and Islam.* New York: Ballantine Books, 1993.

Asad, Talal. *Genealogies of Religion: Discipline and Reasons of Power in Christianity and Islam.* Baltimore: Johns Hopkins University Press, 1993.

Ashley, Kathleen and Pamela Sheingorn. *Writing Faith: Text, Sign, and History in the Miracles of Sainte Foy.* Chicago: University of Chicago Press, 1999.

Athanasius, Saint. *On the Incarnation.* Translated by a Religious of C.S.M.V. [Sr. Penelope Lawson] London: A. R. Mowbray, 1953.

Bailey, Michael D. *Magic and Superstition in Europe: A Concise History from Antiquity to the Present.* New York: Rowman & Littlefield, 2007.

Baumgarten, A. I. "Miracles and Halakah in Rabbinic Judaism." *Jewish Quarterly Review* 73:3 (January 1983).

Bechert, Heinz and Richard Gombrich, editors. *The World of Buddhism.* London: Thames and Hudson, 1984.

The Bhagavad-Gita: Krishna's Counsel in Time of War. Translated by Barbara Stoler Miller. New York: Bantam Books, 1986.

Birnbaum, Ruth. "The Polemic on Miracles." *Judaism* 33:4 (Fall 1984).

Bokser, Baruch M. "Wonder-working and the Rabbinic Tradition: The Case of Hanina ben Dosa." *Journal for the Study of Judaism in the Persian, Hellenistic and Roman Period* 16 (1985).

Borg, Marcus. *Jesus A New Vision: Spirit, Culture, and the Life of Discipleship.* San Francisco: Harper & Collins, 1987.

Brown, Daniel. *Rethinking Tradition in Modern Islamic Thought.* Cambridge: Cambridge University Press, 1996.

Brown, Peter. *The Cult of Saints: Its Rise and Function in Latin Christianity.* Chicago: University of Chicago Press, 1982.

Brown, William Adams. "Permanent Significance of Miracle." *Harvard Theological Review* 8:3 (July 1915).

Buber, Martin. *Tales of the Hasidim: The Early Masters.* New York: Schocken Books, 1947.

———. *Tales of the Hasidim: The Later Masters.* New York: Schocken Books, 1948.

The Buddha-Karita of Asvaghosha (Acts of Buddha). Translated by E. B. Cowell (1894). *The Sacred Books of the East,* volume 49. Reprinted in *Buddhist Mahayana Texts.* New York: Dover Publications, 1969.

Bultmann, Rudolf. *Jesus and the Word*. New York: Charles Scribner's Sons, 1934.

———. *Jesus Christ and Mythology*. New York: Charles Scribner's Sons, 1958.

Burton, John. *Introduction to the Hadith*. Edinburgh: Edinburgh University Press, 1994.

Butte, George. *I Know That You Know That I Know: Narrating Subjects from Moll Flanders to Marnie*. Columbus: Ohio State University Press, 2004.

Śrī Caitanya-caritamrta, *Ādi-līlā*, volume 2. Translated by A. C. Bhaktivedanta Swami Prabhupada. New York: Bhaktivedanta Book Trust, 1973.

Calvin, John. *Institutes of the Christian Religion*. Translated by Ford Lewis Battles. Philadelphia: Westminster Press, 1960.

Campanini, Massimo. *The Basics: The Qur'an*. Translated by Oliver Leaman. New York: Routledge, 2007.

Caputo, John D. and Michael J. Scanlon, editors. *Transcendence and Beyond: A Postmodern Inquiry*. Bloomington: Indiana University Press, 2007.

Cavadini, John C., editor. *Miracles in Jewish and Christian Antiquity: Imagining Truth*. Notre Dame, IN: University of Notre Dame Press, 1999.

Chapple, Christopher and Yogi Anand Viraj. *The Yoga Sutras of Patanjali: An Analysis of the Sanskrit with Accompanying English Translation*. Delhi: Indian Books Centre, 1990.

Ciardi, John. *How Does a Poem Mean?* Boston: Houghton Mifflin, 1959.

Cohn-Sherbok, Dan, editor. *Divine Intervention and Miracles in Jewish Theology*. Lewiston, ME: Edwin Mellen Press, 1996.

Coleman, Simon. *Globalisation of Charismatic Christianity: Spreading the Gospel of Prosperity*. Cambridge: Cambridge University Press, 2000.

Collins, John J. *The Scepter and the Star: The Messiahs of the Dead Sea Scrolls and Other Ancient Literature*. New York: Doubleday, 1995.

Corner, Mark. *Signs of God: Miracles and their Interpretation*. Burlington, VT: Ashgate Publishing, 2005.

A Course in Miracles. Mill Valley, CA: Foundation for Inner Peace, 1992.

Cox, Harvey. *When Jesus Came to Harvard: Making Moral Choices Today*. Boston: Houghton Mifflin, 2004.

Cruz, Joan Carroll. *Mysteries, Marvels, Miracles in the Lives of the Saints*. Rockford, IL: Tan Books and Publishers, 1997.

Cullavagga, The Book of Discipline, volume 5. Translated by I. B. Horner. London: Luzac & Company, 1963.

Davis, Richard H. editor. *Images, Miracles, and Authority in Asian Religious Traditions*. Boulder, CO: Westview Press, 1998.

Dempsey, Corrine G. "Lessons in Miracles from Kerala, South India: Stories of Three 'Christian' Saints." *History of Religions* 39:2 (November 1999).

Denny, Frederick M. *An Introduction to Islam*. New York: Macmillan, 1994.

Descartes, René. "Passions of the Soul." *The Philosophical Writings of Descartes*, volume 1. Translated by J. Cottingham. Cambridge: Cambridge University Press, 1985.

Dhammapada (Path of Teaching). Translated by Irving Babbitt. New York: New Directions, 1965.

Dhammapada Stories. Translated by Daw Mya Tin. Burma Pitaka Association, 1986.

Diamond Sutra. Translated by Edward Conze. *Buddhist Wisdom Books*. London: George Allen & Unwin, 1958.

Doniger, Wendy. *The Implied Spider: Politics and Theology in Myth*. New York: Columbia University Press, 1998.

———, editor. *Merriam-Webster's Encyclopedia of World Religions*. 1999.

Eliach, Yaffa. *Hasidic Tales of the Holocaust*. New York: Vintage Books, 1982.

Eliade, Mircea. *The Sacred and the Profane: The Nature of Religion*. Translated by Willard R. Trask. New York: Harcourt, 1957.

Ernst, Carl W. *The Shambhala Guide to Sufism*. Boston: Shambhala Publications, 1997.

———. *Teachings of Sufism*. Boston: Shambhala Publications, 1999.

Esposito, John. *Islam: The Straight Path*. New York: Oxford University Press, 1998.

Fackenheim, Emil L. *God's Presence in History: Jewish Affirmations and Philosophical Reflections*. New York: Harper Torchbooks, 1972.

Ficocelli, Elizabeth. *Lourdes: Font of Faith, Hope, and Charity*. New York: Paulist Press, 2007.

Fogelin, Robert J. *A Defense of Hume on Miracles*. Princeton, NJ: Princeton University Press, 2003.

Fox, Douglas A. *The Heart of Buddhist Wisdom: A Translation of the Heart Sutra with Historical Introduction and Commentary*. Lewiston, NY: Edwin Mellen Press, 1985.

Friedlander, Shems. *Ninety-Nine Names of Allah*. San Francisco: HarperCollins, 1993.

Gilsenan, Michael. *Recognizing Islam: Religion and Society in the Modern Middle East*. London: I. B. Tauris, 1982.

The Gnostic Scriptures: Ancient Wisdom for the New Age. Translated by Bentley Layton. New York: Doubleday, 1987.

Govinda, Lama Anagarika. *Foundations of Tibetan Mysticism*. San Francisco: Weiser Books, 1969.

Guillaume, Alexander. *The Life of Muhammad: A Translation of Ishāq's Sīrat Rasūl Allāh*. London: Oxford University Press, 1955.

Guttmann, Alexander. "The Significance of Miracles for Talmudic Judaism." *Hebrew Union College Annual* 20 (1947).

Halm, Heinz. *Shi'a Islam: From Religion to Revolution*. Princeton, NJ: Markus Wiener Publishers, 1997.

Handelman, Susan A. *The Slayers of Moses: The Emergence of Rabbinic Interpretation in Modern Literary Theory*. Albany: State University of New York Press, 1982.

HarperCollins Dictionary of Religion. Edited by Jonathan Z. Smith. New York: HarperSanFrancisco, 1995.

Harris, Sam. *The End of Faith: Religion, Terror, and the Future of Reason*. New York: W. W. Norton, 2004.

Harvey, Peter. *An Introduction to Buddhism: Teachings, History and Practices*. New York: Cambridge University Press, 1990.

Hausner, Sondra. *Wandering with Sadhus: Ascetics in the Hindu Himalayas*. Bloomington, IN: Indiana University Press, 2007.

Hillebrand, Hans, editor. *The Encyclopedia of Protestantism*. New York: Routledge, 2004.

Hume, David. "Of Miracles." Tom L. Beauchamp, *An Enquiry Concerning Human Understanding: A Critical Edition*. New York: Oxford University Press, 2000.

Idel, Moshe. *Hasidism: Between Ecstasy and Magic*. Albany: State University of New York Press, 1995.

Iser, Wolfgang. *The Implied Reader: Patterns of Communication in Prose Fiction from Bunyan to Beckett*. Baltimore: Johns Hopkins University Press, 1974.

Jacobs, Lenworth M., Karyl Burns, and Barbara Bennet Jacobs. "Views of the Public and Trauma Professionals on Death and Dying from Injuries." *Archives of Surgery* 143:8 (August, 2008): 730–735.

Jacobs, Louis. *A Concise Companion to the Jewish Religion*. New York: Oxford University Press, 1999.

Jackson, Deirdre. *Marvellous to Behold: Miracles in Medieval Manuscripts*. London: British Library, 2007.

James, William. *The Varieties of Religious Experience: A Study in Human Nature* (1902). New York: Longmans, Green, 1928.

Kant, Immanuel. *Critique of Practical Reason* (1788). Translated by L. W. Beck. Indianapolis: Bobbs-Merrill, 1956.

———. *Religion Within the Limits of Reason Alone* (1793). Translated by T. M. Greene and H. M. Hudson. New York: Harper Torchbooks, 1960.

Kaplan, Mordecai M. *Judaism as a Civilization: Toward a Reconstruction of American-Jewish Life* (1934). New York: Schocken Books, 1967.

Kariyawasam, A.G.S. "The Bodhisattva Concept." Bodhi Leaves Publication No. 157. Sri Lanka: Buddhist Publication Society, 2002.

Kassam, Tazim R. *Songs of Wisdom and Circles of Dance; Hymns of the Satpanth Ismāʿīlī Muslim Saint, Pīr Shams*. Albany: State University of New York, 1995.

Kaufman, Suzanne K. *Consuming Visions: Mass Culture and the Lourdes Shrine*. Ithaca, NY: Cornell University Press, 2005.

Kearney, Richard. *The God Who May Be: A Hermeneutics of Religion*. Bloomington: Indiana University Press, 2001.

Kee, Howard Clark. *Jesus in History: An Approach to the Study of the Gospels*. New York: Harcourt Brace Jovanovich, 1977.

Khuri, Faudi I. *Imams and Emirs: State, Religion, and Sects in Islam*. London: Saqi Books, 1990.

Kierkegaard, Søren. *Training in Christianity* (1850). Translated by Walter Lowrie. Princeton, NJ: Princeton University Press, 1967.

Kleinberg, Avaida. *Prophets in Their Own Country: Living Saints and the Making of Sainthood in the Later Middle Ages*. Chicago: University of Chicago Press, 1992.

———. *Flesh Made Word: Saints' Stories and the Western Imagination*. Translated by Jane Marie Todd. Cambridge, MA: Belknap Press, 2008.

Kołakowski, Leszek. *Metaphysical Horror*. Oxford: Basil Blackwell, 1988.

———. *God Owes Us Nothing: A Brief Remark on Pascal's Religion and the Spirit of Jansenism*. Chicago: University of Chicago Press, 1995.

The Koran. Translated with notes by N. J. Dawood. New York: Penguin Books, 1997.

Krishna: The Beautiful Legend of God, Śrīmad Bhāgavata Purāṇa, Book X. Translated by Edwin F. Bryant. London: Penguin Books, 2003.

Lee, Robert D. *Overcoming Tradition and Modernity: The Search for Islamic Authenticity*. Boulder, CO: Westview Press, 1997.

Lessing, Gotthold Ephraim. *Lessing's Theological Writings*. Translated by Henry Chadwick. Stanford, CA: Stanford University Press, 1957.

Levin, Meyer. *Classic Hasidic Tales* (1932). New York: Penguin Books, 1975.

Lewis, C. S. *Miracles: A Preliminary Study*. New York: Macmillan, 1947.

The Little Flowers of St. Francis of Assisi. London: J. M. Dent, 1973.

The Long Discourses of the Buddha: A Translation of the Dīgha Nikāya. Translated by Maurice Walshe. Boston: Wisdom Publications, 1995.

Lopez, Donald S., Jr., ed. *Buddhist Scriptures*. New York: Penguin Books, 2004.

The Lotus Sutra. Translated by Kubo Tsugunari and Yuyana Akira. Berkeley: Numata Center for Buddhist Translation and Research, 1993.

Mackie, J. L. *The Miracle of Theism*. New York: Oxford University Press, 1982.

The Mahāvastu, volume 3. Translated by J. J. Jones. London: Luzac & Company, 1956.

Maimonides (Moses ben Maimon). *Guide of the Perplexed*. Translated by M. Friedlander. New York: Hebrew Publishing, 1946.

Martin, Charlotte J. *Dynamics of Hope: Eternal Life and Daily Christian Living*. Collegeville, MN: Liturgical Press, 2002.

Martin, Richard C. *Islamic Studies: A History of Religions Approach*. Upper Saddle River, NJ: Prentice-Hall, 1996.

Marty, Martin and Scott Appleby. *The Power and the Glory: Fundamentalisms Project*. Chicago: University of Chicago Press, 1998.

McCrea, Lawrence. "Just Like Us, Just Like Now": The Tactical Implications of the Mīmāmsā Rejection of Yogic Perception." In *Yogic Perception, Meditation, and Altered States of Consciousness*, ed. Eli Franco. Vienna, Austria: Austrian Academy of Sciences, 2009.

McCutcheon, Russell T. *Manufacturing Religion: The Discourse on Sui Generis Religion and the Politics of Nostalgia*. New York: Oxford University Press, 1997.

McPherson, Aimee Semple. *In the Service of the King: The Story of My Life*. New York: Boni and Liveright, 1927.

The Meaning of the Glorious Qur'an. Translated by Abdullah Yusuf Ali. Cairo: Dar Al-Kitab Al-Masri, 1934.

Meri, Joseph. *The Cult of Saints among Muslim and Jews in Medieval Syria*. New York: Oxford University Press, 2002.

Miles, Jack. *God: A Biography*. New York: Vintage Books, 1996.

Miller, Perry. *Errand into the Wilderness*. New York: Harper & Row, 1956.

Miller, Robert Henry. "An Appreciation of the Miracles." *Journal of the National Association of Biblical Instructors* 2:2 (1934).

Mitchell, Robert Allen. *The Buddha: His Life Retold*. New York: Paragon House, 1989.

Moore, R. Laurence. *Touchdown Jesus: The Mixing of Sacred and Secular in American History*. Louisville, KY: Westminster John Knox Press, 2003.

Müller, Max F. *Ramakrishna: His Life and Sayings*. New York: Scribner, 1899.

Mullin, Robert Bruce. *Miracles and the Modern Religious Imagination*. New Haven, CT: Yale University Press, 1996.

The Nag Hammadi Library in English. Edited by James M. Robinson. San Francisco: Harper & Row, 1988.

Narayan, Kirin. *Storytellers, Saints, and Scoundrels: Folk Narrative in Hindu Religious Teaching*. Philadelphia: University of Pennsylvania Press, 1989.

Nasr, Seyyed Hossein. *Ideals and Realities of Islam* (1966). San Francisco: Aquarian, 1994.

———. *The Heart of Islam: Enduring Values for Humanity*. New York: HarperSanFrancisco, 2002.

Nasr, Seyyed Hossein, Hamid Dabashi, and Seyyed Vali Reza Nasr, editors. *Shi'ism: Doctrines, Thought, and Spirituality*. Albany: State University of New York, 1988.

Neusner, Jacob. *Invitation to the Talmud*. New York: HarperCollins, 1973.

———. *Between Time and Eternity: The Essentials of Judaism* (Belmont, CA: Wadsworth Publishing, 1975.

———. *Talmud of Babylonia: An Academic Commentary*, vol. 21:A, University of South Florida Academic Commentary Series. Atlanta: Scholars Press, 1996.

Nhat Hanh, Thich. *The Miracle of Mindfulness: An Introduction to the Practice of Meditation*. Translated by Mobi Ho. Boston: Beacon Press, 1975.

———. *The Heart of the Buddha's Teaching*. New York: Broadway Books, 1998.

Otto, Rudolf. *The Idea of the Holy* (1917). Translated by John W. Harvey. New York: Oxford University Press, 1958.

Paden, William E. *Religious Worlds: The Comparative Study of Religion*. Boston: Beacon Press, 1994.

Pagels, Elaine. *The Gnostic Gospels* (1979). New York: Random House, 2004.

———. *Beyond Belief: The Secret Gospel of Thomas*. New York: Random House, 2005.

Pallares, Jose Cárdenas. *A Poor Man Called Jesus: Reflections of the Gospel of Mark*. Translated by Robert R. Barr. Maryknoll: Orbis Books, 1986.

Parish, Helen L. *Monks, Miracles and Magic: Reformation Representations of the Medieval Church*. New York: Routledge, 2005.

Patanjali's Yoga Sutras with the Commentary of Vyasa and the Gloss of Vachaspati Misra. The Sacred Books of the Hindus, volume 4. Translated by Rama Prasada. Allahabad: Indian Press, 1912.

The Path of Purification, volume 1. Translated by Bhikkhu Ñyāynamoli. Berkeley: Shambala Publications, 1976.

Patton, Kimberly and Benjamin Ray, editors. *A Magic Still Dwells: Comparative Religion in the Postmodern Age*. Berkeley: University of California Press, 2000.

Pechilis, Karen, editor. *The Graceful Guru: Hindu Female Gurus in India and the United States*. New York: Oxford University Press, 2004.

Peters, E. F. *Muhammad and the Origins of Islam*. Albany: State University of New York Press, 1994.

Porterfield, Amanda. *Healing in the History of Christianity*. New York: Oxford University Press, 2005.

Prebish, Charles S. *Buddhist Monastic Discipline*. University Park: Pennsylvania State University Press, 1975.

Qutb, Sayyid. *Social Justice in Islam* (1949). Translated by John B. Hardie. New York: Octagon Books, 1970.

———. *Milestones* (1964). Translated by Ahmad Zaki Hammad. Indianapolis: American Trust Publications, 1990.

Radhakrishnan, Sarvepalli. *The Hindu View of Life*. New York: Macmillan, 1973.

Radner, Ephraim. *Spirit and Nature: The Saint-Médard Miracles in 18th-Century Jansenism*. New York: Crossroad, 2002.

Rahula, Walpola. *What the Buddha Taught*. New York: Grove Press, 1959.

Ravīndra-svarūpa dās (William H. Deadwyler). "The Scholarly Tradition in Caitanyite Vaisnavism: India and America." *ISKCON Review* 1:1 (Spring 1985).

Renard, John. *Friends of God: Islamic Images of Piety, Commitment, and Servanthood.* Berkeley: University of California Press, 2008.

Reps, Paul, editor. *Zen Flesh, Zen Bones: A Collection of Zen and Pre-Zen Writings.* Garden City, NY: Anchor Book, n.d.

The Rig Veda: An Anthology. Translated by Wendy Doniger. New York: Penguin Books, 1981.

Rinpoche, Bokar. *Chenrezig, Lord of Love: Principles and Methods of Deity Meditation.* English edition. San Francisco: ClearPoint Press, 1991.

Rippin, Andrew. *Muslims: Their Religious Beliefs and Practices. Volume 1: The Formative Years.* New York: Routledge, 1990.

———. *Muslims: Their Religious Beliefs and Practices. Volume 2: The Contemporary Period.* New York: Routledge, 1993.

Roberts, Oral Granville. *Don't Give Up! Jesus Will Give You that Miracle You Need!* Tulsa, OK: Oral Roberts Evangelistic Association, 1980.

———. *Deliverance from Fear & Sickness: The Master Key to Your Healing* (1954). Irving, TX: Benny Hinn Ministries, 2007.

Robinson, James. M., editor. *The Nag Hammadi Library in English.* San Francisco: Harper & Row, 1988.

Rozehnal, Robert. *Islamic Sufism Unbound: Politics and Piety in Twenty-First Century Pakistan.* New York: Palgrave Macmillan, 2007.

Rubenstein, Mary-Jane. *Strange Wonder: The Closure of Metaphysics and the Opening of Awe.* New York: Columbia University Press, 2008.

Rubenstein, Richard. *After Auschwitz: Radical Theology and Contemporary Judaism.* Indianapolis: Bobbs-Merrill, 1966.

Rūmī, Jalāl al-Dīn. *The Essential Rumi.* Translated by Coleman Barks. New York: HarperSanFrancisco, 1995.

Russell, D. S. *Divine Disclosure: An Introduction to Jewish Apocalyptic.* Minneapolis: Fortress Press, 1992.

Sacks, Jonathan. *To Heal a Fractured World: The Ethics of Responsibility.* New York: Schocken Books, 2005.

Saddhatissa, Hammalava. *The Life of the Buddha.* New York: Harper & Row, 1976.

Samuel, Simon. *A Postcolonial Reading of Mark's Story of Jesus.* London: T & T Clark, 2007.

Schimmel, Annemarie. *Mystical Dimensions of Islam.* Chapel Hill: University of North Carolina Press, 1975.

———. *And Muhammad Is His Messenger: The Veneration of the Prophet in Islamic Piety.* Chapel Hill: University of North Carolina Press, 1985.

———. *Rumi's World: The Life and Work of the Great Sufi Poet.* Boston: Shambhala Publications, 2001.

Scholem, Gershom. *The Messianic Idea in Judaism.* New York: Schocken Books, 1971.

Schuon, Frithjof. *Sufism: Veil and Quintessence.* Bloomington, IN: World Wisdom Books, 1981.

Secrets of a Soul: Padre Pio's Letters to His Spiritual Directors. Translated by Elvira G. DiFabio. Boston: Pauline Books, 2003.

Selection from Hadith. Edited by Abdul Hamid Siddique. Safat, Kuwait: Islamic Book Publishers, 1983.

Senzaki, Nyogen. *The Iron Flute: 100 Zen Koans.* Boston: Tuttle Publishing, 2000.

Shah, Indries. *The Hundred Tales of Wisdom*. London: Octagon Press, 1978.

Sharma, I. C. *Ethical Philosophies of India*. Lincoln, NE: Johnsen Publishing, 1965.

Smith, Jonathan Z. *Relating Religion: Essays in the Study of Religion*. Chicago: University of Chicago Press, 2004.

Smith, Margaret. *Rabi'a: The Life and Work of Rabi'a and Other Women Mystics in Islam*. Oxford: Oneworld Publications, 1994.

Smith, Morton. *Jesus the Magician*. New York: HarperCollins, 1978.

Spinoza, Benedict. *Theological-Political Treatise* (1670). Edited by Jonathan Israel. New York: Cambridge University Press, 2007.

Stendahl, Krister. *Paul Among Jews and Gentiles*. Philadelphia: Fortress Press, 1976.

Stewart, Matthew. *The Courtier and the Heretic: Leibniz, Spinoza, and the Fate of God in the Modern World*. New York: W. W. Norton, 2006.

Stuckrad, Kocku von, editor. *The Brill Dictionary of Religion*. Leiden: Brill Publications, 2007.

Suttanibhanga, The Book of Discipline, volume 1. Translated by I. B. Horner. London: Luzac & Company, 1970.

Sutton, Matthew Avery. *Aimee Semple McPherson and the Resurrection of Christian America*. Cambridge, MA: Harvard University Press, 2007.

Suzuki, D. T. *Essays in Zen Buddhism*. New York: Grove Press, 1961.

Swami Amritaswarupananda. *Mata Amritanandamayi: A Biography*. Kerala, India: MAM Trust, 1996.

Swami Vivekananda. *The Complete Works of Swami Vivekananda*. Calcutta: Advaita Ashrama, 1964–68.

———. *Rāja-Yoga*. New York: Ramakrishna-Vivekananda Center, 1982.

Swinburne, Richard. *Miracles*. New York: Macmillan, 1989.

Tabātabā'ī, Muhammad Husayn. *Shī'ah*. Translated by S. H. Nasr. Qum, Iran: Ansariyan Publications, 2006.

Talmud of Babylonia: An Academic Commentary, volume 21. Translated by Jacob Neusner. Atlanta, GA: Scholars Press, 1996.

Thondup, Tulke. *Masters of Meditation and Miracles: Lives of the Great Buddhist Masters of India and Tibet*. Boston: Shambhala Publications, 1999.

Trigg, Roger. *Rationality and Religion: Does Faith Need Reason?* Oxford: Blackwell, 1998.

Tweed, Thomas A. and Stephen Prothero, editors. *Asian Religions in America: A Documentary History*. New York: Oxford University Press, 1999.

Wacker, Grant. *Heaven Below: Early Pentecostals and American Culture*. Cambridge, MA: Harvard University Press, 2001.

Walzer, Michael. *Interpretation and Social Criticism*. Cambridge, MA: Harvard University Press, 1987.

Warrier, Maya. *Hindu Selves in a Modern World: Guru Faith in the Mata Amritanandamayi Mission*. New York: RoutledgeCurzon, 2005.

Whitehead, Alfred North. *Process and Reality*. Edited by David Ray Griffin and Donald W. Sherburne. New York: Free Press, 1978.

Wiesel, Elie. *Four Hasidic Masters and Their Struggle with Melancholy*. Notre Dame, IN: University of Notre Dame Press, 1978.

———. *Night* (1960). Translated by Stella Rodway. New York: Bantam Books, 1982.

Woodward, Kenneth L. *The Book of Miracles: The Meaning of the Miracle Stories in Christi-anity, Judaism, Buddhism, Hinduism, and Islam*. New York: Simon & Schuster, 2000.

Zagzebski, Linda Trinkaus. *Philosophy of Religion: An Historical Introduction*. Malden, MA: Blackwell, 2007.

Zornberg, Avivah Gottlieb. *The Particulars of Rapture: Reflections on Exodus*. New York: Doubleday, 2001.

Index

Jacobs, Louis, 72
James, William, 2
Jerusalem, 72, 84, 88–89, 143, 145, 148, 150, 157, 165–166, 228n3; site of Muhammad's Night Journey and Ascent, 1, 7, 190–191
Jesus, 5, 12, 20, 33, 65, 109, 153, 155, 190, 211, 213; as agent of contemporary healings, 166–170; ascension of, 54; as "bread of life," 27; marks (stigmata) of, 157–160; miracles of, xiii, 22, 147–151, 173; miraculous conception and birth of, 145–147; as moral exemplar and teacher, 172, 174–175; pre-existence of, 235n89; restriction on miracles, 13, 184; revelations of, 31, 152; walking on water, 1, 7, 141–144; as witnessing prophet, 202

Kabbalah, 89, 94–95
Kant, Immanuel: compared to Buddha, 111; moral critique of miracles, 172; noumenal freedom as transcendent, 18–20, 174; rationalism challenged by Vivekananda, 65
Kaplan, Mordecai, 99–102
Kariyawasam, A. G. S., 132
karma, 36, 41, 43, 60, 68–69, 113, 211
Kearney, Richard, 221n13
Kee, Howard Clark, 144
Khan, Sayyid Ahmad, 205
Kierkegaard, Søren, 21, 172–173, 217n33
King, Martin Luther, Jr., 125
Kleinberg, Avaida, 156
koan, 5, 132
Kołakowski, Leszek, 214
Krishna, 15, 33, 62, 145; "divine magic" of, 29; miracles of, 1, 37–46; object of devotion, 50–56, 58; revelation to Arjuna, 35–37, 114
Kuan Yin (Japanese name of Avalokiteśvara): miracles of, 122
Kūkai: miraculous effects of meditation, 131

Lessing, Gotthold Ephraim, 172–173, 205, 231n71
Levitation, 6, 27, 30–31, 37, 44–45; of Buddha, 2, 105–106, 114, 118; of Francis of Assisi, 157; of Sufi masters, 209; of Tibetan master, 129–130; of yogis, 47–48

Lewis, C. S., 17
limited age of miracles: in Islamic reform, 205; in Protestant tradition, 164, 205
Lotus Sutra, 119; miracles of Avalokiteśvara in, 120–122
Lourdes, 33; site of apparition of Mary, 160–162, healings at, 162–163, 170

mahāsiddhas: Tibetan miracle workers, 127–128
Mahāyāna (Great Vehicle) Buddhism, 108, 111, 113; different from Theravada, 132; miracles of Bodhisattvas in, 120–126; similar to Vajrayāna, 127; Zen school of, 132–134
Maimonides (Moses ben Maimon), 83, 221n13
Magritte, René, vii–viii
Maitreya, 120, 126
Marty, Martin, 10
māyā (illusion), 29, 41, 57
McCrea, Lawrence, 220n31
McCutcheon, Russell, 213
McPherson, Aimee Semple, 166–168, 170
Meri, Josef, 201
Midrash (exegetical commentary), 77–79, 81
Milarepa: Yoga of Inner Fire, 128
Miller, Perry: "rhetoric of sensation," 167–168
Mīmāmsā, 63–64
Miracle: ambivalence toward in Jewish tradition, 72–73; authority of in Islamic tradition, 181–183; as category of cross-cultural comparison, 25–26; definition of, 3–4, 15–16; distinction from magic, 28–29, 32, 76; inner and outer, 30–32; as occasion of wonder, 21–25; pedagogical purpose in Buddhist tradition, 106–108, 114; as response to human needs, 26–27; as signs of divine presence in Christian tradition, 141; as signs of liberation in Hindu tradition, 37; as transcendent event, 14–21

Renard, John, 191, 200, 202
Ridā, Rashīd, 205
Rippin, Andrew, 185, 207
Roberts, Oral Granville, 168–170
Rozehnal, Robert, 198–199
Rubenstein, Mary-Jane, 217n37
Rubenstein, Richard, 101–102
Rūmī, Jalal al-Dīn, 191; miracles of,
　200–201

Sacks, Jonathan, 80–81
Saint: as "friend of God" in Islamic tradi-
　tion, 183, 197–198; miracles of in Chris-
　tian tradition, 153–164
Śankara, 57, 67–68
Schimmel, Annemarie, 182, 187–188, 190,
　201–202
Scholem, Gershom, 73
Schuon, Frithjof, 178
shakti (feminine divine energy), 56–57
Shams al-Dīn Sabzawārī , Hadrat Pīr:
　miracles of, 195
Sharma, I. C., 63
shaykh (Sufi master), 178–179, 198; as "cen-
　ter of the universe," 182
Shiite Islam, 178–179
Shrīsimha: levitation and translocation, 129
siddhis (paranormal powers): of yogis, 47,
　66; of Buddha, 106, 114–115
Simon, Samuel, 143
Sinai: miracle of revelation, 75, 79–82
Smith, Jonathan Z., 26
Soubirous, Bernadette: vision of Mary,
　160–162
Spinoza, Baruch de, 97–99
Strauss, D. F., 173
Sufi Islam, 178–179, 197–198
Sunni Islam, 178–179; Qur'an the only
　miracle in, 203, 205
śūnyatā (emptiness), 111, 211
Suzuki, Daisetz Teitaro, 135–137
Swamiji (pseudonymous story teller),
　61–63
Swinburne, Richard, 17–18

Tabātabā'ī, Muhammad Husayn, 193
Theravada (Way of Elders) Buddhism, 108,
　120; objections to miracles, 131–132
Thomas of Celano, 154, 157
Tillich, Paul, 174
Torah, 71–73, 80–81, 96, 177, 182; as eternal,
　235n
Transcendent: Buddha's wisdom as, 110–
　112, 114; definition, xi–xii; Jesus's healing
　power as, 148, 151; Kant's noumenal
　freedom as, 18–20; Krishna's reality as,
　35; miraculous events as, 1–4, 6–7, 14–16,
　25–26, 33, 212–214; revelation of Qur'an
　as, 177; Shiite Imams' wisdom as, 193

Vajrayāna (Diamond or Thunderbolt) Bud-
　dhism, 108; supernormal powers in, 127
Vivekananda, Swami: objections to
　miracles, 64–67

al-Wahāb, Muhammad Ibn 'Abd, 205;
　Wahābī rejection of miracles, 206
Walzer, Michael: "connected critic," 13, 102;
　interpretation of Oven of Akhnai, 73
Ward, Benedicta, 218n44
Warrier, Maya, 58, 61
Weinberger, Theodore, 221n23
Whitehead, Alfred North: "ontological
　principle," xii
Wiesel, Elie, 91–92, 101

Yau, Tan Peng, 122
Yoga Sutras, 48–49, 65–66, 106
Yogi: levitation, 46–47; paranormal powers
　of, 48–50, 66–67, 69

Zaddikim (holy ones), 89, 92; as "center of
　the universe," 182
Zagzebski, Linda Trinkaus, 218n51
Zen Buddhism: interpretation of miracle
　story, 123; objections to miracles,
　132–134; Suzuki's modernist interpreta-
　tion of, 135–137
Zornberg, Avivah Gottlieb, 78, 81

About the Author

DAVID L. WEDDLE is the David and Lucile Packard Professor of Religion at Colorado College. He is the author of *The Law as Gospel: Revival and Reform in the Theology of Charles G. Finney.*